e-Learning Ecologi

M000307440

e-Learning Ecologies explores transformations in the patterns of pedagogy that accompany e-learning—the use of computing devices that mediate or supplement the relationships between learners and teachers—to present and assess learnable content, to provide spaces where students do their work, and to mediate peer-to-peer interactions. Written by the members of the "new learning" research group, this textbook suggests that e-learning ecologies may play a key part in shifting the systems of modern education, even as technology itself is pedagogically neutral. The chapters in this book aim to create an analytical framework with which to differentiate those aspects of educational technology that reproduce old pedagogical relations from those that are genuinely innovative and generative of new kinds of learning. Featuring case studies from elementary schools, colleges, and universities on the practicalities of new learning environments, *e-Learning Ecologies* elucidates the role of new technologies of knowledge representation and communication in bringing about change to educational institutions.

Bill Cope is Professor in the Department of Educational Policy Studies at the University of Illinois, USA. He is Principal Investigator in a series of major projects funded by the Institute of Educational Sciences in the US Department of Education and the Bill and Melinda Gates Foundation researching and developing multimodal writing and assessment spaces.

Mary Kalantzis is Dean of the College of Education at the University of Illinois, Urbana-Champaign, USA. She was formerly Dean of the Faculty of Education, Language and Community Services at RMIT University in Melbourne, Australia, and President of the Australian Council of Deans of Education.

e-Learning Ecologies

Principles for New Learning
and Assessment

Edited by
Bill Cope and Mary Kalantzis

Routledge
Taylor & Francis Group

NEW YORK AND LONDON

First published 2017
by Routledge
711 Third Avenue, New York, NY 10017

and by Routledge
2 Park Square, Milton Park, Abingdon, Oxon, OX14 4RN

Routledge is an imprint of the Taylor & Francis Group, an informa business

Library of Congress Cataloging-in-Publication Data
A catalog record for this book has been requested

ISBN: 978-1-138-19371-0 (hbk)
ISBN: 978-1-138-19372-7 (pbk)
ISBN: 978-1-315-63921-5 (ebk)

Typeset in Goudy
by Apex CoVantage, LLC

Contents

1   Conceptualizing e-Learning

Bill Cope and Mary Kalantzis

On Learning Environments

This book explores phenomena we call e-learning ecologies. We use this metaphor because a learning environment is in some senses like an ecosystem, consisting of the complex interaction of human, textual, discursive, and spatial dynamics. These take a coherent, systemic form. Traditional classrooms, with their linear arrangement of seating and desks, their lecturing teachers, their textbooks, their student workbooks, and their classroom discussions are also learning systems. Moving from one of these classrooms to another, the modes of interaction are familiar and predictable because they are so systematically patterned. After a while, they seem "normal." However, these are strange human artifacts that were not put together into this configuration until the nineteenth century. They quickly became universal and compulsory sites of socialization of mass-institutionalized education. In terms of the long arc of human history, it was not until about the time of our great-great-grandparents that we first encountered these modern educational systems. But will these institutional forms survive long into the twenty-first century? Is it time for them to be reformed? And if change is to come, what will be the role of new technologies of knowledge representation and communication in bringing about change?

This book explores transformations in the patterns of pedagogy that accompany e-learning, or the use of computing devices to mediate or supplement the relationships between learners and teachers, to present and assess learnable content, to provide spaces where students do their work, and to mediate peer-to-peer interactions.

Our thesis is this: e-learning ecologies may play a key part in the largest shift in the systems of modern education since their rise to dominance in the nineteenth century. Everything *may* change—configurations of space, learner-to-teacher and learner-to-learner relationships, the textual forms of knowledge to which learners are exposed, the kinds of knowledge artifacts that students create, and the way the outcomes of their learning are measured. Or we may introduce a whole lot of technology into schools and nothing will change in institutional or epistemic senses. Technology is pedagogically neutral.

So our questions of e-learning ecologies become these: How can they be different? And why should they be different?

About This Book

This book is a collaborative work, written by the members of the "new learning" research group coordinated by Bill Cope and Mary Kalantzis, including colleagues, postdoctoral students, and graduate students at the University of Illinois. The group's work has been in part conceptual; to create an analytical framework with which to differentiate those aspects of educational technology that reproduce old pedagogical relations from those that are genuinely innovative and generative of new kinds of learning. However, our work has been in equal measure practical. We have been working in schools, from elementary to college and university, experimenting with the practicalities of new learning ecologies. A focal point of this work for our team has been a research and development program that has resulted in the creation of the *Scholar* platform, supported by a series of research grants from the Institute of Educational Sciences in the US Department of Education and the Bill and Melinda Gates Foundation (see Figure 1.1).[1] Research papers arising from this work are to be found here: http://newlearningonline.com/scholar/references.

The theoretical framework for this book—seven affordances for transformative e-learning ecologies—covers the same territory as the "e-Learning Ecologies" MOOC offered through Coursera. The companion website to this book, http://elearningecologies.com, presents the video mini-lectures that accompany this course. The book also reflects key themes developed for our

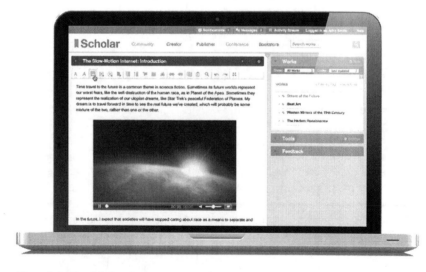

Figure 1.1 The *Scholar* platform

learning design and leadership master's and doctoral programs at the University of Illinois. At our http://elearningecologies.com website, you will also find a rich (and always growing) directory of e-learning case studies created by our graduate students.

Forces of Educational Change

e-Learning environments fall into two categories: new institutional sites of learning and traditional sites of learning that are being transformed by educational technologies. Striking new institutional forms include the rise of purely online learning and "virtual schools" (Molnar et al., 2014), the phenomenon of MOOCs (Knox, 2014; Waldrop, 2013), and "open education" (DeBoer et al., 2014; Peters & Britez, 2008). Traditional sites of learning are also undergoing transformation, including blended and ubiquitous learning (Cope & Kalantzis, 2009b, 2013), extending the range of classical classroom interactions beyond the physical classroom and class times and by one-to-one schools where every student has a device that they can take home.

In both new and traditional sites of learning, a range of new educational technologies is emerging. To a large degree, the same platforms are used in both new and traditional contexts. The following are some of the key educational technologies to emerge since the introduction of computer-mediated and online learning:

1. *Learning management systems.* Older systems include the commercial offering Blackboard and the open source offering Moodle. More recent commercial systems include D2L and Canvas. MOOC platforms, principally Coursera and edX, follow essentially the same pattern. Learning management systems align with the historical genre of the syllabus, laying out content to be covered and activities to be undertaken in a sequence, often ordered by time targets and deadlines. They may include readings, prerecorded videos, discussion areas, tasks, and assessments. A new feature of these systems is the possibility of learning analytics to track learner engagement, including not only traditional assessments and teacher gradebooks but also analyses based on incidental "data exhaust," including keystroke patterns, edit histories, clickstream and navigation paths, and social interaction patterns (Cope & Kalantzis, 2016).
2. *e-Textbooks.* Replacing print textbooks, e-textbooks may include multimedia content and quizzes.
3. *The flipped classroom.* Low cost, easily accessible video recording and web upload of teacher lectures (Bishop & Verleger, 2013).
4. *Intelligent tutors, games, and simulations.* These guide a learner through a body of knowledge, serving content, requesting responses, making hints, offering feedback on these responses, and designing stepwise progression through a domain depending on the nature of these responses (Aleven, Beal, & Graesser, 2013; Chaudhri et al., 2013; VanLehn, 2006).

Underlying intelligent tutors, games and simulations are cognitive models that lay out the elements of a target domain, anticipating a range of learning paths (Conrad, Clarke-Midura, & Klopfer, 2014). Intelligent tutors work best in problem domains where highly structured progressions are possible, such as algebra or chemistry (Koedinger et al., 2013). They are less applicable in areas where progression cannot readily be assembled into a linear sequence of knowledge components (Graesser et al., 2001).

5. *Discussion boards.* These substitute for the oral discussions of the traditional classroom, supporting various forms of conversational interaction. Patterns of peer interaction can be mapped—who is participating, with whom, and to what extent (Speck et al., 2014; Wise, Zhao, & Hausknecht, 2013). Natural language processing methods can be used to parse the content of interactions (Xu et al., 2013).

6. *Web workspaces and e-portfolios.* Contemporary student workspaces differ from traditional pen-and-paper student activity in several key respects, including expansion of the media of knowledge representation, the ease of collaborative work, and the possibility of sharing completed work in e-portfolios. These spaces also support logistically complex, highly structured interactions such as peer review. Using a single cloud-located source, it is possible to manage what is otherwise a difficult-to-administer process of anonymization, randomization, and simultaneous review by multiple reviewers (Abrams, 2013; Cope & Kalantzis, 2013; Kline, Letofsky, & Woodard, 2013; Lammers, Magnifico, & Curwood, 2014; McCarthey et al., 2014).

7. *Adaptive, personalized, and differentiated instruction.* Such systems monitor differential learning progress from student to student and adapt the path and pace of learning to the speed at which the learner is progressing. This represents a break from the logics of one-size-fits-all, everyone-on-the-same-page of traditional classrooms, continuously calibrating learning to individual needs (Conati & Kardan, 2013; Koedinger et al., 2013; Shute & Zapata-Rivera, 2012; Walkington, 2013; Wolf, 2010; Woolf, 2010).

8. *Machine assessments.* Two principal kinds of machine assessment have emerged with the use of computing in education: computer adaptive testing and natural language processing (Cope et al., 2011; Vojak et al., 2011). Computer adaptive testing extends long-standing item response theory, where correct student response to test items varies according to what the student knows or understands (a latent cognitive trait) and the relative difficulty of the item. Computer adaptive tests serve students progressively harder or easier questions depending on whether they answer correctly or incorrectly. Such tests provide more accurately calibrated scores for students across a broader range of capacities, reach an accurate score faster, and are harder to game because no two students end up taking quite the same test (Chang, 2015). One variant of these assessments, computer diagnostic testing, allows for the coding of topic areas within a test and disaggregation of scores within the subdomains addressed by the test (Chang, 2012). In another major form of machine assessment, natural

language processing technologies are today able to grade short-answer and essay-length supply-response assessments with reliability equivalent to human graders (Burstein & Chodorow, 2003; Chung & Baker, 2003; Cotos & Pendar, 2008; Shermis, 2014; Warschauer & Grimes, 2008). Natural language processing offers two types of tools for writing assessment, often used in concert with each other: statistical corpus comparison and analytical text parsing (Cope, Kalantzis, & Magee, 2011). In the case of the corpus comparison, the computer is "trained" by being given a corpus of human-graded texts; the machine compares new texts and grades them based on statistical similarity with the human-graded texts. In the case of text parsing, computers are programmed to search for language features, such as markers of textual cohesion, the range and complexity of vocabulary, and latent semantics based on word clustering and frequencies (Crossley et al., 2015; Landauer et al., 2007; McNamara et al., 2014).

None of these technologies is particularly new. Indeed, in a sense, the future of education represented by these shifts in educational media has been a long time coming. As early as 1959, researchers at the University of Illinois were developing the world's first e-learning system, PLATO (Programmed Logic for Automatic Teaching Operations), connected to the ILLIAC mainframe computer, also developed at the university. Prompted to a large degree by the requirements of an e-learning system, this work spawned pioneering developments, including the plasma screen for a visual interface, a messaging system, synthesized sound, and the first computer games. Half a century later, we are still to realize the full potential of these developments on education (see Figures 1.2 and 1.3).

Figure 1.2 The ILLIAC mainframe computer, c. 1959

Figure 1.3 A PLATO workstation, c. 1980

Paradigms of Learning

We opened this chapter with the provocative proposition that everything might change in education with the application of educational technologies. But also, in a pedagogical sense, nothing might change. Technologies are pedagogically neutral.

To make this case, we need to delineate the main pedagogical alternatives. We have done this in the past several times in historical narratives that distinguish threefold didactic/authentic/transformative pedagogies (Kalantzis & Cope, 2012), fourfold didactic/authentic/functional/critical pedagogies (Kalantzis et al., 2016), or more simply, a twofold distinction of didactic/reflexive pedagogies (Cope & Kalantzis, 2015a; Kalantzis & Cope, 2016b). For our analysis now, we are going to stay with the simpler twofold didactic/reflexive distinction.

The discursive forms of didactic pedagogy are older than mass-institutionalized education, but on the scale of human history, they are not very old. Our reference point for the modern might be Plato's Academy of Athens, where learning was primarily dialogical (Socratic dialogue), rhetorical, and argumentative. The Western universities that arose in the late Middle Ages represented a newly didactic mode of learning, originating as they did from a monastic tradition, where in the words of one of the founders of this tradition, "It belongeth to the master to speak and to teach; it becometh the disciple to be silent and to listen" (Benedictine University, Center for Mission and Identity, 2016). Then, after the rise of the printing press, teacher lectures are supplemented by a novel textual artifact, the textbook. This lays out, in a synoptic, systematically ordered, definite, and seemingly inarguable way, knowledge that students are to acquire, with the aim of optimizing efficient acquisition and retention by learners (Ong, 1958). These modern discursive and pedagogical forms become universal by the end of the nineteenth century (see Figure 1.4).

As early as the eighteenth century, Jean-Jacques Rousseau railed against didactic pedagogy.

> Teach your scholar to observe the phenomena of nature; you will soon rouse his curiosity, but if you would have it grow, do not be in too great a hurry to satisfy this curiosity. Put the problems before him and let him solve them himself. Let him know nothing because you have told him, but because he has learnt it for himself. If ever you substitute authority for reason he will cease to reason, he will be a mere plaything of other people's thoughts.
>
> (Rousseau, 1762/1914)

By the beginning of the twentieth century, educational thinkers and practitioners from John Dewey to Maria Montessori and Rabindranath Tagore were to offer systematic critiques and practical alternatives to didactic pedagogy. We call these reflexive in the sense that they represent a revival of the dialogical, where the agency of the learner is at play in a dialectic between teacher and learner, the to-be-learned and the learning.

In a twenty-first-century version of this debate, Kirschner, Sweller, and Clark (2006) argue in favor of something they term *guided instruction*. The object of their critique is a series of ostensible evils that they label "constructivist, discovery, problem-based, experiential, and inquiry-based teaching." They put the case for "direct instructional guidance, . . . defined as providing information that fully explains the concepts and procedures that students are required to learn." These "procedures of the discipline" are "based on the facts, laws, principles and theories that make up a discipline's content." To what pedagogical end? "Long-term memory is now viewed as the central, dominant structure of human cognition. . . . We are skillful in an area because our long-term memory contains huge amounts of information concerning the area. . . . The

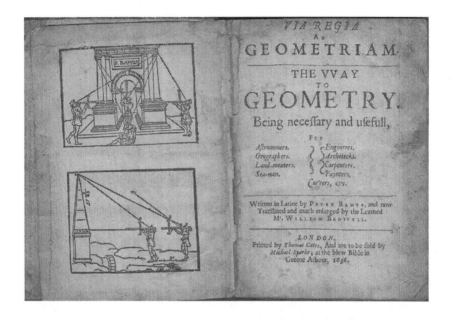

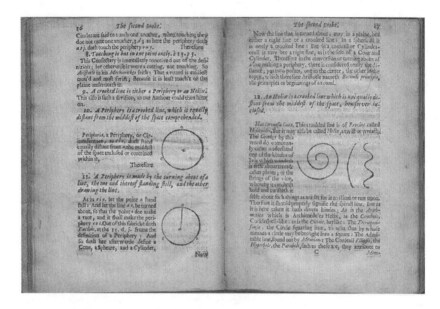

Figure 1.4 Early modern textbook: Petrus Ramus, *The Way of Geometry* (1596; English translation, 1636)

architecture of long-term memory provides us with the ultimate justification for instruction. The aim of all instruction is to alter long-term memory." This is where, according to these authors, fundamental problems arise with the various approaches that they seek to criticize. "Minimal guidance places a huge burden on working memory. . . . Cognitive load theory suggests that the free exploration of a highly complex environment may generate a heavy working memory load that is detrimental to learning" (Kirschner, Sweller, & Clark, 2006, pp. 76–80).

Here are the key features of what we call didactic pedagogy:

1. For there to be "direct instructional guidance," the *balance of control of a learning environment must be with the instructor,* along the lines of Figure 1.5— hence the synoptic, monological artifacts of the lecture and the textbook.
2. There is a *focus on cognition,* and mostly at times, on one particular aspect of cognition, *long-term memory*—measurable per the artifact and ritual of closed-book, summative examination.
3. The focus is on the *individual learner* because long-term memory is singularly individual.
4. There is an emphasis on a narrow range of epistemic processes by means of which learners can *demonstrate that they can replicate disciplinary knowledge*—which in this pedagogical mode is limited to remembering facts, appropriately applying definitions, correctly deducing answers by the application of received theorems, and faithfully applying the "procedures of the discipline." This is pedagogy of mimesis or knowledge replication.

Soon after publication of the Kirschner, Sweller, and Clark (2006) article, there came a rebuttal by Hmelo-Silver, Duncan, and Chinn (2007). They argue that

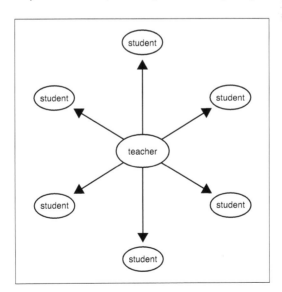

Figure 1.5 Role configurations in didactic pedagogy

pedagogical processes such as problem-based learning and inquiry learning "provide students with opportunities to engage in the scientific practices of questioning, investigation, and argumentation as well as learning content in a relevant and motivating context." This entails "not only learning content but also learning 'softer skills' such as epistemic practices, self-directed learning, and collaboration that are not measured on achievement tests but are important for being lifelong learners and citizens in a knowledge society." This is not to say that learning is without structure. This structure takes the form of "scaffolding [that] makes the learning more tractable for students by changing complex and difficult tasks in ways that make these tasks accessible, manageable, and within student's zone of proximal development" (Vygotsky, 1962/1978). Such pedagogy constitutes a kind of "cognitive apprenticeship, whereby students become increasingly accomplished problem-solvers given structure and guidance from mentors who scaffold students through coaching, task structuring, and hints, without explicitly giving students the final answers" (Hmelo-Silver, Duncan, & Chinn, 2007, pp. 100, 105).

Here now is our gloss on what we call reflexive pedagogy:

1. There is a shift in the balance of agency between an instructor and a learner, where *the learner has considerable scope and responsibility for epistemic action*, albeit within the frame of reference of an activity sequence that has been scaffolded by the instructor. Knowledge activity is dialogical, with backward and forward movement between instructor and students and between students and students—see Figure 1.6. The sources of knowledge are not monological (the artificially singular, synoptic voice

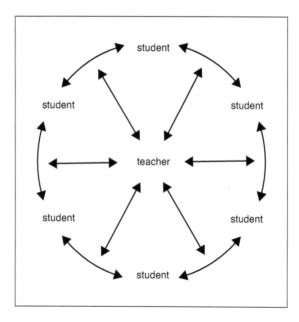

Figure 1.6 Role configurations in reflexive pedagogy

of the lecturer or textbook writer). Rather, they are multiple—the great variety of authentic and problematically varied knowledge sources now immediately accessible in the universal library that is the Internet, and beyond that, the lived experience of learners.

2. The focus is on *the artifacts and knowledge representations constructed by the learner and the processes of their construction.* In an age where knowledge is always accessible via personal digital devices, long-term memory is not so important. Long-term memory will develop, but it will be an incidental and inessential consequence of deep engagement in a discipline. There is no longer a need to emphasize long-term memory in pedagogy. For if a fact cannot for the moment be remembered, then it is always possible to look it up in an instant. If a procedure cannot be remembered, then there is an app that will execute that procedure—a calculation, a series of directions, a data mash-up. The objectives of learning are different in an age where we have these ubiquitous devices, these cognitive prostheses. The measurable object of learning now shifts from long-term memory to knowledge processes and their documentation in the form of epistemic artifacts or knowledge representations—the report, the worked solution, the recorded activity, the model, and the design. This, in other words, involves a shift in emphasis from cognition to epistemic artifacts, a phenomenon that we have elsewhere called ergative pedagogy (Cope & Kalantzis, 2015a).

3. The focus is on *the social sources of knowledge*. Knowledge is not a matter of what I know as an individual. It is my capacity to navigate the wide epistemic world at my fingertips; it is my ability to discern critically what is salient and what is not; it is commitment to acknowledge the social provenance of my knowledge by means such as citations and links; it is my ability to work with others to create collaborative knowledge where the sum of the knowable is greater than the individual contributions of colleagues in-the-knowing; it is my capacity for synthesis; and it is my ability to extend creatively socially acquired knowledge.

4. By now, we will have brought to education *a wider range of epistemic processes*. In a reflexive pedagogy, we don't need to abandon evidence in the form of facts, conceptual clarity with finely calibrated definitions, or deductions grounded in theorems—the things Kirschner, Sweller, and Clark, (2006) value. However, these always sit within a wider epistemic frame of reference, where evidence is contextualized by argument to justify the supportability of a claim, where nontrivial claims are always provisional and open to rebuttal, and where in our disciplinary practice knowledge is dynamic and evolving.

In these four senses, the pedagogy we are describing here is reflexive, by way of contrast with didactic pedagogy, which is essentially mimetic.

The debate between Kirschner, Sweller, and Clark (2006) and Hmelo-Silver, Duncan, and Chinn (2007) has been rehearsed time and time again over the course of the history of modern education, and doubtless it will be rehearsed many times again. Our purpose here has been to use this debate as a symptomatic starting point, as a reference point on which to ground our analysis of e-learning ecologies.

It's Not the Technology That Makes a Difference, It's the Pedagogy

Here are some relatively recent educational technologies and the ways in which, on our four measures, in some fundamental respects, they reinstantiate didactic pedagogies. Perhaps, even at times, they resuscitate them in their moment of imminent decline.

- *The learning management system* reinforces a didactic role for the instructor, reviving a role like that of the textbook as they lay out course content, section by section, delivering content such as video lectures or quasi-textbook reading materials. As the course unfolds week by week, tests of memory may provide a retrospective view of what has been learned. The focus is still individual learning and the replication of disciplinary knowledge. Learning management systems need not be used this way—they can be used in other ways and increasingly are. However, this is commonly the default mode of delivery.
- *The flipped classroom* transfers to a recording of the monological, synoptic lecture form. In this sense, the relationship of teacher to student is exactly what St Benedict had prescribed. Of course, there are differences. The idea behind the flipped classroom is not to waste valuable in-person time and to leave space there for interaction. Learners also have a modicum of control not possible in a live lecture—to play the recording when it suits them, to run the lecture at double speed when the pace of spoken language is slower than the speed of thought, or to go back over bits that they did not fully understand on the first hearing. However, these differences are minor compared to the effect of preserving the lecture medium.
- *The e-textbook* may add a little to the print textbook, such as moving images or adaptive multiple-choice tests at the end of each chapter, but the basic textual form is the same as it was at the time of its invention in the century after the emergence of the printing press. Just as textbooks have for centuries, the e-textbook summarizes knowledge, lays it out in a systematic order, and speaks in the singular, authoritative, teacherly voice of the author.
- *Intelligent tutors and games* march students through domains that require the correct application of procedures—classically and most effectively mathematics, the mechanics of language, or empirical science. To the extent that they are adaptive and personalized, and to the extent that they operate on small cycles of behaviorist response (stimulus-response-sanction/reward), their focus is on individualized cognition. This individualization is heightened when students can work at their own pace, separate from peers. Here the relationship of learning to learnable content is one computer/lone mind.
- *Computer adaptive tests* are extensions of long-standing item-response theory. Items need to be just hard enough to be able to differentiate those students who understand what is being delivered (the concept of "theta," or understanding) and those who don't. But they work on the basis of a simple epistemology: that facts can be only right and wrong; that deductions can

have only one correct answer; that concepts can have only one congruent meaning. In an item, there can be only one correct answer. The other alternatives are "distractors," designed to be plausible but wrong. There is no way of knowing whether the learner's plausible but wrong response is based on thinking that is in a certain sense insightful or whether the student's correct answer was based on false premises or instinct without adequate underlying reasoning. The computational mechanisms of today's psychometrics may be more advanced, but the epistemological premises remain unchanged.

These are just some of the media by means of which didactic pedagogies may be brought back to life. The technology has changed, but this does not change the pedagogy in any fundamental way. To say it again, technology is pedagogically neutral. But it has affordances.

e-Learning Affordances: Toward a Theory

What is potentially new and transformative about e-learning ecologies? We have two "nothing" answers to this question. The first "nothing" we've just addressed—educational technologies can be used as a medium for didactic pedagogy. And for some domains and in some instances, this may not be a bad thing—for example, where repetition and memory are still important: to learn a new language or to get better at arithmetic.

Our second "nothing" answer is that educational technologies at their best can do little more than to realize long-held aspirations for education, traceable from Rousseau to Dewey, Montessori, Tagore, and many others. If they make a difference, then it is just to make these aspirations more practicable or more achievable in practice.

However, we also want to offer an "everything" answer. Educational technologies could support the most fundamental change in ecologies of learning since the invention of the modern school and its mass institutionalization in the nineteenth century. A pedagogical paradigm change is possible—a change from didactic to reflexive pedagogy.

To make a promise of "everything" is not to make a prediction, because who knows? We could easily slip back into a world where didactic pedagogy rules again. To try for "everything" is to set an agenda. It is to make a promise to ourselves as educators. We want to propose that reflexive pedagogy, enabled by an emerging wave of educational technologies, can create e-learning ecologies that will be more engaging for learners, more effective, more resource efficient, and more equitable in the face of learner diversity.

So what is potentially new and transformative about these e-learning ecologies? In the rest of this chapter and in the remaining chapters of this book, we will explore seven "new learning" affordances opened up by digital media: ubiquitous learning, active knowledge production, multimodal knowledge representations, recursive feedback, collaborative intelligence, metacognitive reflection, and differentiated learning (see Figure 1.7 and Table 1.1). This book offers

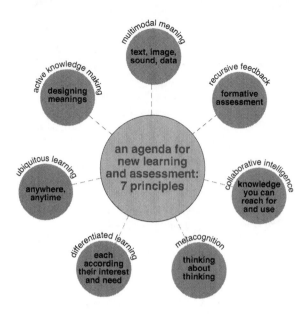

Figure 1.7 e-Learning affordances

Table 1.1 Comparing Didactic and Reflexive Pedagogy

	Didactic Pedagogy	Reflexive Pedagogy
Spatio-temporal dimension	Confined by the four walls of the classroom and the cells of the timetable	Ubiquitous learning: anywhere, anytime, anyhow
Epistemic dimension	The learner as knowledge consumer, passive knowledge acquisition, memorization	Active knowledge making: the learner-as-knowledge producer and discerning knowledge discoverer/navigator
Discursive dimension	Academic literacies: traditional textbooks, student assignments and tests	Multimodal meaning: new media texts, multimodal knowledge representations
Evaluative dimension	Emphasis on summative assessments and retrospective judgments that serve managerial purposes but are not immediately actionable	Recursive feedback: formative assessment, prospective and constructive feedback, learning analytics
Social dimension	The isolated learner, with a focus on individual cognition and memory	Collaborative intelligence: peer-to-peer learning, sourcing social memory, using available knowledge tools appropriately
Cognitive dimension	Focus on facts to be remembered, theories to be correctly applied	Metacognition: thinking about thinking, critical self-reflection on knowledge processes and disciplinary practices
Comparative dimension	Homogenizing, one-size-fits-all curriculum, standardized teaching and assessment	Differentiated learning: flexible, self-expressive, and adaptive learning, addressing each student according to his or her interests, self-identity, and needs

a theoretical overview of the dimensions of new and emerging learning environments, a review of the research evidence of their effectiveness, and a wide variety of examples of learning technologies and technology implementations that demonstrate these affordances in action.

Affordance 1: Ubiquitous Learning

The classroom of mass-institutionalized education is a communications medium. There is nothing of the knowable world outside the classroom that cannot be brought into the classroom via media: about volcanoes or algebra or dentistry or poetry or geometry or spelling or geology. The reference is exophoric, to things outside the classroom. The outside is brought in via media—primarily in the era of didactic pedagogy, teacher lecture, and textbook. These are classical one-to-many media, in their general form not unlike the mass media of pre-digital newspapers, radio, and television. For younger learners, 1-to-20 or 30 seems to work. Much of the time, the teacher speaks, and the students listen. Each student has a limited opportunity to speak during classroom discussion. This is simply a matter of logistical necessity, given the affordances of the media. For college students, a lecture may be one-to-hundreds, with even less or no opportunity for dialogue.

As a communications system, this classical modern classroom requires two kinds of confinement. One is spatial, or what is hearable within the four walls of the classroom. The other is temporal, framed by the cells of the timetable, determined by the necessity to listen together, and to be on the same page of the textbook at the same time.

Just as media in the wider society have changed, so the media of classrooms are changing. Where the mass media were one-to-many, the social media are many-to-many. Where the mass media configured audiences, viewers, and readers as relatively passive recipients, the social media configure "users" simultaneously as readers and writers, viewers and image makers, and media creators and media consumers. Where the mass media assumed an audience that was fundamentally the same (because their message had to be mass produced and mass distributed), the social media express and reflect a panoply of identities and interests depending on a user-selected pattern of friends, likes, or followings. Quietly underlying these transformations are some fundamental technological changes that might variously be named ubiquitous computing (Cope & Kalantzis, 2009b), Web 2.0 (O'Reilly, 2005), cloud computing (Erl, Puttini, & Mahmood, 2013), and semantic publishing (Cope, Kalantzis, & Magee, 2011). But the technologies do not produce the change; they only offer affordances, for the same technologies could with equal force be used for control, command, and social homogenization—and sometimes are. To the extent that there is change, it is fundamentally social, in our everyday communicative relationships (Kalantzis & Cope, 2015).

Figure 1.8 "Hands up!" classical classroom discourse

So what might happen in education that parallels these changes in the wider world of our communications media? To provide an example from the microdynamics of pedagogy, we will examine the subtle but profound changes in classroom discussion that occur when it moves from oral, in-class discussion to online discussion.

In her pathbreaking book *Classroom Discourse*, Courtney Cazden characterizes the classical pattern of classroom discussion as Initiation-Response-Evaluation (IRE) (Cazden, 2001). Teacher initiates: "What's the furthest planet from the sun in the solar system?" Students shoot up their hands, and one responds, a proxy for all the others (see Figure 1.8): "Pluto." Teacher evaluates: "Yes, that's correct!" (Or an alternative ending: "No, that's wrong. Does someone else know the answer?")

To compare this to the dialogue that occurs in discussion boards, they're the same in this respect—a class discussion space that enacts the classic discursive Initiation-Response-Evaluation pattern. And they are utterly different. And they are better in the following ways. We will use examples from the Community space in *Scholar*, illustrated in Figure 1.9 (Kalantzis et al., 2016):

- *Everyone responds*. In classical I-R-E, one person is proxy, answering for all. Instead, in *Scholar*, everyone can respond. In fact, there may be an expectation that everyone must respond. The result: a silent classroom that in classical classroom discourse would have been chaotically noisy as everyone speaks at once or where the class would have to wait an interminably long time for more or all to give their responses. Student A: "I can be sitting next to someone, and we are not even looking face to face but I can know everything that they are saying, and to be able to have everyone do it at once instead of just having one person talk, it's really cool, it's total collaboration."

- *Lowered barriers to response.* Here's a rough rule of thumb—in classical I-R-E, it's usually the wrong person who responds with the proxy answer—the student who has the confidence to shoot up his or her hand first or early, or the person who the teacher can rely on to have the anticipated answer. In *Scholar*, the initiation happens in an "update" and the response in a "comment" on that update. Students often tell us that simply having a few extra moments to look over their responses before pressing the "submit comment" button reduces their anxiety to participate. Student B: "In other classes teacher talks and you get to raise your hand occasionally. I like *Scholar* because you have a better chance of being heard in the classroom. There can be those kids that dominate the conversation, so I think it's cool that we all get to hear what each other really has to say."

- When everyone responds, *differences become visible.* In the classical I-R-E scenario, it is not practicable to get answers from everyone. The expectation is that there is one answer because the person answering for the rest of the class must act as proxy for the others. This becomes an exercise in guessing the answer that the teacher expects. In asking the question, they must have had something particular in mind. If only one person is going to answer, then it must mean there is only one answer. But is Pluto really a planet? Perhaps not, though if it is, might there be other small planets? The definition of planet is not so simple. Most things are interesting enough for there to be more than one answer or differently nuanced answers or different examples that students might give to illustrate a point based on personal interest and experience. Student C: "I think I learn more because I am hearing more perspectives, more opinions, rather than have one student dominate the conversation, hearing from everyone." In the *Scholar* Update <=> Comment dialogue, the univocal response of the proxy in classical I-R-E becomes polyvalent. Distinctive identities and voices come through. Students soon start discussing these differences, addressing one other @Name. Student D: "You could see all the different views from all the different people, it's interesting because a lot of people have different views." If classical I-R-E erases the differences, now they become visible and valued as a resource for intellectual dialogue. This phenomenon we have elsewhere termed *productive diversity* (Kalantzis & Cope, 2016b). Student E: "Sometimes someone will make a comment and it could be something you had never thought about, and once you read it, it changes your view." Also, anxieties to participate and voice one's own view are reduced as others' responses start to come through. Student F: "I get to hear everyone else's opinions and based on theirs, you can create your post."

- *This is highly engaging.* Classical I-R-E is boring—listening to the teacher ask a question and another student give an answer. The cognitive load is suboptimal. Reading lots of answers is much more engaging. Instead of one answer, there may be as many as there are members of the community and more. In the era of Facebook and Twitter feeds, the cognitive load when everyone answers in the discussion thread is about right. And there is a social "stickiness" in the visibility of the discussion—you stay engaged because others will be reading and responding to your updates and comments.

- *The read/write mix and the participation mix is right.* Heritage classrooms had students listening more than speaking, reading more than writing. Like the participatory social media, e-learning environments such as *Scholar* offer a balance of read/write and an expectation of active participation that resonates with the spirit of our times. Also, the text of the discussion is deceptively different from oral language. Linguist Michael Halliday contrasts the grammars of orality and writing—speaking is linear, redundant, and strings of clauses; writing is in sentences, concise, and carefully composed in a nonlinear, backward-and-forward process (Halliday, 1987/2002). Student G: "When you are writing stuff down, instead of speaking where you get jumbled up in your words, you get a chance to lay everything out and see it in front of you, so you can have it all planned out." Looking back over a comment and editing it before submitting moves part way from the grammar of speaking to the grammar of writing—and toward "academic literacy." Student H: "People think about what they say before they say it; it's more concise and more thoughtful conversation, you get a better view of what they want to say than a kind of in-moment answer."

- *We can break out of the four walls of the classroom and the cells of the timetable.* In an environment like *Scholar*, there is no difference between in-person, synchronous classroom discussion and at-a-distance, asynchronous discussion. And there are useful intermediate permutations—"Finish the discussion tonight" or "Not at school today? No problem. Participate anyway."

- *Anyone can be an initiator.* It's not only the teacher who can make updates in *Scholar* or start a classroom discussion. If the teacher choses to open this setting in the Community area, then students can make updates too—and this can comprise any number of media objects, including image, sound, video, and dataset.

- *A new transparency, learning analytics, and assessment.* Whereas discussions in the traditional classroom were ephemeral, online discussions are for-the-record. In the new I-R-E where everyone responds, every response can be seen, and the responses can be parsed using learning analytics (frequency of engagement, extent of engagement, language level, discussion network visualizations, and a myriad of other measures). If you are not participating, then it will be visible to others and to your teachers. It will show up in your results. Teacher A: "The kids like to be able to talk to each other, but they are thinking more than they would in a regular Facebook kind of setting, they realize that the teacher can see this as well. There's a certain helpful guardedness before they post, and thoughtfulness before they post it, which is a good skill for us to teach kids in the technology age."

Figure 1.9 Discussion in *Scholar's* community space

(*Continued*)

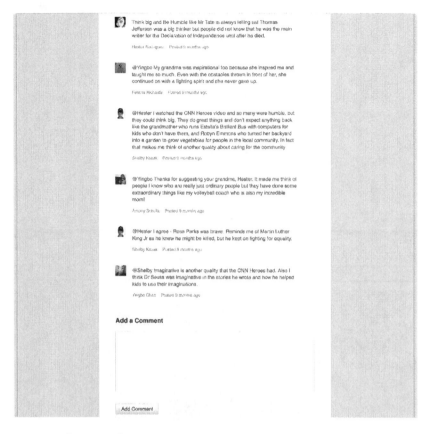

Figure 1.9 (Continued)

Such are the renewed dynamics of classroom discourse in the era of social media.

In these ways, classroom discussion in social media spaces is deceptively the same and totally different from traditional classrooms. In this medium, there is no difference between in-class and out-of-class discussion. Ubiquitous learning means that we have transcended the old pedagogical separations of space (the walls of the classroom) and time (the cells of the timetable). Not that classrooms go away, just that a certain kind of convergence occurs, where there are no discursive differences between in-person and at-a-distance learning. The platforms can be the same. The learner-teacher and learner-learner dynamics can be the same. Gone too is teacher surveillance requiring that students be in the teacher's direct and embodied line of sight, in the fashion of Bentham's panoptical prison (Foucault, 1979). Student work and activity in the cloud is always accessible and always recorded for the purposes of learning analytics and behavior management. A new transparency, as well as insistence on responsible digital citizenship, is accompanied on the flip side of new forms of digital surveillance. In the case of cyberbullying and other forms of antisocial behavior, teachers must exercise new duties of care. Finally, there is a question of scale. For children, traditional classrooms had an optimal scale of 20 or 30 students. In the era of ubiquitous learning, scale is variable—from a teacher working one-to-one with a student while others work autonomously, small groups working together based on activity scaffolds created by teachers, or larger numbers of students across multiple grade levels working in open online spaces. Ubiquitous learning makes possible all of these profound changes in the institutional forms and pedagogical modes of education.

Affordance 2: Active Knowledge Making

e-Textbooks can reproduce the relationships of knowledge and learning that accompanied the invention of the print textbook in the sixteenth century. Characteristically, learners are placed in a relatively passive relation to knowledge, which has been simplified, summarized, and ordered for them in the monological voice of the textbook writer. In the end, there is a test to see what the student has retained in long-term memory. Students are configured as knowledge consumers more than they are knowledge producers. The moral of their learning is that they should comply with epistemic authority.

How could things be different in e-learning ecologies? The key is a pedagogical process we call active knowledge making. We want to allow learners more scope for agency in their learning. Here we want to suggest a recalibration of the balance of agency. It's not that students completely lacked agency in the didactic classroom—listening attentively involves a certain level of agency. Reading the textbook and making some sense of it involves agency, a phenomenon that Barthes and Eco have called the role of the reader (Barthes, 1964/1977; Eco, 1981). On the other hand, learning activities without scaffolds can lack focus, to the point of becoming chaotic (Kalantzis & Cope, 1993). So the agency of learners needs to be within a framework of optimally generative constraint. The art of effective pedagogy is to calibrate just the right balance of openness and structure.

As part of our *Scholar* research and development project, we have designed and trialed as an alternative to the e-textbook an artifact that we call a learning module. The learning module is a hybrid of syllabus, lesson plan, and textbook. It is all of these things and none of them.

To describe the design, a learning module has a two-column format: a "for the member" side where the teacher speaks directly to the student, and a "for the admin" side where the teacher speaks the professional discourse of education, articulating learning aims, curriculum standards, and teaching tips (see Figures 1.10 and 1.11). The learning module offers three modes of interaction with and among students:

1. *Updates* that can be pushed into the student's activity stream, including a wide range of multimedia formats. Each update prompts comments from

students and class discussion. If the teacher selects the "unrestricted" setting, then students can also be asked to make updates that initiate discussions.

2. *Projects*, including a prompt and a rubric for peer, self-, and/or teacher review.

3. *Surveys*, including knowledge surveys that anticipate right and wrong answers, and information surveys that do not have right or wrong answers (such as an opinion survey).

Here are the differences: whereas a textbook summarizes the world, transmitting content to learners in the single voice of the textbook writer, the learning module curates the world—web links to textual content, videos, and other embedded media. It is multimodal. And it uses a variety of sources, requiring

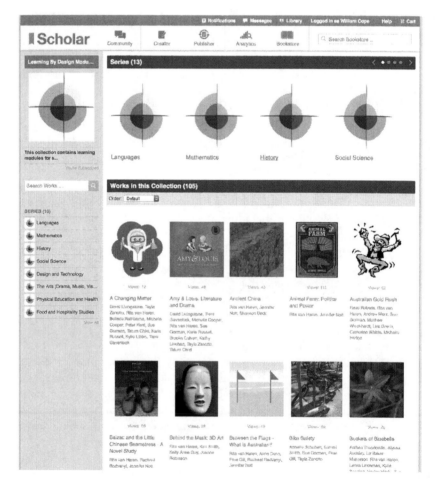

Figure 1.10 Learning modules in the Bookstore area of *Scholar*

Ordinary People, Extraordinary Lives: An Informative Text about a Person Who Makes a Difference

Grade 7 English Language Arts

Creator(s): Rita van Haren
Publisher: Liberacles Learning Module Projects

Produced with **Scholar**

Abstract

Through this Scholar writing project, students develop their reading skills, and build their knowledge of the characteristics of someone who makes a difference. They learn about the structure and language features of informative/explanatory texts before writing a biography about an ordinary person who has led an extraordinary life.

Keywords

Informative, Explanatory, Writing, Research, Structure, Language Features.

1. Overview

For the Student

In this *Scholar* writing project, you are going to create an informative/explanatory text about an ordinary person who has led an extraordinary life. Through online discussion and research, you will learn about the qualities of ordinary people who have led extraordinary lives by making a positive impact on others. You will also learn about the structure and language features of informative/explanatory writing. You will then draft an informative text, give feedback to your peers, revise your own work based on that feedback, and publish.

Focus Questions

In this learning module, we will focus on the following questions:

What are the qualities of ordinary people who lead extraordinary lives?

How do I draw inferences from a text?

How do I write an informative/explanatory text about an ordinary person who has led an extraordinary life?

Comment: Drawing on your background knowledge, post the name of someone who you think is/was an ordinary person who has led an extraordinary life. It could be a famous person such as swimmer, Michael Phelps, or Civil Rights activist, Rosa Parks, or someone you know personally. Then look at the list of people suggested by your peers in their comments.

For the Teacher

Through an online writing project, students develop their reading skills, and build their knowledge of the qualities of ordinary people who lead extraordinary lives. They learn about the structure and language features of informative/explanatory texts, and then through the writing process, they draft, provide peer feedback, revise, and submit their own work for publication.

Main CCSS Focus

W.7.2: Write informative/explanatory texts to examine a topic and convey ideas, concepts, and information through the selection, organization, and analysis of relevant content.

    Post Left-Side Content to a Community

2. Making a Difference

For the Student

Learning Intention: To think, discuss and write about ordinary people who are extraordinary because they have made a difference in other people's lives.

Have you ever thought about what makes an ordinary person extraordinary? Think about all the people who started off as normal people like you and made a difference in people's lives. It could be a famous person in history, science, education, medicine, politics, etc. It could also be a friend, parent, grandparent, teacher, coach, leader, etc.

Watch *Ordinary People Doing Extraordinary Things* YouTube clip.

Media embedded March 12, 2016

For the Teacher

The activity aims to:

- Engage students in the topic by valuing their interest in different kinds of people.

- Develop their confidence to post to the *Scholar* learning community, interact with others, and express their thoughts in full sentences in blog-like interactions.

- Establish working collaboratively, using their collective intelligence in an online learning community.

While students work collaboratively and independently on completing this Community Update, the teacher can support students who require extra help to think about the topic and compose their responses. Encourage students to read other students' posts so they don't repeat comments.

Posting comments is a form of accountability, promotes reflection, and develops students' writing skills and confidence to work in Scholar.

Updates of the CNN Heroes videoclips are available each year.

CCSS Focus

SL.7.1: Engage effectively in a range of collaborative discussions (one-on-one, in groups, and teacher-led) with diverse partners on grade 7 topics, texts and issues, building on others' ideas and expressing their own clearly.

SL.7.1c: Pose questions that elicit elaboration and respond to other questions and comments with relevant observations and ideas that bring the discussion back on topic as needed.

SL.7.1d: Acknowledge new information expressed by others and, when warranted, modify their own views.

    Post Left-Side Content to a Community

Figure 1.11 The two-column format of the learning module

students to critically evaluate sources, not just to memorize content that has been delivered to them to consume. It suggests that learners may also find and curate content. Whereas a syllabus outlines content and topics to be covered, a learning module prompts dialogue—an update prompts class discussion; commencing a project sets in motion the process of drafting, peer reviewing, revising, self- and/or teacher reviewing, and publishing a work; a survey elicits a student response. It is a medium to facilitate active and collaborative learning rather than individualized content acquisition. And whereas a lesson plan is the teacher's private activity outline, the learning module can be shared with the class and optionally published to the web for other teachers to use within a school or beyond, thus building a school-based pedagogical knowledge bank. For professional collaboration and learning, a learning module can be jointly written and peer reviewed before publication.

The underlying shift in textual architecture from a textbook to a learning module reflects a shift in the assumed role of the learner, a recalibration of the balance of learner and teacher agency. Moving away from the content transmission model of the textbook, the learning module sets up a series of reflexive, dialogical relationships with and among learners—the comments they make on an update, the peer and self-reviews, the responses to surveys. This is a move from telling to dialogue in which every learner must participate. The learning module also places responsibility on learners to be knowledge producers: when they make an update to initiate a discussion; when they create a "work" for peer review; and when these works are published and shared in a class knowledge bank. In a sense, instead of reading the textbook, students have been placed by the learning module in a position where they are now in effect writing the textbook. This represents a change in direction of knowledge flows, from hierarchical, top-down knowledge flows to lateral knowledge flows, and a distributed model of learners as co-creators or designers of new knowledge. This aligns with the logic of contemporary, participatory media (Haythornthwaite, 2009) and the skills and sensibilities for a knowledge society and knowledge economy (Peters, Marginson, & Murphy, 2008).

However, the process is highly scaffolded, in the design of open-ended updates, the nature of the requests that students receive to create updates, the project prompts and review rubrics, and the survey instruments. This changes in a fundamental way the nature of the teaching profession from a talking profession (someone else has written the textbook) to a profession where the central medium of interaction with learners is a documented, web-deliverable, interactive learning design.

Affordance 3: Multimodal Meaning

Student I: "With kids in our age group, technology is everything, it gets us to do something better than a student writing on paper and pencil."

Contemporary digital media are multimodal—where text, image, and sound are all manufactured of the same raw material: binary encoding. In the era of analog information and communication technologies (letterpress print, lithography, photography, sound recording, cinema, radio, telephone), media for the production, reproduction, and distribution of knowledge and culture were relatively separate. In the digital era, they are now made of the same stuff and distributed through the shared infrastructure of the Internet. With this transition, we have seen the rise of new multimodal genres where text, image, sound, and data are inseparable: the social media feed, the website, the app, the infographic, the data visualization. Elsewhere, we have called this phenomenon multiliteracies (Cope & Kalantzis, 2009a; Kalantzis et al., 2016). As it happens, the web still tends to separate the media into spaces that have a specialist focus on audio, video, or text. But this need not be the case, and often it is not the case.

Our response in *Scholar* has been to offer expanded tools for knowledge representation and communication through the multimodal editor, Creator (see Figure 1.12). Here, creators can write their text and insert audio, video, image, or any other data type—a manipulable dataset, a 3-D animation, or a mathematical formula, for instance. They can also embed inline external media—a YouTube video, SoundCloud audio, or code in GitHub, for instance.

Creator is a semantic editor (Cope, Kalantzis, & Magee, 2011), so the person producing the work is always prompted to be explicit about his or her meaning. When "emphasis" is added to a word or a phrase, this text is italicized.

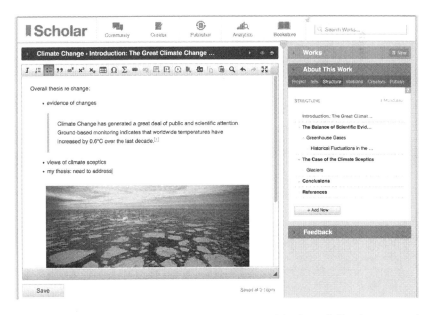

Figure 1.12 Beginning to draft work in the multimodal editor (*left*); planning and navigating its structure (*right*)

When "block quote" is selected, it is indented, and this tells us unequivocally for the purposes of reading and learning analytics to determine the writer's language level, that the creator did not write the selected text. The "structure" tool is for creating sections and headings, which tells us clearly what the creators intend in terms of the architecture of their text. It also prompts the creators to think explicitly about the structure of their text. Having a semantic editor means that the creator's work is more readily analyzable and also allows for flexible rendering to a web portfolio or a PDF. Rendering to different formats varies based on the medium but is always based on the creator's "semantic markup."

This is a fundamental difference between technologies such as the word processor and desktop publishing software, which are based on the typography of the printed page invented in the fifteenth century—fonts, point sizes, type weights, and variable spacing in a million possible combinations, the differences among which don't mean a great deal. There is no directly entered typography in Creator, nor are there in contemporary social media spaces such as Facebook or Twitter. This is how they are able to render effectively to very different devices. Now we also have educational reasons to move to a semantic editor—to prompt students to think explicitly about the form of their text and to make that text more readily analyzable by peers, teachers, and natural language processing technologies.

Affordance 4: Recursive Feedback

What evidence do we have that a student has learned? In didactic pedagogy, the classical answer is to be found in the result of a test. At the end of a period of learning, there is a test, typically "closed book," to see what the student has retained in long-term memory. The focus is essentially cognitive, to draw inferences about an individual's mind. Classical testing logic runs along these lines: cognition developed in learning → observation in a test → interpretation of the test results as evidence of cognition. Cognition itself is inaccessible, so we construct instruments with which we can develop an interpretative argument based on indirect evidence. The process is linear: learn → test. The test is "summative" or retrospective and judgmental. The result is an individualized, "mentalist" (Dixon-Román & Gergen, 2013) construct. Such tests are peculiar artifacts and processes, quite different from the other artifacts and processes of learning, inside and outside school. They are external to the learning process. There is a sharp distinction between times of learning and the time of the test. They are also "standardized" to ensure that all learners are being tested for the same things. Their frame of reference is "normative" to compare students with one another on the assumption that some will prove themselves smarter and others dumber. A "normal" distribution guarantees inequality. In order for the few to be smart, many have to be mediocre and at least some dumb. Comparative inequality among learners is statistically guaranteed (see Figure 1.13).

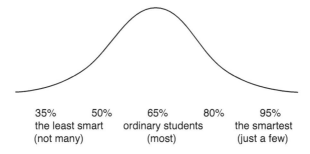

35%	50%	65%	80%	95%
the least smart		ordinary students		the smartest
(not many)		(most)		(just a few)

Figure 1.13 Norm-referenced assessment in standardized tests

Educational technologies can be used to deliver classical tests with no change in their underlying pedagogical and social presuppositions. In fact, they can intensify the process by mechanizing select-response assessments (computer-supported psychometrics) and supply-response assessments (natural language processing). The "standardization" of inequality persists, albeit with ever more obscure algorithmic bases. Mechanization means that educational systems can offer more tests, so teaching comes to be dominated by test prep and the peculiar logic of the test.

But what could be different? How could educational technologies support other ways of measuring evidence of learning? If tests are linear, then how could we create assessment processes that are more reflexive and recursive? In answering this question, we might learn from digital media. Not only are these intrinsically dialogical (captured in the difference between Web 2.0 and its predecessors), but the underlying data systems are recursive. Take, for instance, the mechanisms that underlie "web reputation systems" (Farmer & Glass, 2010)—the recursive reviewing processes that drive e-Bay, Amazon, or YouTube, with their incessant rating, commenting, commenting on comments, and ranking by upvoting those comments that are useful. They are also dialogical. The "stickiness" of social media is in the feedback that comes with quick responses in the form of likes and retweets and then the response to response. Mass media (for instance, newspapers and television) were transmissive rather than dialogical, linear rather than recursive. So was didactic pedagogy. What is going to happen with schooling if we fail to address the disjunction of the traditional didactic discourses of school and the recursive "stickiness" that keeps us engaged with social media? In these media, we have now become active media creators, but we always have a responsive audience. We are always adapting based on friends' or followers' responses. If we don't change our pedagogical ways, then students will become (even more) disaffected with school.

Today's students will not want to wait until the end of the course or the unit of work to be told they have received a grade of B–, which is simply to say something like "you're a bad person; try harder next time." They want and need continuous feedback. Not to be merely retrospective and judgmental, they require feedback that is prospective, constructive, and constitutive of their learning. This may be a machine response in a game or an intelligent tutor, a peer comment against the criterion of a rubric, a select response question where the answer can immediately be checked, a reply in a discussion board, or a review of a work in an e-portfolio. This builds on an older tradition of and literature on "formative assessment" or assessment for learning—though all agree that formative assessment has been badly neglected given the long-standing and ongoing domination of our education systems by summative assessments (Armour-Thomas & Gordon, 2013; Gorin, 2013; Kaestle, 2013; Ryan & Shepard, 2008). The formative/summative distinction was first named by Michael Scriven in 1967 to describe educational evaluation and then applied by Benjamin Bloom and colleagues to the assessment of learning (Airasian, Bloom, & Carroll, 1971; Bloom, 1968). The subsequent literature on formative assessment has consistently argued for its effectiveness (Baker, 2007; Bass & Glaser, 2004; Black & Wiliam, 1998; OECD Centre for Educational Research and Innovation, 2005; Shepard, 2008; Wiliam, 2011).

Moreover, instead of norm-referenced assessment, we might return to some other old but neglected notions. With rich, on-the-fly feedback from multiple sources and perspectives (machine, peers, teacher, self-reflection), it may be more possible for all students to achieve "mastery" (Bloom, 1968). There is no reason why, against the measure of criterion-referenced assessment (see Figure 1.14), that all students in a class should not achieve criterion—particularly with non-standardized instruction (i.e., "differentiated learning"—see affordance 7)—with a lot of formative feedback or interim assessment designed to bring all students up to criterion (see Figure 1.15). In this context, moreover, it is not so relevant whether students meet criterion at a different pace, as long as they do. The measure then is self-referenced or progress assessment. Could we

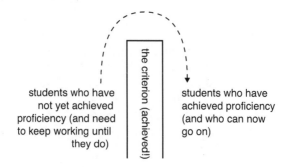

Figure 1.14 Criterion-referenced assessment

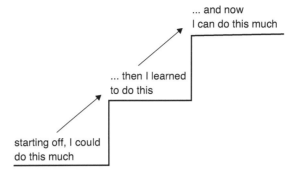

Figure 1.15 Self-referenced or progress assessment

create a no-failure educational paradigm where you can keep taking feedback until you are as good as you are supposed to be? Perhaps this is for the first time possible where the teacher's grade and the test are not the principal forms of feedback. Instead of the B– grade on the test at the end of the term, in the course of that term students may receive tens of thousands of small, incremental pieces of feedback that were responsive to their needs and that they could respond to in turn, realizing the dialogic promise of reflexive pedagogy.

In *Scholar*, over the course of a single project (a piece of writing, documentation of a science experiment, a worked mathematical example), students may receive many hundreds or even thousands of pieces of feedback in a process that is carefully designed by the teacher or the creator of the learning module: a comment from a peer against a criterion in a peer-review rubric, a coded annotation, machine feedback from the natural language processor, an answer to a question in a survey, or a comment in a class discussion (see Figure 1.16). It's not just the teacher who is offering feedback, nor is the feedback coming just at the end. The sources are multiple, incremental, and just-in-time—in fact, there are many more items of peer and teacher feedback than a teacher alone could realistically offer. In the context of Web 2.0, this phenomenon is called crowdsourcing (Surowiecki, 2004)—in this case, crowdsourcing assessment. We have shown that average peer-review ratings across multiple raters in *Scholar* align with expert ratings (Cope et al., 2013).

Feedback is embedded, constructively contributing to the creation of a work during its draft phases (see Figure 1.17). This involves a reframing of learning outcomes as described in standards, from retrospective and judgmental to prospective and constructive, suggesting to reviewers the kinds of feedback that might be most helpful in the revision of the work (see Figure 1.18). Teacher

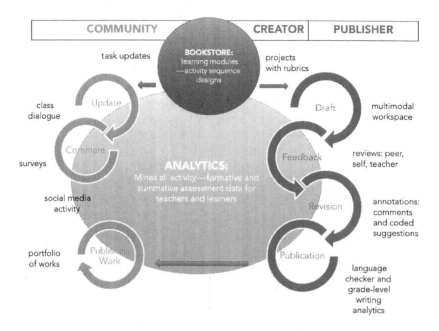

Figure 1.16 The *Scholar* learning and recursive feedback ecology

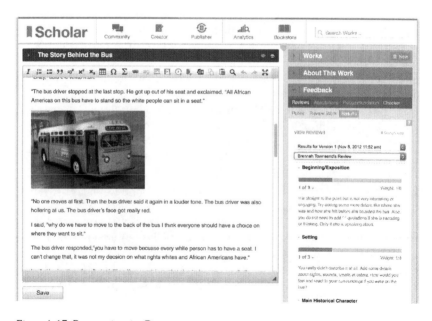

Figure 1.17 Peer review in Creator

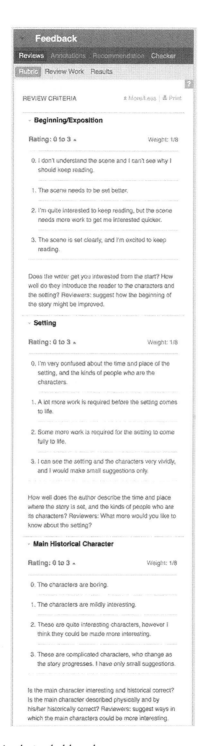

Figure 1.18 Scholar's Analytics dashboard

B: "I think the peer review piece is one of the most important parts of *Scholar*. The students are able to look at a piece of writing and give constructive feedback. Instead of just saying 'good job,' they have a rubric inside of Scholar. I think they really take it seriously because they know that the other student has really put some hard work into their peer review. You can see they are learning from each other. You're learning that we are a team, helping everyone to become a better writer."

The result is an enormous amount of data in different forms and from multiple sources. Figure 1.19 is a snapshot of *Scholar* Analytics in a school with an open-plan learning space where approximately 100 students are writing and offering peer feedback on one another's projects. We have data showing version development, peer/self/teacher assessments, reviews written, annotations made—hundreds of thousands of words, generated over a week of work. It is possible for the teacher to drill down to see every detail, including every piece of feedback and every change the student makes. They can do this at any time during the learning process, not just at the end when papers are turned in. Red warning signs might alert the teacher to a student in need of attention. Teacher C: "Analytics is allowing us to have insights that we never had, when with one teacher and a bunch of papers, it was just too overwhelming."

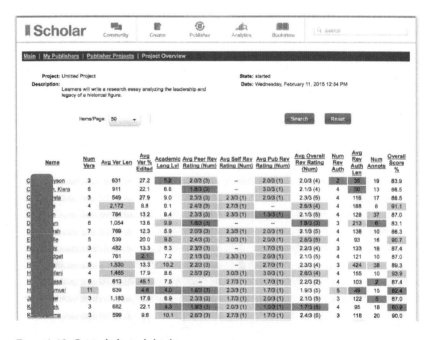

Figure 1.19 Critical clinical thinking peer review

The larger context for these educational technologies has been public discussion of the issue of "big data" in society (Mayer-Schönberger & Cukier, 2013; Podesta et al., 2014) and in education (Cope & Kalantzis, 2015b, 2016; DiCerbo & Behrens, 2014; Piety, 2013). We would like to make a series of propositions toward an agenda for the future of assessment.

1. Assessment can increasingly be *embedded in instruction*, allowing us to realize long-held ambitions to offer richer formative assessment.
2. We may now have so much *interim learning or progress data*, why do we even need these strange artifacts, summative assessments? With the help of data mash-ups and visualizations, the datapoints need only be those located within the learning process. The test is dead; long live assessment!
3. Now that we can assess everything, and there is no learning without reflexive, recursive, machine feedback, peer and teacher feedback, and structured self-reflection, do we even need a distinction between instruction and assessment? There should be no instruction without embedded recursive feedback and no feedback that does not directly and incrementally contribute to learning. Reflexive pedagogy *ends the assessment/instruction distinction*.
4. The focus on what is assessable now shifts from individual cognition to the *artifacts of knowledge representation and their social provenance*. It's not what you can remember but the knowledge artifact you can create, recognizing its sources in collective memory via links and citations and tracing the collaborative construction process via the feedback offered by peers and teachers and the revisions made in response.
5. The focus on what is assessable moves from the repetition of facts and the correct application of theorems to what we call *complex epistemic performance* or the kinds of analytical thinking that characterize disciplinary practices—being a scientist or a writer or applying mathematics to a problem.

Affordance 5: Collaborative Intelligence

Over the course of this analysis, we have been moving away from a focus on individual cognition to a notion of collaborative intelligence. Jim Gee calls this notion the social mind (Gee, 1992/2013). Carl Bereiter calls it distributed cognition (Bereiter, 2002). Perhaps the notion of the individual mind was ever only and at least in part an ideological illusion created by didactic pedagogy and its assessment systems. In e-learning ecologies, it becomes more necessary to recognize the social sources of intelligence. We can also actively nurture the social mind in these environments—hence a renewed focus on collaborative intelligence. There are two fundamental aspects of this new recognition of the sociability of knowledge: a shift away from knowledge memorization toward a culture of knowledge sourcing and developing skills and strategies for knowledge collaboration and social learning.

Today, we have remarkable, world-connected cognitive prostheses at our fingertips, carrying them in our bags or keeping in our pockets. There is no fact that cannot be looked up, no calculation that cannot be made using computational and data access tools in the myriad of apps. Memory may come as an ancillary part of learning and knowledge work, but it need no longer be the central pedagogical concern that it once was. If in everyday life we have ubiquitous access to these cognitive prostheses, then assessments and pedagogies that deny us these lack *validity*, to apply a key term from assessment theory. So replacing the fiction that memory is my personal knowledge, learners must increasingly acknowledge the social sources of their learning, via citations and links, distinguishing clearly their own thoughts from the social knowledge on which those thoughts are built. This is mnemonic work rather than memory work.

The other key aspect of collaborative intelligence is to structure learning systematically around peer collaborations. In Figure 1.20, we see one

Figure 1.20 Cognition (*left*); rubric prompting and metacognition (*right*)

example from *Scholar*—a snapshot of a critical clinical case analysis by a medical student with one of three peers' reviews. This tracks the process of offering a "second opinion," an essential part of the collaborative culture of medicine. In traditional classroom architecture and teacher-coordinated pen-and-paper processes, systematic processes of collaboration are logistically difficult to achieve. However, in e-learning ecologies, it is possible to manage this complexity—random distribution of review requests to a predetermined number of peers, anonymizing creators and reviewers, automatically versioning from draft to revision to publication, and providing data mash-ups that analyze progress. By the time a project has been finished, your work is as good as the collaborations you have had with your peers. All learners have been thinking, but the social provenance of their thinking can be traced in the peer and machine feedback to which they responded in their redrafts as well as their self-reflections on the impact of peer feedback on their revisions. This also shifts the focus of motivation in learning from the grade at the end (an institutional reward, an extrinsic motivation) to the responsibilities of giving feedback and an interest in receiving feedback. This tracks the "stickiness" of digital media—there is a strong motivational force now in the logic of collaboration and task achievement (intrinsic motivation) (Magnifico, Olmanson, & Cope, 2013).

Affordance 6: Metacognition

Metacognition is second-order thinking. It is thinking about thinking. Research shows that metacognitive awareness improves learner performance (Bransford, Brown, & Cocking, 2000). Metacognition can have several meanings. In one, it is psychological: "self-regulation" or to undertake an educational endeavor with self-conscious intent, to focus and to achieve goals (Schunk & Zimmerman, 1994). A broader definition includes thinking that exemplifies disciplinary practice—to think like a historian, writer, or physicist. This requires explicit thinking about the methods of the discipline—for instance, how claims are supported by evidence in history or how persuasion works in writing or to explain mathematical thinking. It also involves theoretical work where learners not only immerse themselves in content, the facts of a topic, but also are able to relate these facts to overall explanatory frameworks, applying facts to frameworks and testing frameworks against facts.

Here we are in *Scholar* again. These students are working on the physics of drag on a cricket ball (see Figures 1.21 and 1.22).

Scholar's Creator space has a temporal structure consisting of several phases (see Figure 1.23). It also has a spatial structure that is designed to support metacognition. The student (or students, in the case of jointly created works) does his or her work in the multimodal editor on the left. Aspects

Figure 1.21 Peer review

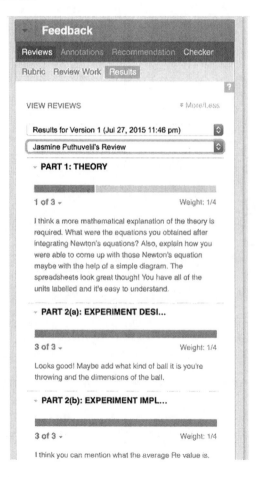

Figure 1.22 The knowledge process: A play between cognition and metacognition

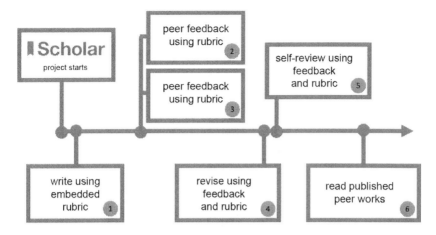

Figure 1.23 Phases in a Scholar project

of metacognition are juxtaposed on the right: a rubric, peer reviews, coded annotations, a natural language processor, dialogue with contributors. In every phase, there is a dialectic between cognition on the left and metacognition on the right:

1. While students create their work on the left, they see the rubric on the right, created by the teacher or learning module designer, specifying disciplinary expectations at a high level of generality.
2. They read their peers' works and review them on the right—the number of reviews having been determined by the teacher/admin, anonymous or named as determined by settings. They may also annotate these works.
3. Feedback is returned, viewable on the right, and the juxtaposed text on the left is revised based on feedback from multiple perspectives and against the same rubric that they have already used intensively in phases 1 and 2.
4. In a self-review on the right, criterion by criterion and against the same rubric, students reflect on the influence of peer feedback on their work and on the changes they have made from version to version, viewable on the left.
5. Finally, the revised work is published to an e-portfolio by the teacher/admin, where further dialogue around the work may occur. The teacher/admin may also review the work at this stage and request revisions before publication. Teacher D: "We see a process of metacognition—I have created a rubric, students are giving feedback to each other, and now we're talking about whether that feedback is worthwhile."

In every phase of this process, there is a play between the left and the right sides of the screen as follows:

Cognition: *Left Side of the Scholar Screen*	Metacognition: *Right Side of the Scholar Screen*
Learning activity: a focus on representation of specific content knowledge	*Self-regulation of learning:* project objectives, phase outline; ongoing dialogue around processes
Disciplinary practice: thinking about a specific topic, its facts and arguments	*Disciplinary thinking:* a focus on the general conditions of insightful work in this discipline; epistemological reflection
Empirical work: outlining specific content and applying disciplinary reasoning to that content	*Theoretical work:* thinking based on the general theoretical precepts of the discipline; a play/dialogue between the particular (thinking about specific details of knowledge) and the general (thinking about conceptual concepts and frameworks that tie this knowledge together)
Individual intelligence: the activity of representing knowledge (including contribution to jointly created works)	*Collaborative intelligence:* structured feedback; productive diversity in learning from varied perspectives
Learning: the knowledge representation made by the student	*Assessment:* formative assessments by peers, teachers, and self; retrospective data analytics

Affordance 7: Differentiated Learning

Traditional educational media were grounded in an architecture of sameness: the whole class listening to the teacher lecture in real time, all the students on the same page of the textbook, and tests that were standardized. New educational media facilitate the management of the complexities of differentiated instruction, where students can be working on different things at the same time. Variants of this notion include adaptive learning, where the environment is responsive to micro-steps made by each student in the learning process, and personalized learning (Conati & Kardan, 2013; Koedinger et al., 2013; McNamara & Graesser, 2012; Wolf, 2010).

To broaden the notion of differentiated learning, we have developed principles for what we call a pedagogy of productive diversity (Kalantzis & Cope, 2016b):

1. *The differentiation principle.* Architectures of pedagogical sameness are no longer logistically necessary, as perhaps they were in the era of didactic pedagogy. It is not necessary that learners do the same tasks

at the same time and in the same way. It is not necessary that they work through and complete a task at the same pace. With today's dashboards, on-the-fly learning analytics, alternative navigation paths, recalibrating systems, and adaptive learning mechanisms, new educational media make the organizational intricacies of productive diversity ever more manageable. In fact, managing learner differences becomes easier than one-size-fits-all teaching because there is not the dissonance of bored or disaffected students for whom the pace of learning may be wrong.

2. *The design principle.* In reflexive pedagogy, learners are positioned as designers of their own knowledge. Students are scaffolded by their teachers and digital learning environments to encounters with available knowledge resources in the world in all of their multivocal and multimodal diversity. They remake that world according to the disciplinary scaffolds that are the studies of science or art or language. They are positioned as disciplinary practitioners—as scientists, as art critics or artists, as critical readers or writers. Now knowledge producers more than knowledge consumers, every artifact of their knowledge (re)making is uniquely voiced—a notion that we have called design (Kalantzis et al., 2016). Learning is no longer a matter of replicating received knowledge from memory. The evidence of learner activity is to be found in designed knowledge artifacts—for instance, students' projects, solutions with workings explained, online discussions, models, or the navigation paths they have taken through games, simulations, or intelligent tutors. As active designers, the world of knowledge is redesigned by learners, revoiced according to the tenor of each learner's interest, identity, and experience.

3. *The collaboration principle.* One unfortunate consequence of personalization with educational technologies can be to individualize the experience of learning, reducing the learning relationship to a lone student with a computer. However, in technology-mediated learning environments designed on social media principles, complex structured social interactions can also be managed. And as soon as the social comes into play, differences become visible and may be deployed as a productive resource. Different perspectives prompt deeper discussion. Providing structured peer feedback exposes learners to different perspectives and ways of thinking. Sharing work in progress and finished work highlights different points of focus and different angles on knowledge. In these ways, learner diversity can be harnessed as a resource for learning.

4. *The comparability principle.* Under the principle of comparability, where assessment rubrics are pitched at a high level of generality, students can be doing different things but of comparable cognitive or practical difficulty. Learners no longer have to be the same to be equal.

Toward Reflexive Pedagogy

In the pages of this book that follow, we will examine these seven pedagogical possibilities in greater detail.

From Didactic Pedagogy	To Reflexive Pedagogy
1. Learning that is institutionally confined in time and space	1. Ubiquitous learning—anytime, anyplace
2. Transmission pedagogy	2. Active knowledge making, where learners are knowledge producers
3. Traditional academic literacies	3. Multimodal meaning and knowledge representations
4. Standardized, summative assessment	4. Recursive feedback
5. Individual memory	5. Collaborative intelligence
6. Single-level content focus	6. Metacognition, double-level thinking
7. One-size-fit-all curriculum	7. Differentiated learning

Educational technologies, as we have argued, can reproduce didactic pedagogies, even to give them an aura of newness that affords them a new life. Meanwhile, the principles of reflexive pedagogy are by no means new. Many of these things we have aspired to do in education for a long time. But now, with educational technologies, they become feasible. The result, we contend, will be learning that is more engaging, more effective, more resource efficient, and more equitable in the face of learner diversity. If anything has decisively changed with the emergence of new educational media, it is to offer a new economy of effort that makes long-held pedagogical ambitions more practicable. Because now that we can, we should.

Note

1. US Department of Education, Institute of Education Sciences: "The Assess-as-You-Go Writing Assistant: A Student Work Environment That Brings Together Formative and Summative Assessment" (R305A090394); "Assessing Complex Performance: A Postdoctoral Training Program Researching Students' Writing and Assessment in Digital Workspaces" (R305B110008); "u-Learn.net: An Anywhere/Anytime Formative Assessment and Learning Feedback Environment" (ED-IES-10-C-0018); "The Learning Element: A Lesson Planning and Curriculum Documentation Tool for Teachers" (ED-IES-10-C-0021); and "InfoWriter: A Student Feedback and Formative Assessment Environment for Writing Information and Explanatory Texts" (ED-IES-13-C-0039). Bill and Melinda Gates Foundation: "Scholar Literacy Courseware." *Scholar* is located at cgscholar.com.

References

Abrams, S. S. (2013). Peer review and nuanced power structures: Writing and learning within the age of connectivism. *e-Learning and Digital Media, 10*, 396–406.

Airasian, P. W., Bloom, B. S., & Carroll, J. B. (1971). *Mastery learning: Theory and practice*. Edited by J. H. Block. New York: Holt, Rinehart & Winston.

Aleven, V., Beal, C. R., & Graesser, A. C. (2013). Introduction to the special issue on advanced learning technologies. *Journal of Educational Psychology, 105*, 929–931.

Armour-Thomas, E., & Gordon, E. W. (2013). *Toward an understanding of assessment as a dynamic component of pedagogy*. Princeton, NJ: The Gordon Commission.

Baker, E. L. (2007). *Moving to the next generation system design: Integrating cognition, assessment, and learning*. Los Angeles: National Center for Research on Evaluation, Standards, and Student Testing, University of California.

Barthes, R. (1977). *Elements of semiology*. New York: Hill and Wang. (Original work published 1964)

Bass, K. M., & Glaser, R. (2004). *Developing assessments to inform teaching and learning*. Los Angeles: National Center for Research on Evaluation, Standards, and Student Testing.

Benedictine University, Center for Mission and Identity. (2016). *The holy rule of St. Benedict*. Retrieved from http://www.ben.edu/center-for-mission-and-identity/resources/rule-of-st-benedict.cfm

Bereiter, C. (2002). *Education and mind in the knowledge age*. Mahwah, NJ: Lawrence Erlbaum.

Bishop, J., & Verleger, M. (2013, June). *The flipped classrom: A survey of the research*. Paper presented at the 120th ASEE Annual Conference and Exposition, Atlanta, GA.

Black, P., & Wiliam, D. (1998). Assessment and classroom learning. *Assessment in Education, 5*, 7–74.

Bloom, B. S. (1968). Learning for mastery. *Evaluation Comment, 1*, 1–2.

Bransford, J. D., Brown, A. L., & Cocking, R. R. (2000). *How people learn: Brain, mind, experience and school*. Edited by N. R. C. Commission on Behavioral and Social Sciences and Education. Washington, DC: National Academy Press.

Burstein, J., & Chodorow, M. (2003). Directions in automated essay scoring. In R. Kaplan (Ed.), *Handbook of applied linguistics* (pp. 529–538). New York: Oxford University Press.

Cazden, C. B. (2001). *Classroom discourse: The language of teaching and learning*. Portsmouth, NH: Heinemann.

Chang, H.-H. (2012). Making computerized adaptive testing diagnostic tools for schools. In R. W. Lissitz & H. Jiao (Eds.), *Computers and their impact on state assessment: Recent history and predictions for the future* (pp. 195–226). Charlotte, NC: Information Age.

Chang, H.-H. (2015). Psychometrics behind computerized adaptive testing. *Psychometrika, 80*, 1–20.

Chaudhri, V. K., Gunning, D., Lane, H. C., & Roschelle, J. (2013). Intelligent learning technologies: Applications of artificial intelligence to contemporary and emerging educational challenges. *AI Magazine, 34*, 10–12.

Chung, G.K.W.K., & Baker, E. L. (2003). Issues in the reliability and validity of automated scoring of constructed responses. In M. D. Shermis & J. C. Burstein (Eds.),

Automated essay scoring: A cross-disciplinary assessment (pp. 23–40). Mahwah, NJ: Lawrence Erlbaum.

Conati, C., & Kardan, S. (2013). Student modeling: Supporting personalized instruction, from problem solving to exploratory open-ended activities. *AI Magazine, 34*, 13–26.

Conrad, S., Clarke-Midura, J., & Klopfer, E. (2014). A framework for structuring learning assessment in a massively multiplayer online educational game: Experiment centered design. *International Journal of Game Based Learning, 4*, 37–59.

Cope, B., & Kalantzis, M. (2009a). "Multiliteracies": New literacies, new learning. *Pedagogies: An International Journal, 4*, 164–195.

Cope, B. & Kalantzis, M. (2009b). Ubiquitous learning: An agenda for educational transformation. In B. Cope & M. Kalantzis (Eds.), *Ubiquitous learning*. Champaign: University of Illinois Press.

Cope, Bill, & Kalantzis, Mary. (2013). Towards a new learning: The "scholar" social knowledge workspace, in theory and practice. *e-Learning and Digital Media, 10*, 334–358.

Cope, B., & Kalantzis, M. (2015a). Assessment and pedagogy in the era of machine-mediated learning. In T. Dragonas, K. J. Gergen, S. McNamee, & E. Tseliou (Eds.), *Education as social construction: Contributions to theory, research, and practice* (pp. 350–374). Chagrin Falls, OH: Worldshare Books.

Cope, B., & Kalantzis, M. (2015b). Sources of evidence-of-learning: Learning and assessment in the era of big data. *Open Review of Educational Research, 2*, 194–217.

Cope, B., & Kalantzis, M. (2016). Big data comes to school: Implications for learning, assessment and research. *AERA Open, 2*, 1–19.

Cope, B., Kalantzis, M., Abd-El-Khalick, F., & Bagley, E. (2013). Science in writing: Learning scientific argument in principle and practice. *e-Learning and Digital Media, 10*, 420–441.

Cope, B., Kalantzis, M., & Magee, L. (2011). *Towards a semantic web: Connecting knowledge in academic research*. Cambridge: Elsevier.

Cope, B., Kalantzis, M., McCarthey, S., Vojak, C., & Kline, S. (2011). Technology-mediated writing assessments: Paradigms and principles. *Computers and Composition, 28*, 79–96.

Cotos, E., & Pendar, N. (2008). Automated diagnostic writing tests: Why? How? In C. A. Chapelle, Y. R. Chung, & J. Xu (Eds.), *Towards adaptive CALL: Natural language processing for diagnostic language assessment* (pp. 65–81). Ames: Iowa State University.

Crossley, S., Allen, L. K., Snow, E. L., & McNamara, D. S. (2015). Pssst . . . textual features . . . there is more to automatic essay scoring than just you! In *Proceedings of the Fifth International Conference on Learning Analytics and Knowledge* (pp. 203–207). New York: ACM.

DeBoer, J., Ho, A. D., Stump, G. S., & Breslow, L. (2014). Changing "course": Reconceptualizing educational variables for massive open online courses. *Educational Researcher, 43*, 74–84.

DiCerbo, K. E., & Behrens, J. T. (2014). *Impacts of the digital ocean on education*. London: Pearson.

Dixon-Román, E. J., & Gergen, K. J. (2013). *Epistemology in measurement: Paradigms and practices*. Princeton, NJ: The Gordon Commission.

Eco, U. (1981). *The role of the reader: Explorations in the semiotics of texts*. London: Hutchinson.

Erl, T., Puttini, R., & Mahmood, Z. (2013). *Cloud computing: Concepts, technology and architecture.* Upper Saddle River, NJ: Prentice Hall.

Farmer, F. R., & Glass, B. (2010). *Web reputation systems.* Sebastapol, CA: O'Reilly.

Foucault, M. (1979). *Discipline and punish: The birth of the prison.* New York: Vintage Books.

Gee, J. P. (2013). *The social mind: Language, ideology, and social practice.* Champaign, IL: Common Ground. (Original work published 1992)

Gorin, J. S. (2013). *Assessment as evidential reasoning.* Princeton, NJ: The Gordon Commission.

Graesser, A. C., VanLehn, K., Rosé, C. P., Jordan, P. W., & Harter, D. (2001). Intelligent tutoring systems with conversational dialogue. *AI Magazine, 22*(4), 39–51.

Halliday, M.A.K. (2002). Spoken and written modes of meaining. In J. J. Webser (Ed.), *On grammar: The collected works of M.A.K. Halliday* (Vol. 1, pp. 323–351). London: Continuum. (Original work published 1987)

Haythornthwaite, C. (2009). Participatory transformations. In B. Cope & M. Kalantzis (Eds.), *Ubiquitous learning* (pp. 32–37). Champaign: University of Illinois Press.

Hmelo-Silver, C. E., Duncan, R. G., & Chinn, C. A. (2007). Scaffolding and achievement in problem-based and inquiry learning: A response to Kirschner, Sweller, and Clark. *Eductional Psychologist, 42,* 99–107.

Kaestle, C. (2013). *Testing policy in the United States: A historical perspective.* Princeton, NJ: The Gordon Commission.

Kalantzis, M., & Cope, B. (1993). Histories of pedagogy, cultures of schooling. In B. Cope & M. Kalantzis (Eds.), *The powers of literacy: A genre approach to teaching literacy* (pp. 38–62). London: Falmer Press.

Kalantzis, M., & Cope, B. (2012). *New learning: Elements of a science of education.* Cambridge: Cambridge University Press.

Kalantzis, M., & Cope, B. (2015). Learning and new media. In D. Scott & E. Hargreaves (Eds.), *The Sage handbook of learning* (pp. 373–387). Thousand Oaks, CA: Sage.

Kalantzis, M., & Cope, B. (2016a). Learner differences in theory and practice. *Open Review of Educational Research, 3,* 85–132.

Kalantzis, M., & Cope, B. (2016b). New media and productive diversity in learning. In S. Barsch & S. Glutsch (Eds.), *Diversity in der LehrerInnenbildung* (pp. 310–325). Münster, Germany: Waxmann.

Kalantzis, M., Cope, B., Chan, E., & Dalley-Trim, L. (2016). *Literacies* (2nd ed.). Cambridge: Cambridge University Press.

Kirschner, P. A., Sweller, J., & Clark, R. E. (2006). Why minimal guidance during instruction does not work: An analysis of the failure of constructivist, discovery, problem-based, experiential, and inquiry-based teaching. *Educational Psychologist, 41,* 75–86.

Kline, S., Letofsky, K., & Woodard, B. (2013). Democratizing classroom discourse: The challenge for online writing environments. *e-Learning and Digital Media, 10,* 379–395.

Knox, J. (2014). Digital culture clash: "Massive" education in the e-learning and digital cultures MOOC. *Distance Education, 35,* 164–177.

Koedinger, K. R., Brunskill, E., Baker, R.S.J.D., & McLaughlin, E. (2013). New potentials for data-driven intelligent tutoring system development and optimization. *AI Magazine, 34,* 27–41.

Lammers, J. C., Magnifico, A. M., & Curwood, J. S. (2014). Exploring tools, places, and ways of being: Audience matters for developing writers. In K. E. Pytash &

R. E. Ferdig (Eds.), *Exploring technology for writing and writing instruction* (pp. 186–201). Hershey, PA: IGI Global.

Landauer, T. K., McNamara, D. S., Dennis, S., & Kintsch, W. (2007). *Handbook of latent semantic analysis*. New York: Routledge.

Magnifico, A., Olmanson, J., & Cope, B. (2013). New pedagogies of motivation: Reconstructing and repositioning motivational constructs in new media-supported learning. *e-Learning and Digital Media, 10*, 484–512.

Mayer-Schönberger, V., & Cukier, K. (2013). *Big data: A revolution that will transform how we live, work, and think*. New York: Houghton Mifflin Harcourt.

McCarthey, S. J., Magnifico, A., Woodard, R., & Kline, S. (2014). Situating technology-facilitated feedback and revision: The case of Tom. In K. E. Pytash & R. E. Ferdig (Eds.), *Exploring technology for writing and writing instruction* (pp. 152–170). Hershey, PA: IGI Global.

McNamara, D. S., & Graesser, A. C. (2012). Coh-Metrix: An automated tool for theoretical and applied natural language processing. In P. M. McCarthy & C. Boonthum-Denecke (Eds.), *Applied natural language processing: Identification, investigation and resolution* (pp. 188–205). Hershey, PA: IGI Global.

McNamara, D. S., Graesser, A. C., McCarthy, P. M., & Cai, Z. (2014). *Automated evaluation of text and discourse with Coh-Metrix*. New York: Cambridge University Press.

Molnar, A., Rice, J. K., Huerta, L., Shafer, S. R., Barbour, M. K., Miron, G., Gulosino, C., & Horvitz, B. (2014). *Virtual schools in the U.S. 2014: Politics, performance, policy and research evidence*. Boulder, CO: National Education Policy Center.

OECD Centre for Educational Research and Innovation. (2005). *Formative assessment: Improving learning in secondary classrooms*. Paris: Organisation for Economic Co-operation and Development.

Ong, W. J. (1958). *Ramus, method and the decay of dialogue*. Cambridge, MA: Harvard University Press.

O'Reilly, T. (2005, September 30). What is Web 2.0? Design patterns and business models for the next generation of software. *O'Reilly Media*. Retrieved from http://www.oreilly.com/pub/a//web2/archive/what-is-web-20.html

Peters, M. A., & Britez, R. G. (2008). *Open education and education for openness*. Rotterdam: Sense.

Peters, M. A., Marginson, S., & Murphy, P. (2008). *Creativity and the global knowledge economy*. New York: Peter Lang.

Piety, P. J. (2013). *Assessing the big data movement*. New York: Teachers College Press.

Podesta, J., Pritzker, P., Moniz, E., Holdern, J., & Zients, J. (2014). *Big data: Seizing opportunities, preserving values*. Washington, DC: Executive Office of the President.

Rousseau, J.-J. (1914). *Emile, or education*. Translated by B. Foxley. London: J. M. Dent & Sons Ltd. (Original work published 1762)

Ryan, K. E., & Shepard, L. A. (2008). *The future of test-based accountability*. New York: Routledge.

Schunk, D. H., & Zimmerman, B. J. (1994). *Self-regulation of learning and performance: Issues and educational applications*. Hillsdale, NJ: Lawrence Erlbaum.

Shepard, L. (2008). Formative assessment: Caveat emperator. In C. A. Dwyer (Ed.), *The future of assessment* (pp. 279–304). Mahawah, NJ: Lawrence Erlbaum.

Shermis, M. D. (2014). State-of-the-art automated essay scoring: Competition, results, and future directions from a United States demonstration. *Assessing Writing, 20*, 53–76.

Shute, V., & Zapata-Rivera, D. (2012). Adaptive educational systems. In P. Durlach & A. Lesgold (Eds.), *Adaptive technologies for training and education* (pp. 7–27). New York: Cambridge University Press.

Speck, J., Gualtieri, E., Naik, G., Nguyen, T., Cheung, K., Alexander, L., & Fenske, D. (2014, March). *ForumDash: Analyzing online discussion forums.* Paper presented at the first annual meeting of the ACM Conference on Learning at Scale, Atlanta, GA.

Surowiecki, J. (2004). *The wisdom of crowds: Why the many are smarter than the few and how collective wisdom shapes business, economies, societies and nations.* New York: Doubleday.

VanLehn, K. (2006). The behavior of tutoring systems. *International Journal of Artificial Intelligence in Education, 16,* 227–265.

Vojak, C., Kline, S., Cope, B., McCarthey, S., & Kalantzis, M. (2011). New spaces and old places: An analysis of writing assessment software. *Computers and Composition, 28,* 97–111.

Vygotsky, L. S. (1978). *Mind in society: The development of higher psychological processes.* Cambridge, MA: Harvard University Press. (Original work published 1962)

Waldrop, M. M. (2013, March 13). Massive open online courses, aka MOOCs, transform higher education and science. *Scientific American.* Retrieved from https://www.scientificamerican.com/article/massive-open-online-courses-transform-higher-education-and-science/

Walkington, C. A. (2013). Using adaptive learning technologies to personalize instruction to student interests: The impact of relevant contexts on performance and learning outcomes. *Journal of Educational Psychology, 105,* 932–945.

Warschauer, M., & Grimes, D. (2008). Automated writing assessment in the classroom. *Pedagogies: An International Journal, 3,* 22–36.

Wiliam, D. (2011). *Embedded formative assessment.* Bloomington, IN: Solution Tree Press.

Wise, A. F., Zhao, Y., & Hausknecht, S. N. (2013). Learning analytics for online discussions: A pedagogical model for intervention with embedded and extracted analytics. In D. Suthers, K. Verbert, E. Duval, & X. Ochoa (Eds.), *Proceedings of the Third International Conference on Learning Analytics and Knowledge* (pp. 48–56). New York: ACM.

Wolf, M. A. (2010). Innovate to educate: System [re]design for personalized learning, a report from the 2010 symposium. Washington, DC: Software and Information Industry Association.

Woolf, B. P. (2010). A roadmap for education technology. GROE. http://www.cra.org/ccc/docs/groe/GROE%20Roadmap%20for%20Education%20Technology%20Final%20Report.pdf

Xu, X., Murray, T., Woolf, B. P., & Smith, D. (2013, July). *Mining social deliberation in online communication: If you were me and I were you.* Paper presented at the 6th International Conference on Educational Data Mining, Memphis, TN.

2 Ubiquitous Learning

Spatio-Temporal Dimensions of e-Learning

Samaa Haniya and Adam Rusch

While riding the car with her parents going on a family trip, 10-year-old Banan accessed Google from her tablet while sitting in the back seat: "OK Google, how old is the universe?" she asked. Google instantly responded: "Age may only be a number, but when it comes to the age of universe, it's a pretty important one. According to research, the universe is approximately, 13.8 billion years old."

This information opened the door for informal family discussion and a new journey of knowledge discovery for Banan. How was the universe first created? How big is it? Why does it keep evolving? How long will it last? From here, the conversation continued with Banan, her little sister, Foziea, and her parents.

This scenario represents a moment of daily life common for a vast majority of the new generation in the digital era. Digital technologies are at the forefront of our world today, and individuals are able to explore a world of knowledge with the click of the mouse, tap of a finger, hand gesture, or voice command. Technology can take you back in time or forward to possible or imagined futures; it can let you travel to any place in a virtual world while you are sitting in your seat; it can take you up to space, help with your homework, or entertain you with the latest movie. New forms of digital media applications and recent technology devices provide seemingly limitless resources and unlimited information. Billions of people across the globe have come to rely on this information.

People rely on these technologies because they save them time and effort and provide for their information needs effectively and efficiently (Burbules, 2006). Consequently, technology is becoming an essential part of our lives, and devices keep evolving to ensure more convenient use. This growing ubiquity of new media applications and portable devices and the instant learning opportunities they offer raises questions about our traditional teaching and learning models.

With new generations immersed in virtual environments and the learning opportunities they offer on a daily basis, we must ask ourselves how education and schools will be affected. What is the purpose and role of the curriculum when knowledge and information are freely shared and curated online? Our students have access to blogs, wikis, apps, and social network platforms. Open resources such as Khan Academy, edX, and Coursera MOOCs provide an exponentially growing number of educational resources on every imaginable subject, including courses from prestigious institutions and scholars that were previously only accessible to a privileged few in the ivory tower. Siri, Galaxy, and OK Google voice search apps answer students' inquiries instantly. Apps like Starfall help children learn how to read. Design platforms like Minecraft allow users to construct their own games. And 3-D printers let individuals create physical models of their own bodies.

This is not simply an expanded exposure to information. It is a new kind of intellectual interaction characteristic of what is being recognized as a knowledge society and a knowledge economy (Peters, Marginson, & Murphy, 2009). Popular media is quick to declare the demise of the old institutions of learning. We are told that public libraries will be replaced by Google and Amazon, colleges will be replaced by MOOCs, and even K–12 schools will be replaced with . . . something, we just don't know what yet. Are our old institutions truly going the way of the dinosaurs or can they be used to create methods of instruction that serve the twenty-first-century learner?

This chapter aims to address these questions by analyzing the affordances of ubiquitous learning and what they mean for learners. We will explore implications of ubiquitous learning for more effective learning, grounded in ever-evolving technologies. Following that, we will address the challenges of facilitating ubiquitous learning through schools and propose some ways to negotiate changing technologies in learning. More examples and case studies of applying ubiquitous learning can be found on our website at newlearning online.com/e-learning.

The Meaning of Ubiquitous Learning

As educational institutions developed in modern societies, something curious happened. We began to see education as a field set apart from real-world problems and everyday life experiences—a place where we talk about the real world in the abstract. The school becomes defined by its spatial and temporal dimensions: a building with four walls, containing blackboards, desks, textbooks, students, and teachers. Teachers impart knowledge to students between the opening and closing bells, assign homework, and then students display mastery of knowledge through essays, quizzes, and tests (Kalantzis & Cope, 2012). This view of education fails to take into account the multiplicity of ways that society and education influence each other—especially in a time of technological innovation and the proliferation of affordable digital devices.

It is important to note that this is not a new idea. Educational philosophers have long sought to rethink education in ways that recognize society's ongoing changes, especially to promote more meaningful learning that connects informal experiences with formal learning (Dewey, 1907). We can see ubiquitous learning as a form of learning on-demand. Digital technologies afford the opportunity to engage in learning anytime, anyplace, and in almost any way that we prefer more easily than ever. This type of learning goes beyond the restrictions of the timetable cells and the physical boundaries of traditional school settings and the didactic pedagogies.

Although older communication technologies, such as the textbook, met the criteria of being portable, they didn't allow for interpersonal interaction where learners can instantly communicate with others. Over the past 20 years, the emergence of ubiquitous computing has led to digital devices becoming more mobile, less expensive, and more accessible to the general public (Burbules, 2009, 2011; Ratner, 2012). Learners can stay engaged with the world through laptops, smartphones, tablets, or even wearable technologies such as smartwatches. Most likely, they have multiple devices. These items have become so ingrained as a part of our lives that we often take them for granted and find it hard to imagine what life would be like without them.

Living in a world of ubiquitous computing means that those who don't have a device with an Internet connection are disadvantaged. They are "located as a 'have not' on the wrong side of the 'digital divide'" (Kalantzis & Cope, 2008, p. 576). They are not able to fully participate in the new world of information. Today, this is considered so important that the United Nations deems access to the Internet to be a human right (United Nations, 2011). The Internet not only provides individuals with a source of essential information but also allows them to collaborate, create, and disseminate their own content through websites and social media platforms, such as blogs, wikis, video sharing sites, and web applications (O'Reilly, 2005). The Internet has become an essential medium of free speech. "From the late 1990s onward, Blogger (1999), Wikipedia (2001), Myspace (2003), Facebook (2004), Flickr (2004), YouTube (2005), Twitter (2006), and a wide array of ensuing platforms began to offer web tools that sparked old and new online communication tactics" (Van Dijck, 2013, p. 7). By September 2016, approximately two billion people were using social networks around the world (Statista, 2016).

The rise of these technologies and the variety of ways people use them has led to a shift in the landscape of information and learning. Students don't need to carry physical papers home from school because their homework assignments are stored online and can be accessed from their home computers. Cloud computing allows shared processing resources and ubiquitous access to information that can promote collaboration and improve productivity among learners online (Reese, 2009; Stohl, 2014). All of these rapid technological developments in hardware and software innovations bring with them potential learning opportunities to understand what is happening in the world around us, have a voice with respect to others, and connect knowledge to real-life problems.

Given this reality of technology innovations, learning happens all day long and takes place in multiple different settings not only in formal institutions but also in informal settings (home, workplace, coffeehouse, etc.). Ubiquitous learning is, then, the ability to take full advantage of ubiquitous technologies as a medium for structured learning opportunities as well as unstructured learning; it is about connecting formal learning institutions with informal learning experiences. It is to grant students of all ages the ability to collaborate, participate, discover, and learn in a global, digital small world and become active citizens.

Implications for Education

Adopting the concept of ubiquitous learning has the potential to be a disruptive force in K–12 schools, higher education institutions, and the workplace. These practices can be used to empower students' learning capabilities. Next we propose four major implications for ubiquitous learning that shift the structure of formal education; these implications are adapted from the frameworks of Burbules (2009) and Cope and Kalantzis (2008). These shifts are (1) transforming when and where we are able to learn, (2) reconfiguring the teacher-student power relationship, (3) rethinking the ways we develop and assess knowledge, and (4) recognizing the way we build organic and collaborative knowledge cultures.

Transforming When and Where We Are Able to Learn

One of the distinguishing features of ubiquitous learning is to break down the confinements of time and space that characterize the traditional classroom. Earlier efforts have been made to bridge these boundaries with the emergence of distance education. An innovation of the twentieth century, distance education was meant to deliver educational content, textbooks, lectures, and assignments to individuals who were geographically distant from formal educational institutions or unable to attend classes by day because of work or family commitments. Communication could occur via postal services with course books and taped audio/visual resources or via broadcast media, such as radio or television (McGorry, 2003; Moore, Dickson-Deane, & Galyen, 2011). However, this type of learning did not include the kinds of synchronous and asynchronous personal interaction that we have seen in online education. Now, ubiquitous learning can go much further in blurring the spatial and temporal boundaries of learning. Learning software platforms regularly include online meeting rooms, bulletin boards, and resource libraries to facilitate live and ongoing interactions among students and instructors.

Even though technology will naturally help informal learning that happens all the time and anywhere, institutional learning often lags far behind. In fact, much of the time, institutional technologies are designed to do the same old things—textbooks and tests can become e-books and e-tests, but the teacher can still stay at the center of a transmission pedagogy. What good does it do for students to have an endless repository of information at their fingertips if they are forbidden to visit any site that isn't on the school's approved list?

The good news is that there are alternatives. In the context of ubiquitous learning, Burbules (2009, 2011) envisions the school to be a hub that connects formal learning to informal learning opportunities outside the school (home, workplace, library, coffee shop, etc.). For example, a teacher doesn't have to just give a lecture about different kinds of trees. He or she could, instead, introduce resources that help students identify trees themselves and then show them how to find lists of parks and forests in their area—perhaps with a website or an app. Their assignment could be to collect the leaves of several varieties of trees over the weekend and then give presentations at the next class meeting. Teachers in this model act as the "equalizers," facilitating the learning process to ensure that the appropriate information connects to the right students with the right technology tools. Learning is seen as a process of acquiring knowledge produced and reproduced through multiple resources. The keys to success rely heavily on interactions and socialization in the co-construction of knowledge.

Many efforts have been made to bring all the connections together from inside and outside classrooms in different learning contexts utilizing ubiquitous technology, such as blended and online learning. Early results look promising. Evidence from a meta-analysis of more than a thousand empirical studies from 1996 to 2008 conducted by the US Department of Education found:

> On average, students in online learning conditions performed modestly better than those receiving face-to-face instruction. The difference between student outcomes for online and face-to-face classes—measured as the difference between treatment and control means, divided by the pooled standard deviation—was larger in those studies contrasting conditions that blended elements of online and face-to-face instruction with conditions taught entirely face-to-face.
>
> (Means et al., 2009, p. ix)

However, having access to technology tools and online learning tools per se does not always lead to any learning improvement if they are not associated with effective implementation and good teacher preparation. In another research study, Hattie (2009) synthesized more than 70 meta-analyses to examine the relation between students' achievement and computer access. He found that the "computer can increase the probability of learning, but there is no necessary relation between having computers, using computers and learning outcomes" (p. 220). Using computers can enhance learning—but only when teachers are well trained on how to use the technology appropriately, utilize a variety of effective strategies such as peer learning or feedback, and when students take responsibility for their learning.

Furthermore, some theorists have begun to explore creative strategies to immerse students in simulation technologies and interactive game-based learning that take students beyond the school walls, virtually at least. Depending on the game's design principles, games can be interactive, engaging, exciting, and multimodal. They engage students in learning while they are following game logic. This learning can be associated with problem-solving techniques and reasoning strategies while the player is playing the game (Gee, 2007). Because learning is embodied and situated within the game and its activities (Lave & Wenger, 1991), effective educational games can empower students' critical thinking abilities and motivate their learning. Clark, Tanner-Smith, and May (2013) examined 77 meta-analyses conducted from 2000 to 2012 to study the effects of digital games on learning compared with traditional instruction. They reported that digital games have a positive effect on students' learning, especially on cognitive competencies. It is important to mention, though, that this effect size can vary according to the game design and principles. In other words, a certain game design can increase or decrease the learning outcomes relative to cognitive competence.

When access to schooling in some parts of the world is limited by poverty, gender inequality, or war, mobile technologies can serve as an equalizing force. These devices have been especially valuable when put in the hands of girls who face the most risk and discrimination. In a global effort, UNESCO has invested heavily in an endeavor to utilize mobile learning technologies in North Africa and the Middle East to achieve the UN Millennium Development Goals in order to alleviate poverty, promote equity, and harness the right to education for all (United Nations, 2012).

Higher education is also moving in this direction via the utilization of e-learning tools (Haythornthwaite & Andrews, 2011; NMC Horizon Report, 2014; Siemens, Gašvić, & Dawson, 2015). Learning in higher education is becoming more flexible and affordable than ever before. Students who cannot attend higher education institutions physically due to work or household responsibilities are now capable of earning their degrees without having to leave their homes. Innovative e-learning applications allow students from anywhere in the world to learn and work collaboratively via synchronous and asynchronous sessions at their convenience (Haythornthwaite & Andrews, 2011).

Some institutions are even distributing their educational materials and course content freely online in order to reach out to a greater number of prospective students. This phenomenon is often called open education. MIT OpenCourseWare was an early example of the open education phenomenon (Bishop & Verleger, 2013; Carson, 2009), which has evolved into MOOCs (Daniel, 2012; Siemens, 2012). MOOCs have received a great deal of media attention as a disruptive force (Christensen, Horn, & Johnson, 2008) in higher education. They offer high-quality online courses free of charge with professors from elite universities. Generally, only students who are seeking a certificate will pay a fee. Evidence from Eckerdal et al. (2014) indicates that the most common effective feature for students in MOOCs is the freedom to learn at anytime and from anywhere.

As good as these open courses and MOOCs seem in theory, though, they are not perfect. Critics point out that despite the lofty goals of providing elite knowledge to everyone, these courses are mostly taken by individuals who are already well educated and credentialed. About 80% of those who completed MOOCs offered by Harvard and MIT in their first year already had bachelor degrees. However, researchers contend that small percentages do not equate to small numbers, and not everyone must complete the course to gain useful knowledge. While only 2.7% of the course registrants (not all of whom completed) came from the UN's list of least developed countries, that accounted for more than 20,000 learners who were at least exposed to the course materials (Ho et al., 2014).

Reconfiguring the Teacher-Student Power Relationship

Perhaps more important than choosing what technology to adopt is understanding that ubiquitous learning changes the power relationship between students and teachers. Ubiquitous learning aims to break down the banking model of education described by Freire (1970). In this model, education is visualized as "an act of depositing, in which the students are the depositories and the teacher is the depositor" (p. 72). Teachers are seen as transmitters of knowledge while students are seen as passive recipients. Students are expected to listen, repeat, and memorize the information that is transmitted from their teachers. Sometimes models are made of assignments or testing regimes that help with the memorization, but it is always the teacher who is expected to remain the agent in charge of the learning opportunity.

This type of relationship is anachronistic to the extent that it does not also reflect the sociocultural changes of our new media times and the sensibilities of a new generation of learners. New media technologies are breaking down the mass media conglomerate that dominated the twentieth century and are enabling renewed forms of participatory culture that transcend geographic boundaries (Jenkins, 2006; Jenkins, Ito, & Boyd, 2016). Fans of *Star Wars*, *Twilight*, or *Harry Potter* don't just read the books and watch the movies, they write their own fan-fiction stories and create super-cut video edits.

Indeed, all generations are becoming more active communicators and cultural producers than ever before, as they participate in an increasingly connected culture (Ito et al., 2013). People now integrate technology seamlessly into everyday life activities. Young children are immersed in the world of games and educational apps (Gee, 2013). Youth are socializing on Facebook; they are critically commenting on a political debate on Twitter; they are sharing their opinions; they are uploading videos of their interest to YouTube (Herrera, 2012). Older people are online for civic engagement, professional development, or to work remotely (Hobbs, 2010).

In the context of ubiquitous learning, pedagogy is moving away from a teacher-centered relationship to a more student-centered relationship (Kalantzis & Cope, 2008, 2012). New forms of relationships between teacher and students are being enacted to reflect what is now the mainstream of socio-cultural change. With the assistance of digital media tools, these forms of relationship are built on mutual collaboration and active learning. This "involves backwards and forwards dialogue" (Cope & Kalantzis, 2008, p. 201) between students and teachers to construct and reconstruct knowledge.

Students are no longer passive learners; they are "co-organizers"— teachers and students work together to achieve the learning goal (Kalantzis & Cope, 2008, 2012). With the massive information knowledge economy, the boundaries between what teachers know and what students know are being blurred. In order to guide students to become agents of learning, teachers may need to let go of the traditional view that they hold full control of a classroom. In some cases, teachers are becoming learners themselves as they learn new tricks and techniques from students (Burbules, 2011). No one has optimal expertise in everything; we are all students and teachers, employees and directors, males and females, young and old, abled and disabled, domestic and international. Individuals are all experts in certain ways (Eubanks, 2011).

Nationally and globally, promising policies and standards have been formed to encourage and reinforce this type of relationship that engages students in active learning through technology mediated environments. One recent example of these standards is the National Education Technology Plan developed by the US Department of Education in 2016. This plan puts out a new set of technology standards and principles to reimagine the role of technology in education. It aims to empower teaching and learning and to promote active leadership and better assessments while also shedding light on digital access and active use of technology for all learners regardless of their backgrounds and grade levels (US Department of Education, 2016). To name other examples, consider the case of the Common Core State Standards Initiative (2009), the Partnership for 21st Century Skills learning frameworks (2002), and the International Society for Technology in Education's standards for teachers (2008).

With the affordances of ubiquitous technologies, teachers are able to scaffold learning, enriching classroom practices with constructive online class discussions, peer-to-peer evaluation, and posing critical thinking problems. In this new dialogical relationship between teachers and learners, knowledge is not something that is imposed on students for them to memorize. Instead, this model allows learning to be customized according to individuals' unique interests in what in the final chapter of this book we call differentiated learning (Kalantzis & Cope, 2012). Students are encouraged to share their own knowledge and distinctive experiences and to think critically toward solutions to problems via digital media tools. As a result, students develop accumulative knowledge. In fact, these collaborative relationships and gained skills are significant to prepare students for the workplace in the future as they grow up in a complex and diverse society based on knowledge economy.

One of the most common teaching strategies to change the student-teacher relationship is the flipped learning approach. Instead of having teachers lecture to students in the class, this approach allows students to view the educational content and video lectures online outside the classroom and to use class time for reflection, discussion, and collaborations (Bergmann & Sams, 2014; Bishop & Verleger, 2013). A good example of flipped learning can be seen in MOOCs offered by the Coursera platform. Generally, in this type of MOOC, learners first explore the subject matter more deeply via watching a set of instructional, recorded videos online. Then they utilize wikis, forums, blogs, and learning management systems for completing assignments, facilitating class discussion, and increasing the breadth of content interactions among peers via active learning (Viberg & Messina Dahlberg, 2013; Yousef et al., 2014).

In addition to the MOOC model, there are also other technology tools and e-learning platforms that promote student-centered relationships, such as the case of *Scholar*. *Scholar* is an e-learning platform developed to translate into practice ideas from the research group that wrote this book. It is equipped with technology features and interconnected spaces to facilitate digital writing and active learning between the learners and the instructors in K–12 and higher education settings. Several research studies have attempted to examine the use of the *Scholar* platform in different contexts to support engaged learning. The findings reveal that platforms like this have a potential value to enhance students' writing through collaboration, active learning, peer review, and formative evaluation (Ahn & Greene, 2013; Cope et al., 2011; Lammers, Magnifico, & Curwood, 2014; McCarthey et al., 2013).

As shown in the earlier examples, well-designed platforms and effective teaching strategies offer ubiquitous learning opportunities to promote a more student-centered relationship and to foster collaborative learning between students and teachers.

Rethinking the Way We Develop and Assess Knowledge

One of the biggest breaks that ubiquitous learning brings to the structure of education in our society is in the way we conceptualize and develop knowledge. The concept of universal education is built on the premise that all young people will attend formal schools (or at least engage in a formal educational system involving tutors or study materials). With the development of formalized schooling, education has embraced a transmission model of knowledge from the teacher to the student. Benedict of Nursia, patron saint of Europe and founder of Western monasticism, said in his rules for monastic life that "it belongeth to the master to speak and to teach; it becomes the disciple to be silent and to listen" (Benedictine University, Center for Mission and Identity, 2016). This monastic system is credited as being the precursor to modern schools and university systems (Cope & Kalantzis, 2015b).

It is only in the last century that different scholars have been able to gain traction in challenging this idea. Dewey (1907) advocated that the separation of schooling from daily life was a problem. Students go to school to learn academic subjects, but these subjects are separate from the environment around their community, the work they do at their parents' shops, or the daily household chores they are assigned. The alternate to schooling could be an apprenticeship, where a student learns how to practice a trade through the mentorship of a master. Instead of thinking of learning as either at school or through work apprenticeship with life happening in between, we should look for every opportunity to connect learning to all aspects of everyday life. Dewey believes that by doing this we will not only improve the education of our students but also have the opportunity to enact real social reforms.

Technology allows students, first of all, to take their learning materials with them wherever they go. Students don't just have to read about different kinds of trees in a textbook, they can go into the woods and identify different kinds of trees with a smartphone app. Or, conversely, if a student is at home and asked to make dinner for his or her family, then he or she can look up cooking class videos on YouTube. Lifelong learners can also use technology for their personal interests, perhaps listening to an informative podcast while commuting to work.

The problem is that even with all of these technological advancements that afford us the opportunity to enact academic reform, we often use technologies simply to replicate traditional practices. For instance, a traditional way to make sure that students have done an assigned reading is to quiz them on key points of the text. We can find many variations of quiz software that can serve this function online. The assumption is that if students have memorized the key points of the reading, then they have learned something valuable.

In an age of ubiquitous computing and ubiquitous learning, however, we may need to rethink some of these assumptions. Is memorization of key material essential for a student who is able to have constant access to knowledge repositories through electronic devices? Burbules (2009) points out that our devices serve as memory enhancement tools, which can allow us to look up far more information than we would ever be able to memorize. He uses the term *extensible intelligence* to describe how students' memory and processing powers are enhanced by the ability to supplement their own memory as well as participate in networked intelligence through these devices (Burbules, 2009).

If technology is causing students to access information and develop knowledge in new ways, then we need to find new ways to assess what and how well they are learning. Instead of just quizzing students or looking for ways to gauge their level of memorization, we should examine the knowledge artifacts that they are able to produce. In an online learning environment, discussion boards are often used to take the place of in-person discussion. Online essays don't need to be restricted to just text and figures printed on paper, they can also include multimedia and links to related materials. It is now easier than ever for individuals to create their own multimedia thanks to smartphones and inexpensive digital camcorders.

We are also developing tools to help us sort through all these materials on a meta level thanks to the "big data" captured by learning tools. The software we use to facilitate learning environments can keep track of keystrokes, clicked links, word count, language level, cross-references, and many other factors (Baker & Siemens, 2014). Seeing what knowledge the students produce, as well as when they are not participating, can help educators determine their level of accomplishment and what areas need improvement.

Unlike in the conventional approach to learning, where learning outcomes are only measured once or twice a year via high-stakes standardized testing, ubiquitous technologies can support high-quality learning outcomes. It has been argued widely that standardized testing does not do a good job of measuring learning outcomes. These tests are only able to determine whether students can recall a standard repertoire of information; they cannot show how well students are developing or sharing knowledge.

Instead of stressing knowledge development and improving learning, standardized testing problematizes the educational process. Teachers will be under pressure to teach for the purpose of students just passing the exams without a focus on how they are developing knowledge. The biggest lesson that students learn is that the point of their schooling is to be able to simply repeat back key bits of information. According to Wiggin and McTighe (2007), "effective assessment involves a synthesis of valid information from a variety of resources – a photo album not a single snapshot" (p. 230). Shifting the educational system to a ubiquitous learning model where information is constantly being engaged and numerous knowledge artifacts are being produced is a better way to get this essential collection of assessment resources.

A system like this will hold students more accountable for their learning. Knowledge artifacts can be shared among students to inform peers of interesting information or show off what they have learned. Also, learning systems can include Educational Data Mining tools, which capture all students' activities and every keystroke they hit immediately and visualize it in one screen. Their voices are always heard, their actions are always seen, and their assignments are always stored in the cloud. All data points and clickstream patterns can be mapped and clustered in crowdsourced platforms (Baker & Siemens, 2014; Cope & Kalantzis, 2015a).

Being aware of this fact, students take their learning more seriously. Consequently, this information will in turn help teachers to refine their teaching practices to optimize the best learning practices possible for all students. A systematic review of an empirical research study on Learning Analytics and Educational Data Mining during from 2008 to 2013 reveals that these techniques add value to students' interaction and that they can help students to adapt and personalize learning according to their needs (Papamitsiou & Economides, 2014).

Recognizing the Way We Build Organic and
Collaborative Knowledge Cultures

When we move beyond the traditional boundaries of education needing to occur in a prescribed fashion, we see that a learning outcome does not end at a certain point. Burbules (2009) describes this phenomenon as a change in worldview called lifelong learning. The old worldview posits that children first engage in learning through elementary and secondary schools. They move on to colleges, trade schools, or workforce development training, and are finally done with their education and ready to become workers. Perhaps they have some continuing education, but it is all focused around extrinsic motivations of proficiency. Lifelong learning, on the other hand, is about the intrinsic motivation of growth, whether that can happen in structured or unstructured settings. In other words, learning is constant, or as Burbules puts it, "to be is to learn" (p. 20).

Lave and Wenger (1991) put forward that a more natural form of learning happens in communities of practice, where like-minded people form groups to mentor new members and collaborate to advance a common practice. Like Dewey, they take issue with the separation of academic learning from everyday life experiences. Too often, formal schooling focuses on the individual students learning set materials and assesses them on the ability to recall the knowledge. Lave and Wenger show how collaboration as part of a community united in common practice provides opportunities for novices to gain knowledge through mentorship, become mentors themselves once they have learned enough, and then work with others to help create new knowledge that will advance the practice for the community.

Ultimately we find that the lines between formal and informal learning become blurred with ubiquitous learning. Formal learning systems have become less didactic, with students engaging in work outside the classroom as well as bringing their interests into the classroom. At the same time, technologies allow interested people to come together online in ways that transcend time and space to engage in communities and courses like MOOCs that build on traditional academic models.

The rise of MOOCs can be seen as a way for traditional educational institutions to expand their course offerings to larger audiences. What distinguishes a MOOC from a traditional academic class is the scale of the participating membership. While a course offered by a university (even an online course) may be limited to as few as a dozen or as many as a couple hundred students, a comparable MOOC could have thousands or tens of thousands of people participating. Many major universities have come together to form consortiums such as edX (MIT, Harvard, Berkeley), Coursera (Stanford, Princeton, Michigan), and others (Yousef et al., 2014).

Most MOOCs follow the model that the information is free, but a fee will be charged to receive credentials that the course was completed. Assessment is generally automated through electronic quizzes, text analysis of discussion boards, or peer-reviewed essay assignments. Credentialing generally requires a registration fee and an extra step to verify the student's identity, such as the Coursera Signature Track system that takes your picture with a web cam and records your unique typing pattern with a writing sample (see https://www.coursera.org/signature/). The sponsor of a MOOC course may also be trying to entice students to sign up for a degree program, such as the University of Illinois iMBA program. Students in this program complete much of their work through the verified Coursera courses but also have additional assignments directly through the university that will allow them to earn the MBA degree (see https://onlinemba.illinois.edu/faq/).

Other traditional academic models that take advantage of technology to offer lifelong learning opportunities include TED Talks (see https://www.ted.com/talks), self-described as "a nonprofit devoted to Ideas Worth Spreading"; Khan Academy (see https://www.khanacademy.org/), a nonprofit offering short lecture videos mostly on mathematics and STEM topics; and The Great Courses (see http://www.thegreatcourses.com/), a subscription service of academic lectures. While many of the materials offered in these services may be academic in nature, the learners are engaging for personal motivation rather than for a credential or program requirement.

Engagement with lifelong learning materials such as these becomes an integral part of organic and collaborative learning cultures. In an organic culture, the community will draw from all sorts of different sources to find interesting information that can be discussed among members. There may also be planned learning cultures surrounding these materials—such as the discussion boards that accompany online offerings—but we will find them to be collaborative as well when interested individuals offer their own interpretations or ideas spurred from the materials.

The Challenges and Concerns of Ubiquitous Learning

For all good things, there are also pitfalls, challenging issues, and limitations that may hinder the successful deployment of ubiquitous learning models in an educational context. Too often, people assume that simply bringing new technologies into the classroom will also bring the learning advancement being sought. They do not realize that technological tools have their own inherent biases and may create unforeseen circumstances, even when implemented with care (Burbules, Callister, & Taaffe, 2006).

Similarly, Gee (2013) writes,

> I want to warn that digital tools are no salvation. They can make things worse just as easily as they can make things better. They are great tools with which to become dumber just as they are great tools with which to become smarter. It all depends on how they are used. . . . And key to their good use is that they be subordinated to ways of connecting humans for

rich learning and that they serve as tools human learners own and operate and do not simply serve.

(p. xiii)

In other words, technology can be either completely benign or actively harmful instead of helpful if it is not used properly. Even when some technological tool does offer a solution to a previous problem, it will also introduce new problems that must be addressed. Next we outline three major challenges that may influence the successful deployment of ubiquitous learning in any educational context.

Validity and Safety of Online Content

Online safety is one of the main concerns when integrating technology in education. In 2001, the US Congress enacted the Children's Internet Protection Act that required schools and libraries to adopt an Internet safety policy in exchange for discounted costs on Internet access. The Federal Communications Commission has set the requirements to include blocking minors' access to sites that have obscene, pornographic, or harmful materials. They are also required to have education programs that teach minors how to safely access and appropriately interact with others on the web. (See www.ala.org/advocacy/advleg/federallegislation/cipa for more information.)

Safety is not the only concern for minors who use the Internet. The massive information available online makes it difficult for individuals, especially younger or newer users, to distinguish between valid and invalid information. This is in addition to the chances of having students accidentally or knowingly browse inappropriate web content. Goodison and Herald (2007) described how a program was put at risk when students in Nigeria used donated XO laptops to view inappropriate websites. Students may also intentionally or unknowingly get around safety filters to access sites with pornography, hate sites, or be contacted by people who are looking to prey upon them. "It is precisely those new users to whom we are trying to provide greater access who are at the greatest risk of being abused or exploited by online content" (Burbules, Callister, & Taaffe, 2006, p. 92).

Without guidance and scaffolding, learning in ubiquitous digital environments may lead students away from desired educational goals. To avoid such a problem, there is a need to develop awareness among students and teachers of such dilemmas. Both students and teachers should understand the way that search engines like Google and Bing track user activity and use the data to push custom advertisements and site suggestions into search results. In addition, there is a need to increase awareness among parents, teachers, and the community by holding technology workshops or training sessions. This may be a way to help parents and community members feel more confident about engaging in discussions with their children about safe technology usage instead of feeling like it is a subject that is far above their understanding.

Challenges With Teachers' Preparation

According to Rogers (1962) in his theory of diffusion of innovation, when new innovations emerge, not everyone in society will be able to adopt the innovation to the same extent. Some people will be skeptical (34%) and laggards (16%) to new innovations. In a previous study, Cuban (2001) found that some teachers were resistant to using technology in teaching methods because they did not have enough time to learn new technology applications, let alone integrate them into teaching practices. Consequently, some teachers may reject using new technology applications in teaching and learning processes and prefer to teach based on the traditional pedagogical practices—the way they have been taught.

Yet new generations of students will not accept this kind of traditional teaching. These students have become fast learners. They like to get information quickly, with less time and less effort, often multitasking their work (Prensky, 2001). Through ongoing professional development programs, teachers can find a way to deal with these novice students. They can be trained on how to catch up with recent technology in order to best teach these digital students how to focus their energies in ways that result in real learning from the classroom, to the home, and into their professional careers in the future.

Digital Divide Concerns

Although we have spent much of this chapter talking about the digital generation immersed in technologies, it is important to recognize that serious inequalities still exist in our society. The phrase *digital divide* captures the idea that people who do not have access to the Internet and to computing devices are being left behind in the proliferation of information access. Students on the wrong side of the digital divide will have a major disadvantage when it comes to collaboration and learning. Stakeholders and policy makers need to ensure digital inclusion and that all students have access to modern technologies regardless of their backgrounds (Crawford, 2013).

Eubanks (2011) problematized the notion of the digital divide, not so much as a matter of inequality of access to the devices and conduits but as related to learning the skills of how to use these tools to achieve social justice and digital citizenship. Other researchers identified different forms of digital divides, with some relating it to gender (Sullivan, 2002), race (Watkins, 2012), or students with disabilities (Jaeger, 2014). There is also a global digital divide among developing and developed countries (Burbules, Callister, & Taaffe, 2006). With that said, teachers need to consider these challenges when planning any ubiquitous learning environments so as to find ways to bridge the digital divide in the classroom as much as possible to support learning for all students.

Conclusion

In a time of rapidly changing technological tools, no single device or technique will be the perfect fit to ensure a successful learning practice. The structure and practice of the traditional education system arose with the use of tools that had been available for hundreds of years. Whether they were the best approach is debatable, but the stability offered by tried-and-true methods of instruction gave a sense of order to the process of formal education.

With the advent of ubiquitous computing, we now are able to enact many of the educational reforms that have long been proposed but difficult to achieve. We have the opportunity to move past the idea that learning happens only within the confines of formal schooling and that a one-size-fits-all approach will give our students the education they deserve. Our teaching approaches must be as diverse as the tools that enable ubiquitous computing so that our students learn to live in a world of ubiquitous learning.

References

Ahn, J., & Greene, J. C. (2013). Evaluating the developmental stages of digital educational programs: Challenges and opportunities. *e-Learning and Digital Media, 10*(4), 470–482.

Baker, R.S.J.D., & Siemens, G. (2014). Educational data mining and learning analytics. In K. Sawyer (Ed.), *Cambridge handbook of the learning sciences* (2nd ed., pp. 253–274). New York: Cambridge University Press.

Benedictine University, Center for Mission and Identity. (2016). *The rule of St. Benedict.* Retrieved from http://www.ben.edu/center-for-mission-and-identity/resources/rule-of-st-benedict.cfm

Bergmann, J., & Sams, A. (2014). *Flipped learning: Gateway to student engagement.* Arlington, VA: International Society for Technology in Education.

Bishop, J. L., & Verleger, M. A. (2013, June). *The flipped classroom: A survey of the research.* Paper presented at the 120th ASEE Annual Conference and Exposition, Atlanta, GA.

Burbules, N. (2006). Self-educating communities: Collaboration and learning through the Internet. In Z. Bekerman, N. Burbules, & D. Silberman-Keller (Eds.), *Learning in places: The informal education reader* (pp. 273–284). New York: Peter Lang.

Burbules, N. (2009). Meanings of "ubiquitous learning." In B. Cope & M. Kalantzis (Eds.), *Ubiquitous learning* (pp. 15–20). Urbana: University of Illinois Press.

Burbules, N. (2011). Ubiquitous learning as a social foundations issue. In S. Tozer, B. P. Gallegos, & A. M. Henry (Eds.), *Handbook of research in the social foundations of education* (pp. 527–533). New York: Routledge.

Burbules, N. C., Callister, T. A., Jr., & Taaffe, C. (2006). Beyond the digital divide. In S. Y. Tettegah & R. C. Hunter (Eds.), *Technology and education: Issues in administration, policy and applications in K–12 schools* (pp. 85–99). St. Louis, MO: Elsevier.

Carson, S. (2009). The unwalled garden: Growth of the OpenCourseWare Consortium, 2001–2008. *Open Learning: The Journal of Open, Distance and e-Learning, 24*(1), 23–29.

Christensen, C. M., Horn, M. B., & Johnson, C. W. (2008). *Disrupting class: How disruptive innovation will change the way the world learns* (Vol. 98). New York: McGraw-Hill.

Clark, D. B., Tanner-Smith, E. E., & May, S. K. (2013). *Digital games for learning: A systematic review and meta-analysis*. Menlo Park, CA: SRI International.

Cope, B., & Kalantzis, M. (2008). Ubiquitous learning: An agenda for educational transformation. In V. Hodgson, C. Jones, T. Kargidis, D. McConnell, S. Retalis, D. Stamatis, & M. Zenios (Eds.), *Proceedings of the Sixth International Conference on Networked Learning 2008* (pp. 576–582). Lancaster, UK: Lancaster University.

Cope, B., & Kalantzis, M. (2015a). Assessment and pedagogy in the era of machine-mediated learning. In T. Dragonas, K. J. Gergen, & S. McNamee (Eds.), *Education as social construction: Contributions to theory, research, and practice* (pp. 350–374). Chagrin Falls, OH: Worldshare Books.

Cope, B., & Kalantzis, M. (2015b). Sources of evidence-of-learning: Learning and assessment in the era of big data. *Open Review of Educational Research, 2*(1), 194–217.

Cope, B., Kalantzis, M., McCarthey, S., Vojak, C., & Kline, S. (2011). Technology-mediated writing assessments: Principles and processes. *Computers and Composition, 28*(2), 79–96.

Crawford, S. P. (2013). *Captive audience: The telecom industry and monopoly power in the new gilded age*. New Haven, CT: Yale University Press.

Cuban, L. (2001). *Oversold and underused: Computers in the Classroom*. Cambridge, MA: Harvard University Press.

Daniel, J. (2012). Making sense of MOOCs: Musings in a maze of myth, paradox and possibility. *Journal of Interactive Media in Education, 3*, 18. http://doi.org/10.5334/2012-18

Dewey, J. (1907). *The school and society*. Chicago: University of Chicago Press.

Eckerdal, A., Kinnunen, P., Thota, N., Nylén, A., Sheard, J., & Malmi, L. (2014, June). *Teaching and learning with MOOCs: Computing academics' perspectives and engagement*. Paper presented at the 19th Annual Conference on Innovation and Technology in Computer Science Education, Uppsala, Sweden.

Eubanks, V. (2011). *Digital dead end: Fighting for social justice in the information age*. Cambridge, MA: MIT Press.

Freire, P. (1970). *Pedagogy of the oppressed*. Translated by Myra Bergman Ramos. New York: Continuum.

Gee, J. P. (2007). *Good video games plus good learning*. New York: Peter Lang.

Gee, J. P. (2013). *The anti-education era: Creating smarter students through digital learning*. New York: Palgrave Macmillan.

Goodison, D., & Herald, B. (2007, July 23). XXX-tracurricular activities: Kids use donated laptops to find porn. *Wicked Local*. Retrieved from http://cambridge.wickedlocal.com/x113133218

Hattie, J. (2009). *Visible learning: A synthesis of over 800 meta-analyses relating to achievement*. New York: Routledge.

Haythornthwaite, C., & Andrews, R. (2011). *E-learning theory and practice*. Thousand Oaks, CA: Sage.

Herrera, L. (2012). Youth and citizenship in the digital era: A view from Egypt. *Harvard Educational Review, 82*(3), 333–352.

Ho, A. D., Reich, J., Nesterko, S., Seaton, D. T., Mullaney, T., Waldo, J., & Chuang, I. (2014). *HarvardX and MITx: The first year of open online courses* (HarvardX and MITx Working Paper No. 1). Cambridge, MA: Harvard University.

Hobbs, R. (2010). *Digital and media literacy: A plan of action: A white paper on the digital and media literacy recommendations of the Knight Commission on the information needs of communities in a democracy*. Washington, DC: Aspen Institute.

Ito, M., Gutiérrez, K., Livingstone, S., Penuel, B., Rhodes, J., Salen, K., . . . & Watkins, S. C. (2013). *Connected learning: An agenda for research and design*. Irvine, CA: Digital Media and Learning Research Hub.

Jaeger, P. T. (2014). Internet justice: Reconceptualizing the legal rights of persons with disabilities to promote equal access in the age of rapid technological change. *Review of Disability Studies: An International Journal, 9*(1), 39–59.

Jenkins, H. (2006). *Convergence culture: Where old and new media collide*. New York: New York University Press.

Jenkins, H., Ito, M., & Boyd, D. (2016). *Participatory culture in a networked era*. Malden, MA: Polity Press.

Kalantzis, M., & Cope, B. (2012). *New learning: Elements of a science of education*. Cambridge: Cambridge University Press. (Original work published 2008)

Lammers, J. C., Magnifico, A. M., & Curwood, J. C. (2014). Exploring tools, places, and ways of being: Audience matters for developing writers. In K. Pytash & R. Ferdig (Eds.), *Exploring technology for writing and writing instruction* (pp. 186–201). Hershey, PA: IGI Global.

Lave, J., & Wenger, E. (1991). *Situated learning: Legitimate peripheral participation*. New York: Cambridge University Press.

McCarthey, S., Magnifico, A., Woodard, R., & Kline, S. (2013). Situating technology-facilitated feedback and revision: The case of Tom. In K. E. Pytash & R. E. Ferdig (Eds.), *Exploring technology for writing and writing instruction* (pp. 152–170). Hershey, PA: IGI Global.

McGorry, S. Y. (2003). Measuring quality in online programs. *The Internet and Higher Education, 6*(2), 159–177.

Means, B., Toyama, Y., Murphy, R., Bakia, M., & Jones, K. (2009). *Evaluation of evidence-based practices in online learning: A meta-analysis and review of online learning studies*. Washington, DC: US Department of Education.

Moore, J. L., Dickson-Deane, C., & Galyen, K. (2011). e-Learning, online learning, and distance learning environments: Are they the same? *The Internet and Higher Education, 14*(2), 129–135.

NMC Horizon Report. (2014). *Higher education edition*. Austin, TX: The New Media Consortium.

O'Reilly, T. (2005, September 30). What is web 2.0: Design patterns and business models for the next generation of software. *O'Reilly Media*. Retrieved from http://www.oreilly.com/pub/a/web2/archive/what-is-web-20.html

Papamitsiou, Z., & Economides, A. (2014). Learning analytics and Educational Data Mining in practice: A systematic literature review of empirical evidence. *Educational Technology & Society, 17*(4), 49–64.

Peters, M. A., Marginson, S., & Murphy, P. (2009). *Creativity and the global knowledge economy*. New York: Peter Lang.

Prensky, M. (2001). Digital natives, digital immigrants. *On the Horizon, 9*(5), 1–6.

Ratner, H. (2012). Living online: Anytime, anywhere, any device. *Information Services and Use, 32*(1), 49–54.

Reese, G. (2009). *Cloud application architectures: Building applications and infrastructure in the cloud*. Sebastopol, CA: O'Reilly Media.

Rogers, E. M. (1962). *Diffusion of innovations*. New York: Free Press.

Siemens, G. (2012, July 25). MOOCs are really a platform. *Elearnspace*. Retrieved from http://www.elearnspace.org/blog/2012/07/25/moocs-are-really-a-platform

Siemens, G., Gašvić, D., & Dawson, S. (2015). *Preparing for the digital university: A review of the history and current state of distance, blended, and online learning*. Retrieved from http://linkresearchlab.org/PreparingDigitalUniversity.pdf

Statista. 2016. *Most famous social networks worldwide as of September 2016, ranked by number of active users (in millions)*. Retrieved from http://www.statista.com/statistics/272014/global-social-networks-ranked-by-number-of-users/

Stohl, C. (2014). Crowds, clouds, and community. *Journal of Communication*, 64(1), 1–19.

Sullivan, P. (2002). "It's easier to be yourself when you are invisible": Female college students discuss their online classroom experiences. *Innovative Higher Education*, 27(2), 129–144.

United Nations. (2011). *Promotion and protection of all human rights, civil, political, economic, social and cultural rights, including the right to develop*. Retrieved from http://www2.ohchr.org/english/bodies/hrcouncil/docs/17session/A.HRC.17.27_en.pdf

United Nations. (2012). *United Nations Millennium Development Goals*. Retrieved from http://www.un.org/millenniumgoals/

US Department of Education. (2016). *Future ready learning: Reimagining the role of technology in education*. Retrieved from http://tech.ed.gov/files/2015/12/NETP16.pdf

Van Dijck, J. (2013). *The culture of connectivity: A critical history of social media*. Oxford: Oxford University Press.

Viberg, O., & Messina Dahlberg, G. (2013, November). MOOCs' *structure and knowledge management*. Paper presented at the 21st International Conference on Computers in Education, Denpansar, Indonesia.

Watkins, S. (2012). Digital divide: Navigating the digital edge. *International Journal of Learning and Media*, 3(2), 1–12.

Wiggins, G., & McTighe, J. (2007). *Schooling by design: Mission, action, and achievement*. Alexandria, VA: Association for Supervision and Curriculum Development.

Yousef, A., Chatti, M., Schroeder, U., Wosnitza, M., & Jakobs, H. (2014, April). MOOCs: *A review of the state-of-the-art*. Paper presented at the 6th International Conference on Computer Supported Education, Barcelona, Spain.

3   Active Knowledge Making

Epistemic Dimensions of e-Learning

Tabassum Amina

Tell me and I will forget; show me and I may remember; involve me and I will understand.

—Confucius, 450 BC

Acquisition of knowledge has been structured into a recognizable and mostly consistent format since the introduction of mass-institutionalized education. This predictable and straightforward configuration includes a bureaucratic apparatus that prescribes content areas to be learned in the syllabus, textbooks that lay out the content, teacher recitation that includes teacher-student question-and-answer routines, filling out answers in workbooks, reading texts and answering comprehension questions, and writing short texts to check what had been learned. In this knowledge system, students are primarily expected to be passive knowledge consumers. It is declarative knowledge that is transmitted to learners as univocal narrative with the expectation of unquestioned compliance to epistemic authority. The learner's role is limited to receiving the knowledge that is directly given to pass tests that are structured on the preset information already provided in the classroom. This role mostly excludes any expectation or space for making any critical active involvement. Such has been the norm since the beginnings of the modern era of industrial discipline and mass conformity. However, with the advancement of technology and easier access to knowledge, this traditional orientation is changing. It is now possible to position learners as more active knowledge makers. This chapter defines active knowledge making and explains what it encompasses in contrast to the more didactic pedagogies of our recent past. It positions active learning in the history of education and its evolving branches over time. This chapter also explains the benefits of incorporating active learning into the teaching and learning process, presents a summary of how valuable it could be for learners, and provides examples of practical interventions that exemplify active processes of knowledge development and learning.

Defining Active Knowledge Making

Active learning is generally defined as any instructional method that engages students in the learning process, requiring them to do meaningful learning activities and think reflexively about what their knowledge processes. The core difference from traditional learning lies in student activity and engagement in the learning process—students are no longer passive listeners receiving information from the instructor. Active learning is an approach that shifts pedagogy from instructor-focused teaching to a student-focused learning paradigm. This is achieved by foregoing didactic and more passive modes of information delivery and replacing them with active and experiential approaches centered on the learning needs of students (Barr & Tagg, 1995; Donahue, 1999).

Active learning can seem like a complex idea since it can happen in a multiple context and in different learning environments. A student can remain a passive learner and go through the motions of learning through worksheets and collaboration. At the same time, a student can listen passively in a classroom but still make meaning and actively learn. Variations of active learning include collaborative, cooperative, and project-based learning. These approaches overlap to some degree with the notion of active knowledge making. However, the terms are not synonymous. In collaborative work, active learning occurs when students are encouraged to explore new solutions based on existing knowledge, share ideas with group members, and participate, understand, and completely submerge themselves in the process of learning. Collaborative learning (Dillenbourg, 1999; Vygotsky, 1997) refers to students working together in small groups toward a shared goal—interaction is the key feature of this kind of learning activity. Similarly, cooperative learning (Slavin, 1990) is group work with a common end goal where the assessment is individual. Although assessment is individual, in this form of learning, cooperation is encouraged rather than competition. Project-based learning is grounded in John Dewey's "learning by doing" and requires self-directed learning. It can be cooperative or collaborative but also often individual. All three approaches encourage students to be involved actively in the learning process. However, each prioritizes different factors in learning.

In a didactic classroom, the communication technology is set within the walls of a classroom where the teacher or one of the students speak one at a time. The characteristic textual forms are monologues by the teacher or lecturer or the synoptic voice of the textbook author. In each case, the student's goal remains to memorize the facts or determine the correct answers based on the application of theorems. In this kind of a classroom setting, only students who volunteer or are called on answer questions. In classroom discussion, a few students become representative of the whole class, leaving the other students as listeners rather than assuming a participatory role in the interactive process of learning. Although listening can also be part of the active learning process, it is necessary to ensure that the listeners are also making meaning of what is being transferred to them. Discursive participation is mostly vicarious. Students are placed in a passive position as knowledge consumers. The knowledge receivers have limited opportunity to express their thoughts or views or to lead a conversation. Only once in a while do they have the opportunity to speak—to put forward their opinions and interpretations.

New media provide us with the opportunity to create e-learning environments for participatory learning in schools where students are no longer mainly consumers of knowledge. The new digital media are characteristically more interactive than the previous generation of broadcast, analog media. The challenge for education is to remain in sync with the technological advancements of today and to align with the media sensibilities of the new generations of learners (Cope & Kalantzis, 2015). Online learning and new media support active engagement because, in these platforms, users not only consume the information but also exchange and modify it. Each individual brings his or her own personal past experiences and influence and contributes to class discussion and the production of the final product. Although this can happen in both traditional- and e-learning-based classrooms, it is more possible to link valid sources from the online resources and find answers in real time. For instance, in a classroom discussion on historical artifacts, students can use the new media to find images of historical artifacts from museums across the globe to support their claims from existing knowledge acquired from previous classes, sociocultural experiences, and nationality. As a consequence, there is greater scope for expression of diverse identities and perspectives and for creativity in connecting multiple sources.

As knowledge producers, learners search and analyze multiple sources with differing and contradictory perspectives and develop their own observations and conclusions. In this process, they become researchers themselves and learn to collaborate with peers in knowledge production. Collaboration gives learners the opportunity to work with others as coauthors, peer reviewers, and discussants to completed works. Because learners brings their own views, outlooks, and past experiences, the work they create is likely to be uniquely voiced rather than a templated "correct" response.

Evolution of Learning Environments and Emergence of e-Learning

From its inception in the mid-nineteenth century, modern education was didactic, with a vision to achieve cultural uniformity and create dutiful citizens. Diversity and critical thinking were not priorities. The education system was founded on competitive meritocracy, creating a well-disciplined though mainly low-skilled workforce to serve the needs of the expanding industrial economy.

"Progressive" thinking came into focus in the early twentieth century when the social factors in education began to gain more attention. Although progressive thinkers come from a variety of perspectives and disciplines, they have all emphasized the ideas and practices of democracy and the active participation of citizens in the social, political, and economic decisions that affect their lives. In this view, education is expected to incorporate both respect for diversity and the development of critical, socially engaged intelligence that builds the skills to understand and participate in the betterment of their own communities for the common good. Progressive education is developed with ideas and practices aiming to create schools that were effective agents in the creation of a democratic society. With John Dewey (1916, 1938) as a main advocate, progressive educators critiqued an educational system whose aims were purely functional—to educate an elite while relegating the masses to learning minimal "basics," sometimes supplemented by vocational training. Progressives emphasized the importance of the artistic, creative, and emotional aspects of human development. Dewey (1902) explains how children learn naturally through the process of experiencing life. Unlike adults, children's interests lie in the people surrounding them in their work and relationships with them rather than the concrete facts alone. He stated that curriculum needs to provide space to learn, observe, and construct worldviews. The goal should be teaching the child, not teaching the subject. Progressive education has also been called a child-centered approach and sometimes also a social reconstructionist approach. Open classrooms, cooperative learning, the social curriculum, experiential learning, and active knowledge making are examples of alternative learning methods with roots in progressive education. Although the arguments of the progressive educators have been widely disputed, over the years these ideas come up over and over again in various modified versions to address the changing needs of school, children, and society as a whole.

Social learning theories explain how people learn from one another (social contexts) and how teachers can build active learning communities to incorporate this skill into the educational setting. Vygotsky (1962) was one of the pioneers in establishing the theory that people learn from interaction and communication with others, accounting for the ways in which our social environments influence our learning process. He advocated for a collaborative learning environment where teachers encourage interaction, discussion, and feedback, and students have opportunities to exercise interaction with peers. Vygotsky (1962) also identified culture as a determining factor of knowledge construction. When students have the opportunity to think and reflect on existing knowledge and experiences, their approach to problems and asking questions will vary based on their cultural backgrounds. Each person's skills, languages, and experiences is shaped by his or her own culture, and peer-to-peer and teacher-student collaborative work can build on that difference (Vygotsky, 1978). Instructional strategies that promote collaborative work to understand, analyze, and solve a problem will create a community of learners who support and build on one another's skills and knowledge.

In the classic format of teaching, teachers tell students where the information is and what to read, and at the end of a chapter or topic, the assessment is completed through a structured exam or quiz prepared by the instructor. This exam is based on the textbook students read, and throughout the process, they are only knowledge receivers. By contrast, in active knowledge making, students are given a topic, presented with a format or structure, and required to find the information on their own using resources that are available to them. They are not restricted to the class textbook alone. The

Internet has become a definitive resource for information on almost anything, and a student can access this resource from any web-enabled device at any time. Sourcing from the web entails a process of developing and completing a work that inevitably makes learners knowledge producers as long as they can navigate and critically discern the value of multiple sources. This is a skill that must be learned, as many sources that provide information are not valid, reliable, or authentic. When incorporating e-learning, understanding the different sources and identifying the more reliable ones are essential for effective teaching and learning. This is a critical aspect to e-learning because the inability to cite properly or to use reliable resources provides learners with misconstrued information and ideas.

When learning was only textbook focused, the output in the works was limited and may have been repetitive, as everyone was working from a single source. As knowledge producers in an e-learning context, learners become more engaged and have the flexibility to choose how much information to take from the wide array of sources that are available to them. The learning may also involve interaction with peers who may have chosen to focus on other aspects of the same or different resources. In this way, knowledge sharing from multiple resources may increase knowledge production in a continuous process where everyone participates in sourcing and sharing knowledge.

Constructivism for Knowledge Creation and e-Learning

Constructivism is a theory that highlights learning as an active process where learners come to understand by constructing meanings for themselves. The learner is a knowledge maker because people actively construct and build knowledge based on their existing knowledge and own subjective representation of objective reality. Vygotsky (1978) and Piaget (1976) have contributed greatly to the development of this paradigm. Constructivism is an active, contextualized process of constructing knowledge, whereas didactic approaches are more about acquiring knowledge. Personal experiences, cultural factors, and one's outlook and ideas influence the learner's interpretation and construction of the knowledge. Constructivism assumes that all knowledge is constructed from existing knowledge regardless of how or what is taught. Learners come with knowledge, and they are active participants in creating meaning. It suggests that knowledge is created as learners attempt to understand their experiences (Driscoll, 2000, p. 376). People reflect on those experiences and in the process create an understanding of a concept, idea, and the world in general. When new information is encountered, learners may choose to accept it and add onto their existing knowledge, modify the existing knowledge, or discard the new information as unnecessary or irrelevant. Irrespective of how much information is provided or taught, existing knowledge will influence new knowledge making. This is a process by means of which we create our knowledge. Teachers who follow a constructivist approach in teaching encourage students to question how new activities are affecting their learning and what may or may not be working for them. In the process, they learn how to learn, not just what they have been given to learn. A classroom can provide an environment that prepares them for life-long learning.

A teacher can implement a constructivist approach by encouraging students to play an active role in learning through observation and trying to find solutions with hands-on activities, experiments, or real-world problems while referring to existing experiences. As students arrive at solutions that they think are suitable, they can be guided to reflect on the experience and understand how their knowledge is changing. Teachers will need to have a clear idea of students' present knowledge and build on that with new activities. This can be challenging for teachers given that students can come to class with large variations in preexisting knowledge. In a science class, for instance, a teacher knows the correct "answer" to a physics problem but will not give students the answer. Rather, the teacher will play a hands-off role in the process but can help to re-form the question so that the problem to be addressed is clear to students. The teacher can prompt students to connect their existing knowledge on that issue and come up with possible answers or paths to the solution but will not provide any leads or answers. The teacher can also suggest alternative sources of information in the e-learning environment that students may use to find a solution. As students ponder the challenge, if one of them is able to identify a productive line of thinking, then the teacher can encourage others to consider looking in that direction. Following that, the class can come together to discuss what they have learned in the process and what could have helped their learning further. This post-analysis is crucial to understand how effective the constructivist approach is in the classroom and how to incorporate it successfully into an e-learning environment.

When learners are provided with sources to assist in the construction of knowledge, they are expected to construct and find other essential information for themselves. Here preliminary guidance can be defined as a space where learners discover or construct their information with minimal guidance from the instructor or teacher. Findings show that, with minimal guidance, people learn best and are more creative in finding relevant information and knowledge to enrich their own work (e.g., Bruner, 1961; Papert, 1980; Steffe & Gale, 1995). Multiple terms are used to define minimal guidance, including discovery learning (Anthony, 1973; Bruner, 1961), problem-based learning (Barrows & Tamblyn, 1980; Schmidt, 1983), inquiry learning (Papert, 1980; Rutherford, 1964), experiential learning (Boud, Keogh, & Walker, 1985; Kolb & Fry, 1975), and constructivist learning (Jonassen, 1991; Steffe & Gale, 1995). All of these are broadly similar pedagogic approaches where students are immersed into an experiential learning environment and encouraged to rediscover the established principles of a discipline through investigatory activities (Van Joolingen et al., 2005).

Knowledge construction or representation is a process whereby learners construct knowledge when given adequate conceptual and informational resources. Access to more information allows for a better and more accurate representation of knowledge. Research has shown that knowledge construction and instruction methods that may be effective for novices may become less effective as they gain expertise in their fields (Cronbach & Snow, 1977; Kyllonen & Lajoie, 2003; Snow, Corno, & Jackson, 1996). Roblyer, Edwards, and Havriluk (1997) reported that when students have prerequisite knowledge and some prior structured learning experience, they are more successful in discovery learning. Constructivist, discovery, problem-based, experiential, and inquiry-based learning have often been classified as minimally guided instruction. In a minimally guided discovery approach, learners are expected to explore and find answers to problems and/or phenomena mostly on their own. Because constructivist theories of learning emphasize on learners engagement in constructing knowledge, often it is assumed that this is only possible in a minimally guided approach. This is not necessarily the case (Mayer, 2004). For instance, problem-based learning (PBL) and inquiry-based learning (IL) are constructivist approaches to learning that require substantial guidance and facilitation.

In PBL, students learn content, strategies, and self-directed learning skills by collaboratively solving problems, reflecting on their experiences, and engaging in self-directed inquiry. In IL, students learn content as well as discipline-specific reasoning skills and practices (often in scientific disciplines) by collaboratively engaging in investigations. Both PBL and IL address real-world problems or questions and place heavy emphasis on collaborative learning and activity. In both, teachers are facilitators and provide content and information when needed, but students are cognitively engaged in developing evidence-based explanations and communicating their ideas. Hmelo-Silver, Duncan, and Chinn (2007) summarize IL and PBL approaches as ones that "involve the learner, with appropriate scaffolding, in the practices and conceptualizations of the discipline and in this way promote the construction of knowledge we recognize as learning" (p. 105).

Active learning strategies can be supplemented by scaffolding, such as direct instruction offered on a just-in-time basis (Edelson, 2001). Quintana et al. (2004) identified scaffolding as a key element for cognitive apprenticeship where teachers provide guidance and coaching but no explicit final answer. Scaffolding supports students' learning of both how to do a task and why to do it in a certain way (Hmelo-Silver, 2006). Scaffolding also reduces cognitive load, provides expert guidance, and helps students acquire disciplinary ways of thinking and acting (Hmelo-Silver, Duncan, & Chinn, 2007).

Research on PBL shows it is effective in different fields of education. Vernon and Blake (1993) found that medical students in PBL curricula performed better on clinical test knowledge in comparison to traditional medical students. Patel, Groen, and Norman's (1993) research found that PBL students are able to transfer their hypothesis-driven reasoning strategy to new problems—a skill many students in the traditional curriculum did not master as well. Similar findings emerge in Schwartz and Martin's (2004) research on ninth graders. PBL enhanced future learning because it equipped them cognitively to solve new problems based on the previously learned problem-solving skills.

Mergendoller, Maxwell, and Bellisimo (2006) also found that students in PBL courses gained more knowledge in comparison to their traditional course students, and this was true across multiple schools.

Kirschner, Sweller, and Clark (2006) claimed that IL disadvantages weaker performing students. However, this claim was challenged in the Hickey et al. (1999) study where students from general science and biology classrooms were able to complete more sophisticated reasoning in comparison to college-prep and honors students when immersed in an IL environment. Geier et al. (2008) also found IL to have a positive effect, which can be cumulative, with higher levels of participation leading to greater gains. They also found that the influence of IL can be seen even a year and a half after the participation. Another significant finding from this research was that the achievement gap experienced by urban African American boys declined with IL instruction. Lynch et al. (2005) found IL-based curriculum to be more effective than didactic instruction for all diversity groups, and IL increases motivation and engagement among historically disadvantaged learners. Hmelo-Silver, Duncan, and Chinn (2007) conclude from their meta-analysis that multiple studies have shown significant learning gains in IL and PBL methods, and disadvantaged students benefit particularly in the process. They draw the conclusion that "learning situations should provide students with opportunities to engage in the scientific practices of questioning, investigation, and argumentation as well as learning content in a relevant and motivating context" (p. 105).

Connectivism, Collaborative Learning, and e-Learning

Active knowledge making and PBL are not new concepts (Kilpatrick, 1918; Waks, 1997), and collaborative learning has also been an area of extensive research over the years. Connectivism (Siemens, 2005) is a more recent model of learning, acknowledging that the changing society has led to a rise in learning environments that are interconnected with a larger universe of knowledge that extends far beyond teacher and classroom. Siemens (2005) dubbed connectivism as "the learning theory for the digital age," built on the underlying assumption that knowledge is distributed and can exist outside the individual mind. Downes (2007) argues that knowledge is distributed over a network of connections, and learning occurs by building connections and traversing those networks.

Technology can play a defining role in the collaborative learning process, as it influences cognitive operations previously performed by the learner, such as retrieving, organizing, and storing information. As technology advances, new tools are becoming applicable in the educational setting, such as apps that link to and mash-up data sources. The process of teaching and learning changes as new tools are incorporated. Although the field of education has been slow to recognize the effect of and changes from the inclusion of new learning tools, connectivism provides insight into learning skills and tasks needed for learners to flourish in a digital era. In this process, know-where to find knowledge is supplementing know-how and know-what.

Connectivism can also be incorporated into collaborative learning. When students are formed into groups to work collaboratively to solve a problem or explore a question, this collaboration can now happen within the classroom or with students from different schools in the same country or even between countries. Here connectivism in the form of online learning becomes a significant factor in minimizing the effects of distance.

Twenty-first-century learners have the advantage of living in an age of ubiquitous learning where they can access information anywhere and anytime. Collaborative projects are much easier to conduct and complete, as students are no longer required to collaborate within the walls of a classroom. They can collaborate and work on projects at anytime if connected over the Internet. Our "real-time" world allows individuals to be connected, responsive, and collaborative. For instance, wiki pages can be used in education as project-based collaborative learning. In the classroom, teachers can have students create wiki pages or wiki-like pages collaboratively with their classmates. The active process of creating a wiki page with other group members allows students to use their individual ideas and perspectives to contribute to a final completed work. The final project that emerges from multiple views, discussions, and cultural influences is much more elaborate, comprehensive, and thorough. In these kinds of collaborative projects, students learn to do peer reviews, discuss their ideas and findings, and self-assess their work. Students can be assigned specific roles toward the completion of the group work to ensure that everyone works together. In this workspace, students can track their progress and understand their specific roles, and the teacher can also check each student's progress in real time, provide feedback, and guide them with just-in-time assistance. Google Hangouts, wikispaces.com, Weebly, and Google sites are examples of online web portals that can be used in an education setting as collaborative learning spaces.

When developing a "work," for instance in PBL or IL, students go through the active process of knowledge design, from conception to realization. Irrespective of the discipline or format of work, any work has a staged beginning-middle-end narrative structure. This is true for finding a mathematical solution, conducting a historical analysis, and building a business proposal—in short, in the making of any knowledge artifact. The final product represents and documents these stages of knowledge development, where students can be creators as well as consumers of knowledge. They build the knowledge artifacts by figuring themselves as knowledge workers, developing the work through the conceptualization, planning, drafting, peer feedback, revision, and publication stages. Learners are assessed not only on cognitive abstraction but also on the final products they have crafted and the process of making them. As Cope and Kalantzis (2015) stated, "By your works, you shall be known" (p. 359).

Active learning incorporates a social and collaborative experience. Instead of memory-based exams and testing of individualized cognition, students can develop knowledge projects and link their course materials as references and acknowledgements. Peer feedback can make this a systematically collaborative activity, where peer support and working together is encouraged and acknowledged. The creative path is not an individual and lonely road. Today's online writing and assessment environments facilitate collaborative knowledge work. They also nurture a culture of recognition of the social, distributed, and collaborative nature of intelligence. This is how new media can supplement traditional hierarchical knowledge flows (expert to novice, authority to authorized, teacher to student) with relations of lateral knowledge co-creation (Kalantzis & Cope, 2015). When making knowledge is implemented through active learning-focused pedagogy, individual voices come through. Because no two knowledge expressions are the same, the differences themselves become a productive resource for learning (Kalantzis & Cope, 2009).

Changing the Balance of Agency

The traditional classroom is a hierarchically ordered social setting where the teacher controls activity sequences and knowledge flows, and the students are subordinates. Even in a classroom group work setting, there may be one student in charge and others of the group are followers. In recent times, this structure has changed to a more cooperative and collaborative work environment where group members work on projects together, not in a hierarchical way but in a setting of more equal participation. The agency has shifted to a more equal distribution rather than a single dominant force. With this shift, everyone plays a more active role both collaboratively and independently. The final work may be collaborative or the product of an individual with established connections to reliable resources and clearly stated references. Everyone is expected to be innovative, involved, and participating in developing their own work and in providing concrete and useful feedback to others in a collaborative work. This leads to a balance in agency where everyone is participating equally and receiving due credit for the work. This horizontal system moves agency from a centralized source to distributed sources where everyone can play an equally participatory role in building and expanding knowledge.

In a classroom, students can be divided into groups to develop a work independently but with initial sharing of ideas and in-group discussion. In this discussion group, students can benefit from exchange of knowledge where all students bring with them their socioeconomic and cultural experiences that influence their outlook on a problem and possible solutions. If the students developed the work completely independently, then they would only bring in their own ideas and perspectives, but when sharing of ideas occur in a group, they can learn from one another and incorporate that shared knowledge into their own work and acknowledge peers' influence on their thinking process. In this way, students become knowledge distributors for their peers and knowledge consumers from their peers.

Another example of a shift in agency can be seen with the availability of information on the Internet. Teachers are no longer required to provide comprehensive information and theories to students in the classroom, and learners are encouraged to access sources beyond their designated textbooks. Although the textbook can be a starting point, the broad range of information that is now accessible to students through the Internet creates an opportunity for them to become immersed into information that is no longer limited within the walls of a classroom or the pages of a textbook.

With situations like these in the classroom, active learning causes a shift in the balance of agency. Didactic classrooms had a set structure where the teacher was an authority figure and had more control in comparison to the students who were passive learners. However, with active learning, students have more control to choose reading materials, watch podcasts and YouTube videos, and access more resources online than can possibly be provided in a single textbook or classroom that is not e-learning friendly. This leads to the distribution of roles that is distinctly different from the preconceived traditional classroom roles of teachers and learners. Kalantzis and Cope (2012b) have identified these learners as "prosumers" who are no longer consumers of knowledge only. In 1980, Toffler coined the term *prosumers* to define those who have blurred the distinct lines of consumers and producers. Kalantzis and Cope (2012b) define today's learners as prosumers because they develop their own products and works, and these creations are a combination of consumption (reading) with production (writing) in the new media. New media platforms like Wikipedia and blog sites make it difficult to maintain the distinction between the amateurs and the professionals in these spaces. Unlike movies, television, and radio, where one participates vicariously, the new media provide spaces that allow one to put forward thoughts, views, and ideologies. A journalist may present a sensational news story from the sources she has, but her readership today has access to multiple other sources with the ability to correct, disagree, and disprove their reasoning with their own views and information resources. Similarly, instructors cannot always pre-decide the correct answer to a set of questions because the sources for information are no longer limited to what is provided in the classroom.

Accessing Multiple Knowledge Resources

Information is now so readily accessible that it is no longer necessary to remember the information. However, knowing the source, finding the source, and using the information aptly is important to learn and know now more than ever before. Learning today is more about navigation, discernment, induction, and synthesis and less about memory and deduction (Cope & Kalantzis, 2013). Learners must know the social sources of knowledge and understand and correctly use quotations, paraphrases, remixes, links, citations, and the like in the works they develop. The collaborative intelligence of a working group is a vital factor in understanding the process a work has gone through. Recognizing, acknowledging, and giving credit to those involved in the peer feedback is necessary to ensure that the collaborative process is highlighted and everyone's role is clearly defined. Along with this, for a more detailed understanding of each individual's role in the editing, tracking contributions of the joint collaborators in a single work via edit histories can be a great source to understand collaborative intelligence and active knowledge making. It is also more than likely today that learners will be multitasking, accessing multiple resources simultaneously when working on a task. Multimodality in learning is also an essential part of the multitasking, as using different types of resources collaboratively on the Web 2.0 is a skill they have acquired and may even have mastered.

Drucker (1969) termed the twenty-first century societies as *knowledge society* to describe economies and social conditions that are heavily influenced by knowledge workers and that citizens access and create. Today, knowledge is one of the most distinctive factors in shaping individuals and society. In the current knowledge society, employers want to hire people with skills and sensibilities that will make them proactive and use their own thinking in bringing change and developing the company and self. Along with this, they look for workers who can work in a team and develop products and ideas that are better than what exists in the market. Active knowledge making encourages these characteristics, and the earlier one starts thinking in this way, the more prepared he or she will be when approaching the job market. In the active learning process, students become knowledge designers and no longer remain just consumers. They may not design something from scratch but instead take something that exists and modify and develop it further into a new artifact representing something that did not exist before. This remix prompts critical thinking, creativity, and adds their own voice into their artifacts (Kalantzis & Cope, 2012a)—all qualities that are in high demand in the twenty-first-century knowledge society. Knobel and Lankshear (2008) also argue that such a remix culture draws the young generation's interest to invest their time and energy.

Active Knowledge and Retention

Active knowledge making can be a collaborative process, and past research endorses that collaboration reduces attrition and improves memory retention, even in underrepresented groups (Berry, 1991; Fredericksen, 1998; Springer, Stanne, & Donovan, 1999). Collaboration positively influences student learning outcomes, achievement, attitudes, and retention (Prince, 2004). PBL also improves long-term retention of knowledge (Gallagher, 1997; Martensen, Eriksson, & Ingleman-Sundberg, 1985; Norman & Schmidt, 1993) and develops problem-solving and lifelong learning skills. Prince (2004) includes findings from empirical research demonstrating that cooperative learning is more effective than competition and promotes positive learning outcomes. Cooperative learning provides an environment that encourages interpersonal relationships, effective teamwork, stronger social support, and more self-esteem. The wide range of research supporting PBL, collaboration, and cooperative learning strongly suggests that it enhances critical thinking, and inclusion of these in the learning process can be highly beneficial to the learner. Experiential learning, also a form of active learning, increases long-term memory of the experience, student comprehension of the subject matter being taught, and retention of lessons learned (Fox & Ronkowski, 1997; Hertel & Millis, 2002; Jensen, 1998; Krain & Nurse, 2004; Silberman, 1996; Stice, 1987). In researching first-year undergraduate students, Campisi and Finn (2011) found that students claim to have enjoyed the active teaching style more than the traditional style in a post-course survey. Students engaging in active learning projects have a positive outlook on the content (Prince, 2004). Their perception and attitude toward the subject of study improves, and greater learning and development occurs (Astin, 1996; Morgan, 2003). In their research on higher education, Hohmann and Weikart (2002) found that students actively participated in the learning process if the tasks had an empirical component and if they saw a simulation of their future professional lives. Active knowledge making may not be the answer to all educational problems, but it is a way to include different learning styles, incorporate the needs of the learners, and help to develop skills that will be useful in their professional and personal lives.

Assessment in New Media

New media-based learning environments offer students multiple opportunities to master skills at their own pace. The criteria for assessing learning outcomes have changed as active knowledge making has emerged as an alternative to didactic teaching methods. In traditional education, learning outcomes were measured on the basis of long-term memory. However, in active knowledge making, the final work can be proof of the learning outcome and represent a student's ability to use the resources that are available. This shows a shift in pedagogy and assessment and an increase in personalization and individualization of learning (Pea, 2014). Memorizing the information on a topic is less important than the writing, synthesis, and analysis of the available information that has been referenced in the work. This shifts the focus of assessment to the quality of the artifacts and the processes of their construction. Moreover, as technology increases the ability to capture detailed data from formal and informal learning activities, it can give us a new view of how learners progress in acquiring knowledge, skills, and attributes (DiCerbo & Behrens, 2014). Because learning is a continuous process, these advanced, technologically enhanced assessments are more useful in understanding the learning process and knowledge development. Such digitally mediated learning environments are suitable sites for criterion-referenced rather than norm-referenced assessment (Kalantzis & Cope, 2012b). Such assessment tools are well aligned to connectivist and collaborative learning.

Dispersing Knowledge Outside the Classroom

The Common Core State Standards Initiative (www.corestandards.org/read-the-standards/) offers a series of learning goals that are designed to assist educators to prepare students for college, career, and life. Education needs to grow learning habits that can be transferred in future years into college study, workplace, and community settings. The knowledge that is acquired should not be limited to a single subject, class or even the classroom itself. It can be difficult for an instructor to concentrate equally on all students because one person cannot monitor all that is happening among multiple students and sharing it with a much larger and broader audience outside of a classroom. In this condition, digital spaces can capture the contributions of multiple people on multiple topics at the same time. They support the recording, sharing, and incorporating of activities, projects, and works of all students. Not only are teachers and classmates accessing this knowledge and learning from their immediate school settings but also from others across the globe. In this way, knowledge can go beyond the classroom walls and across the borders of countries and continents. This is ubiquitous learning—learning everywhere, all the time, and in multiple ways (Burbules, 2009; Cope & Kalantzis, 2009).

Didactic education focused on strengthening long-term memory so that one can repeat what has been learned and use it at a later stage. The role of the mind in memorizing played an integral part in learning in the past. This scenario has changed, and the importance of memorizing has declined because it is no longer necessary for the mind to remember so much. As more and more information becomes accessible and available through the Internet, and with more affordable devices and connections, remembering the information by heart is no longer necessary. With the decline in emphasis on memorizing, there is a shift from cognition (memorizing) to knowledge representation (artifacts) (Cope & Kalantzis, 2013). Artifacts have been identified as knowledge representations in the form of works that have been developed based on the information one has access to. This information is not from a single book or article or from memory but from a mix of resources that can be anything from a book to a website to a blog or even a podcast. The creator independently taps into different resources and finds the information. Because the searching is part of the process of developing a work, artifacts are no longer dependent on what one has been able to store in the memory but on what one has been able to access as sources of valid information. The final work or knowledge artifact is developed by identifying and referencing the sources that have been used and finishing off the work with much richer information, covering a wider array of sources than would be possible from a single textbook. Moreover, these works can represent information with references to media files, blog posts, and YouTube videos, and this makes the works more accessible to learners with diverse learning abilities. The final artifact becomes a unique product that represents the learner's engagement in the knowledge process and the result of active knowledge making.

Active knowledge may also involve self- or peer evaluation—an assessment tool that can replace or complement testing. Self-grading is a metacognitive process that can improve a student's understanding of subject matter (Sadler & Good, 2006). Peer evaluation can stimulate senses of responsibility, reflective thinking, collaboration, and discussion (Birenbaum, 1996; Boud, 1990; Orsmond, Merry, & Callaghan, 2004; Sambell & McDowell, 1998). Peers can also learn from one another's work and provide substantial feedback that highly improves the quality of a work. This kind of collaborative work can take the form of crowdsourcing assessment, where the "wisdom of crowds" (Surowiecki, 2004) can be considered equivalent to that of experts. Here it is not necessary that someone in the same classroom conduct the peer review; it can be anyone who is interested in and has access to the document through the Internet. In this way, learning can expand outside the four walls of a classroom, and people from across the globe can give valuable feedback. Cope et al. (2013) found that quality of nonexpert raters' feedback can be comparable to expert raters, and diverse reviewers provide rapid qualitative feedback from multiple viewpoints. Another study of fan-fiction reviews, however, found that most reviews added little value and were more focused on praising the authors (Magnifico, Curwood, & Lammers, 2015). Because there is a possibility of distortion and to enhance fairness in grading, the teacher's role can become that of a moderator to overcome any biases or distortions (Boud, 1989).

Shifts in Learning Outcomes

In their literature review on active learning, Bonwell and Eison (1991) conclude that it leads to better student attitudes and improved thinking and writing. Discussion, as a form of active learning, motivates students for further study and develops critical thinking skills. Active learning is also included as one of the "seven principles for good practice" (Chickering & Gamson, 1987) and is recommended as a teaching method because learners need to feel what they learn is a part of themselves. Instructional practices and tools that engage students and create opportunities for active participation are the defining features of active learning (Di Vesta & Smith, 1979). In a study of 6,000 students in introductory physics courses, Hake (1998) found that compared to traditional methods, interactive engagement substantially improves student performance in classrooms and enhances problem-solving ability. Redish, Saul, and Steinberg (1997) and Laws, Sokoloff, and Thornton (1999) also found that deeper learning occurs as a consequence of active engagement. PBL nurtures positive student attitudes (Vernon & Blake, 1993) and a more challenging, motivating, and enjoyable approach to education (Norman & Schmidt, 2000). An active learning exercise is a valuable pedagogical tool when integrated into the larger lesson or curriculum. Lack of substantial and reliable data could have been a barrier to accepting the positive results on active learning research in the past (McKeachie, 1972; Sorcinelli, 1991). However, recent studies (Campisi & Finn, 2011; Prince, 2004) strongly suggest that positive outcomes emerge from incorporating active learning.

Factors Deterring Active Learning

Some studies have continued to highlight the necessity of direct instructional guidance in a disciplined and systematic manner for novice learners so that they do not have to reconstruct knowledge on their own (e.g., Cronbach & Snow, 1977; Klahr & Nigam, 2004; Mayer, 2004; Shulman & Keisler, 1966; Sweller, 2003). Direct instructional guidance can be broadly defined as providing comprehensive yet synoptic theories and information to learners. The expectation then is that students will learn, and learning is defined by a new addition to the existing long-term memory. Over the last few decades, there has been a continuous debate on how extensive is the influence of guidance during teaching on learners (Ausubel, 1964; Craig, 1956; Mayer, 2004; Shulman & Keisler, 1966).

In some fields, researchers note resistance on the part of learners to engage in active learning. In engineering, students may be less interested to search for answers than to be given them (Prince, 2004), although in professional practice, engineers work with real problems. It has been documented that active learning pedagogy requires a significant time commitment, and this is higher in comparison to a didactic lecture-based approach (Casem, 2006; Weimer, 2002). When investment is large but research results show minimal change in learning achievements, this lowers interest to incorporate active learning into the classroom. Moreover, some research indicates that standard academic achievement is not sensitive to any change in instructional approach (Dubin & Taveggia, 1968). However, even minor shifts may be significant, and there may also be long-term benefits in the form of students' better understanding of materials in subsequent courses in the same subject area in comparison to their peers who learned in a didactic classroom (Schwartz & Martin, 2004).

Some researchers have endorsed a guided approach and have distanced themselves from active learning. Evidence from empirical research findings lean toward favoring guided approaches (Mayer, 2004), and multiple researchers showed students learn more from strongly guided learning as opposed to discovery (Chall, 2000; Klahr & Nigam, 2004; McKeough, Lupart, & Marini, 1995; Moreno, 2004; Schauble, 1990; Singley & Anderson, 1989). The argument here is that if the level of information that is provided is reduced to a minimum, then one's ability to represent quality information also declines (Kirschner, Sweller, & Clark, 2006). Systematic and highly structured scaffolding is found to be more beneficial to less able learners in comparison to more able learners (Kyllonen & Lajoie, 2003). However, Clark (1982) concluded that less able learners chose less guided methods and enjoyed the experience more, even if they learned less. Kirschner, Sweller, and Clark (2006) compared the findings from a range of studies on minimally guided instructional approaches and direct instructional approaches and their effect on learning and concluded that direct, strong instructional guidance is most appropriate for novice and intermediate learners. The authors also noted that constructivist views epistemologically and ideologically have become opposed to the presentation and explanation of knowledge and that minimally guided instructional approaches are ineffective and inefficient (Hmelo-Silver, Duncan, & Chinn, 2007).

Conclusion

Digital learning ecologies oriented to active learning offer workspaces that allow learners to bring their own interests and experiences to bear on their learning. Students can use their own identities to influence the digital ecology classroom through shared experiences and knowledge exchange while contributing to the knowledge that is being collaboratively produced. This impacts their agency as they can choose how much and when to contribute and the flexibility is important to create the qualities that will be useful in the long run. e-Learning platforms have the potential to afford space for knowledge creation as well as knowledge consumption. Current generations of learners are so familiar with computers and the Internet that they expect classroom activities and learning resources to be available on demand (Hohmann & Weikart, 2002). Children now have a keen interest in and fascination with technology. This can be channeled to learning by creating a learning environment that uses these capacities and interests. Observing such learning environments can be a window into understanding children's interests and involving them in constructive educational activities that can lead to an increase in their motivation (Huffaker & Calvert, 2003). e-Learning is the use of network technologies that can foster sharing and transfer of information anywhere and at anytime (Huffaker & Calvert, 2003), and this can be a technology-savvy way to create works. Student projects can foster learning using the same technologies they use in their everyday lives and free time.

Students learn more when they are mentally involved and engaged in the process of inquiry, discovery, investigation, and interpretation. Learning is enhanced when students are able to present information in their own words. Passive minds are unable to effectively process and retain information. Learning requires reflection on what is learned, and this step does not necessarily exist when one is memorizing and repeating what has been remembered.

When individuals can choose, search, and combine available information from different sources, they become actively involved in the process of knowledge construction. From early on, children enjoy creating new things, and when they are physically and mentally involved in the process, it gives them a sense of pride and ownership. By being involved and actively participating in creating new things, they can be proud of the manifest products of their activity. Active participatory knowledge making allows students to become more involved in the process of learning and encourages them to take it a step further and be producers and not just consumers of knowledge. However, it is also important for learners to know how to find reliable and valid sources. Instructors can play the connecting role, exploring various ways to identify the validity of sources.

To build the skills of today's learners with the qualities they can use in the future, active participation in knowledge making is crucially important. Active knowledge making can play an important and transforming role in education and knowledge expansion. It is necessary to develop in post-millennial learners the skills of how to know and where to look when they do not know something. They will be individual learners who advance at their own pace but also "prosumers" who enjoy the benefits of active knowledge making. They also need to learn how to document their knowledge and work in collaborative knowledge environments where the total of what is known is greater than the sum of individual minds.

References

Anthony, W. S. (1973). Learning to discover rules by discovery. *Journal of Educational Psychology, 64*, 325–328.

Astin, A. (1996). Involvement in learning revisited: Lessons we have learned. *Journal of College Student Development, 37*, 123–134.

Ausubel, D. P. (1964). Some psychological and educational limitations of learning by discovery. *The Arithmetic Teacher, 11*, 290–302.

Barr, R. B., & Tagg, J. (1995). From teaching to learning—A new paradigm for undergraduate education. *Change, 27*, 12–25.

Barrows, H. S., & Tamblyn, R. M. (1980). *Problem-based learning: An approach to medical education*. New York: Springer.

Berry, L., Jr. (1991). *Collaborative learning: A program for improving the retention of minority students*. Retrieved from ERIC database. (ED384323)

Birenbaum, M. (1996). Assessment 2000: Towards a pluralistic approach to assessment. *Alternatives in Assessment of Achievements, Learning Processes and Prior Knowledge, 42*, 3–29. doi:10.1007/978-94-011-0657-3_1

Bonwell, C. C., & Eison, J. A. (1991). *Active learning: Creating excitement in the classroom* (ASHE-ERIC Higher Education Report No. 1). Washington, DC: The George Washington University, School of Education and Human Development.

Boud, D. (1989). The role of self-assessment in student grading. *Assessment and Evaluation in Higher Education, 14*, 20–30.

Boud, D. (1990). Assessment and the promotion of academic values. *Studies in Higher Education, 15*(1), 101–111.

Boud, D., Keogh, R., & Walker, D. (Eds.). (1985). *Reflection: Turning experience into learning*. London: Kogan Page.

Bruner, J. S. (1961). The art of discovery. *Harvard Educational Review, 31*, 21–32.

Burbules, N. C. (2009). Meanings of "ubiquitous learning." In B. Cope & M. Kalantzis (Eds.), *Ubiquitous learning* (pp. 15–20). Champaign: University of Illinois Press.

Campisi, J., & Finn, K. E. (2011). Does active learning improve students' knowledge of and attitudes toward research methods? *Journal of College Science Teaching, 40*(4), 38–45.

Casem, M. (2006). Active learning is not enough. *Journal of College Science Teaching, 35*(6), 52–57.

Chall, J. S. (2000). *The academic achievement challenge*. New York: Guilford Press.

Chickering, A., & Gamson, Z. (1987). Seven principles for good practice in undergraduate education. *AAHE Bulletin, 39*, 3–7.

Clark, R. E. (1982). Antagonism between achievement and enjoyment in ATI studies. *Educational Psychologist, 17*, 92–101.

Cope, B., & Kalantzis, M. (2009). Ubiquitous learning: An agenda for educational transformation. In B. Cope & M. Kalantzis (Eds.), *Ubiquitous learning* (pp. 1–14). Champaign: University of Illinois Press.

Cope, B., & Kalantzis, M. (2013). Towards a new learning: The "scholar" social knowledge workspace, in theory and practice. *e-Learning and Digital Media, 10*(4), 332–356.

Cope, B., & Kalantzis, M. (2015). Assessment and pedagogy in the era of machine-mediated learning. In T. Dragonas, K. J. Gergen, & S. McNamee (Eds.), *Education as social construction: Contribution to theory, research and practice* (pp. 350–374). Chagrin Falls, OH: Worldshare Books.

Cope, B., Kalantzis, M., Abd-El-Khalick, F., & Bagley, E. (2013). Science in writing: Learning scientific argument in principle and practice. *e-Learning and Digital Media, 10*(4), 420–441.

Craig, R. (1956). Directed versus independent discovery of established relations. *Journal of Educational Psychology, 47,* 223–235.

Cronbach, L. J., & Snow, R. E. (1977). *Aptitudes and instructional methods: A handbook for research on interactions.* New York: Irvington.

Dewey, J. (1902). *The child and the curriculum.* Chicago: University of Chicago Press.

Dewey, J. (1916). *Democracy and education: An introduction to the philosophy of education.* New York: Macmillan.

Dewey, J. (1938). *Experience and education.* New York: The Macmillan Company.

DiCerbo, K. E., & Behrens, J. T. (2014). *Impacts of the digital ocean on education.* London: Pearson.

Dillenbourg P. (1999) What do you mean by collaborative learning? In P. Dillenbourg (Ed.), *Collaborative-learning: Cognitive and computational approaches* (pp. 1–19). Oxford: Elsevier

Di Vesta, F., & Smith, D. A. (1979). The pausing principle: Increasing the efficiency of memory for ongoing events. *Contemporary Educational Psychology, 4*(3), 288–296.

Donahue, L. M. (1999). *What is an experiential learner? Selected Monographs from the Association for Experiential Education International Conference.* Boulder, CO: Association for Experiential Education.

Downes, S. (2007, February 3). What connectivism is [Web log post]. Retrieved from http://halfanhour.blogspot.com/2007/02/what-connectivism-is.html

Driscoll, M. (2000). *Psychology of learning for instruction.* Needham Heights, MA: Allyn & Bacon.

Drucker, P. (1969). *The age of discontinuity: Guidelines to our changing society.* New York: Harper and Row.

Dubin, R., & Taveggia, T. (1968). *The teaching-learning paradox: A comparative analysis of college teaching methods.* Eugene: University of Oregon, Center for the Advanced Study of Educational Administration.

Edelson, D. C. (2001). Learning-for-use: A framework for integrating content and process learning in the design of inquiry activities. *Journal of Research in Science Teaching, 38,* 355–385.

Fox, R. L., & Ronkowski, S. A. (1997). Learning styles of political science students. *PS: Political Science and Politics, 30,* 732–737.

Fredericksen, E. (1998). *Minority students and the learning community experience: A cluster experiment.* Retrieved from ERIC database. (ED216490)

Gallagher, S. (1997). Problem-based learning: Where did it comes from, what does it do and where is it going? *Journal for Education of the Gifted, 20*(4), 332–362.

Geier, R., Blumenfeld, P., Marx, R., Krajcik, J., Fishman, B., & Soloway, E. (2008). Standardized test outcomes for students engaged in inquiry based science curriculum in the context of urban reform. *Journal of Research in Science Teaching, 45*(8), 922–939.

Hake, R. (1998). Interactive-engagement vs. traditional methods: A six-thousand-student survey of mechanics test data for introductory physics courses. *American Journal of Physics, 66,* 64–74.

Hertel, J. P., & Millis, B. J. (2002). *Using simulation to promote learning in higher education.* Sterling, VA: Stylus.

Hickey, D. T., Kindfeld, A.C.H., Horwitz, P., & Christie, M. A. (1999). Advancing educational theory by enhancing practice in a technology supported genetics learning environment. *Journal of Education, 181,* 25–55.

Hmelo-Silver, C. E. (2006). Design principles for scaffolding technology based inquiry. In A. M. O'Donnell, C. E. Hmelo-Silver & G. Erkens (Eds.), *Collaborative reasoning, learning and technology* (pp. 147–170). Mahwah, NJ: Lawrence Erlbaum.

Hmelo-Silver, C., Duncan, R., & Chinn, C. (2007). Scaffolding and achievement in problem-based and inquiry learning: A response to Kirschner, Sweller, and Clark (2006). *Educational Psychologist, 42*(2), 99–107. doi:10.1080/00461520701263368

Hohmann, M., & Weikart, D. P. (2002). Active learning: The way children construct knowledge. *Journal of At-Risk Issues, 8*(1), 25–28.

Huffaker, D. A., & Calvert, S. L. (2003). The new science of learning: Active learning, metacognition, and transfer of knowledge in E-learning applications. *Journal of Educational Computing Research, 29*(3), 325–334.

Jensen, E. (1998). *Teaching with the brain in mind.* Alexandria, VA: Association for Supervision and Curriculum Development.

Jonassen, D. (1991). Objectivism vs. constructivism. *Educational Technology Research and Development, 39*(3), 5–14.

Kalantzis, M., & Cope, B. (2009). Learner differences: Determining the terms of pedagogical engagement. In S. Mitakidou, E. Tressou, B. B. Swadener, & C. A. Grant (Eds.), *Beyond pedagogies of exclusion in diverse childhood contexts* (pp. 13–30). New York: Palgrave Macmillan.

Kalantzis, M., & Cope, B. (2012a). *Literacies.* Cambridge: Cambridge University Press.

Kalantzis, M., & Cope, B. (2012b). *New learning: Elements of a science of education* (2nd ed.). Cambridge: Cambridge University Press.

Kalantzis, M., & Cope, B. (2015). Learning and new media. In D. Scott & E. Hargreaves (Eds.), *The Sage handbook of learning* (pp. 373–387). Thousand Oaks, CA: Sage.

Kilpatrick, W. H. (1918). The project method: The use of the purposeful act in the educative process. *Teachers College Record, 19*(4), 319–335.

Kirschner, P. A., Sweller, J., & Clark, R. E. (2006). Why minimal guidance during instruction does not work: An analysis of the failure of constructivist, discovery, problem-based, experiential, and inquiry-based teaching. *Educational Psychologist, 41,* 75–86.

Klahr, D., & Nigam, M. (2004). The equivalence of learning paths in early science instruction: Effects of direct instruction and discovery learning. *Psychological Science, 15,* 661–667.

Knobel, M., & Lankshear, C. (2008). Remix: The art and craft of endless hybridization. *Journal of Adolescent & Adult Literacy, 52,* 22–33.

Kolb, D. A., & Fry, R. (1975). Toward an applied theory of experiential learning. In C. Cooper (Ed.), *Studies of group process* (pp. 33–57). New York: Wiley.

Krain, M., & Nurse, A. (2004). Teaching human rights through service learning. *Human Rights Quarterly, 26,* 189–207.

Kyllonen, P. C., & Lajoie, S. P. (2003). Reassessing aptitude: Introduction to a special issue in honor of Richard E. Snow. *Educational Psychologist, 38,* 79–83.

Laws, P., Sokoloff, D., & Thornton, R. (1999). Promoting active learning using the results of physics education research. *UniServe Science News, 13.* Retrieved from http://science.uniserve.edu.au/newsletter/vol13/sokoloff.html

Lynch, S., Kuipers, J., Pyke, C., & Szesze, M. (2005). Examining the effects of a highly rated science curriculum unit on diverse students: Results from a planning grant. *Journal of Research in Science Teaching, 42,* 921–946.

Magnifico, A. M., Curwood, J. S., & Lammers, J. C. (2015). Words on the screen: Broadening analyses of interactions among fanfiction writers and reviewers. *Literacy, 49*(3), 158–166.

Martensen, D., Eriksson, H., & Ingleman-Sundberg, M. (1985). Medical chemistry: Evaluation of active and problem-oriented teaching methods. *Medical Education, 19,* 34–42.

Mayer, R. (2004). Should there be a three-strikes rule against pure discovery learning? The case for guided methods of instruction. *American Psychologist, 59,* 14–19.

McKeachie, W. (1972). Research on college teaching. *Educational Perspectives, 11*(2), 3–10.

McKeough, A., Lupart, J., & Marini, A. (Eds.). (1995). *Teaching for transfer: Fostering generalization in learning.* Mahwah, NJ: Lawrence Erlbaum.

Mergendoller, J. R., Maxwell, N. L., & Bellisimo, Y. (2006). The effectiveness of problem-based instruction: A comparative study of instructional methods and student characteristics. *Interdisciplinary Journal of Problem-Based Learning, 1*(2). http://dx.doi.org/10.7771/1541–5015.1026

Moreno, R. (2004). Decreasing cognitive load in novice students: Effects of explanatory versus corrective feedback in discovery-based multimedia. *Instructional Science, 32,* 99–113.

Morgan, A. L. (2003). Toward a global theory of mind: The potential benefits of presenting a range of IR theories through active learning. *International Studies Perspectives, 4,* 351–371.

Norman, G., & Schmidt, H. (1993). The psychological basis of problem-based learning: A review of evidence. *Academic Medicine, 67,* 557–565.

Norman, G., & Schmidt, H. (2000). Effectiveness of problem-based learning curricula: Theory, practice and paper darts. *Medical Education, 34,* 721–728.

Orsmond, P., Merry, S., & Callaghan, A. (2004). Implementation of a formative assessment model incorporating peer and self-assessment. *Innovations in Education and Teaching International, 41*(3), 273–290.

Papert, S. (1980). *Mindstorms: Children, computers, and powerful ideas.* New York: Basic Books.

Patel, V. L., Groen, G. J., & Norman, G. R. (1993). Reasoning and instruction in medical curricula. *Cognition and Instruction, 10,* 335–378.

Pea, R. (2014). *The learning analytics workgroup: A report on building the field of learning analytics for personalized learning at scale.* Stanford, CA: Stanford University.

Piaget, J. (1976). *Piaget's theory.* Berlin: Springer.

Prince, M. (2004). Does active learning work? A review of the research. *Journal of Engineering Education, 93*(3), 223–231.

Quintana, C., Reiser, B. J., Davis, E. A., Krajcik, J., Fretz, E., Duncan, R. G., . . . Soloway, E. (2004). A scaffolding design framework for software to support science inquiry. *Journal of the Learning Sciences, 13,* 337–386.

Redish, E., Saul, J., & Steinberg, R. (1997). On the effectiveness of active-engagement microcomputer-based laboratories. *American Journal of Physics, 65*(1), 45–54.

Roblyer, M. D., Edwards, J., & Havriluk, M. A. (1997). *Integrating educational technology into teaching* (2nd ed.). Upper Saddle River, NJ: Prentice Hall.

Rutherford, F. J. (1964). The role of inquiry in science teaching. *Journal of Research in Science Teaching, 2,* 80–84.

Sadler, P. M., & Good, E. (2006). The impact of self- and peer-grading on student learning. *Educational Assessment, 11*(1), 1–31.

Sambell, K., & McDowell, L. (1998). The value of self and peer assessment to the developing lifelong learner. In C. Rust (Ed.), *Improving student learning—Improving students as learners* (pp. 56–66). Oxford: Oxford Centre for Staff and Learning Development.

Schauble, L. (1990). Belief revision in children: The role of prior knowledge and strategies for generating evidence. *Journal of Experimental Child Psychology, 49,* 31–57.

Schmidt, H. G. (1983). Problem-based learning: Rationale and description. *Medical Education, 17,* 11–16.

Schwartz, D. L., & Martin, T. (2004). Inventing to prepare for future learning: The hidden efficiency of encouraging original student production in statistics instruction. *Cognition and Instruction, 22,* 129–184.

Shulman, L., & Keisler, E. (Eds.). (1966). *Learning by discovery: A critical appraisal.* Chicago: Rand McNally.

Siemens, G. (2005). Connectivism: A learning theory for the digital age. *International Journal of Instructional Technology and Distance Learning.* Retrieved from http://er.dut. ac.za/bitstream/handle/123456789/69/Siemens_2005_Connectivism_A_learning_ theory_for_the_digital_age.pdf?sequence=1

Silberman, M. (1996). *Active learning: 101 strategies to teach any subject.* Boston: Allyn & Bacon.

Singley, M. K., & Anderson, J. R. (1989). *The transfer of cognitive skill.* Cambridge, MA: Harvard University Press.

Slavin, R. E. (1990). *Cooperative learning.* New York: Prentice Hall.

Snow, R. E., Corno, L., & Jackson, D. (1996). Individual differences in affective and conative functions. In D. Berliner & R. Calfee (Eds.), *Handbook of educational psychology* (pp. 243–310). New York: Simon & Schuster.

Sorcinelli, M. (1991). Research findings on the seven principles. In A. W. Chickering & Z. F. Gamson (Eds.), *New directions in teaching and learning, No. 47: Applying the seven principles for good practice in undergraduate education* (pp. 13–25). San Francisco: Jossey-Bass.

Springer, L., Stanne, M., & Donovan, S. (1999). Effects of small-group learning on undergraduates in science, mathematics, engineering and technology: A meta-analysis. *Review of Educational Research, 69*(1), 21–52.

Steffe, L., & Gale, J. (Eds.). (1995). *Constructivism in education.* Mahwah, NJ: Lawrence Erlbaum.

Stice, J. E. (1987). Using Kolb's learning cycle to improve student learning. *Engineering Education, 77,* 291–296.

Surowiecki, J. (2004). *The wisdom of crowds: Why the many are smarter than the few and how collective wisdom shapes business, economies, societies and nations.* New York: Doubleday.

Sweller, J. (2003). Evolution of human cognitive architecture. In B. Ross (Ed.), *The psychology of learning and motivation* (Vol. 43, pp. 215–266). San Diego: Academic.

Van Joolingen, W. R., de Jong, T., Lazonder, A. W., Savelsbergh, E. R., & Manlove, S. (2005). Co-Lab: Research and development of an online learning environment for collaborative scientific discovery learning. *Computers in Human Behavior, 21*, 671–688.

Vernon, D., & Blake, R. (1993). Does problem-based learning work? A meta-analysis of evaluative research. *Academic Medicine, 68*(7), 550–563.

Vygotsky, L. S. (1962). *Thought and language.* Cambridge, MA: MIT Press. (Original work published 1934)

Vygotsky, L. S. (1978). *Mind in society: The development of higher psychological processes.* Cambridge, MA: Harvard University Press.

Vygotsky, L. S. (1997). The historical meaning of the crisis in psychology: A methodological investigation. In R. W. Rieber & J. Wollock (Eds.), *The collected works of L. S. Vygotsky, Vol. 3: Problems of the theory and history of psychology* (pp. 233–344). New York: Plenum.

Waks, L. J. (1997). The project method in postindustrial education. *Journal of Curriculum Studies, 29*(4), 391–406.

Weimer, M. (2002). *Learner centered teaching: Five key changes to practice.* San Francisco: Jossey-Bass.

4 Multimodal Meaning

Discursive Dimensions of e-Learning

Anna Smith and Katrina Kennett

From graphic organizers to 3-D models of cellular structure to choreographed performances of Shakespearean sonnets, multimodal objects and practices are not uncommon in traditional schooling. However, these expressions are often presented as accompaniments to the central, dominant evidence of knowledge and learning—language in the form of print text (Bezemer & Kress, 2008; Jewitt, 2005; Kress & van Leeuwen, 2001). All too often, learning activities and assessments are reduced to alphabetic expressions that can be collected and counted. This holds true for teacher planning materials as well, such as in the prescribed talking points and quiz questions in annotated textbooks. However, the rapid changes to the communicative practices brought on by the sweep of the digital era—including the prevalence of screens, the interactive and social nature of media composition, distribution, and consumption—have created an expanse between the practices of schooling and the practices of daily life, civic engagement, disciplinary study, and professional careers. More often than not, the texts we encounter in daily life are multimodal (Kress, 2003), and we are expected to digitally design multimodal texts in return. Miller and McVee (2012) argue that "integrating the dramatic broadening of purposeful literacies and practices of knowing to include multimodal systems beyond print text for all students may be *the* essential task for schools in the 21st century" (p. 6). In this chapter, we further argue that when educational spaces and practices are reimagined with the affordances of multimodal meaning making foregrounded—particularly those made available by digital tools and interfaces—the potential for reshaping many of the assumed building blocks of educational design and experience in e-learning ecologies is realized.

By multimodal we mean the multiple modes of communication, such as visual, linguistic, spatial, gestural, and aural (Silverstone, 2007), that work in concert with one another to express, create, and represent meaning (see also Scollon, 2001). According to Jewitt (2013), focusing on multimodality in educational spaces draws attention to forms of communication and representation including and beyond language and print—to the full "range of forms of making meaning" (p. 250) that humans use. Multimodality refers to a variety of disciplinary and theoretical approaches, such as semiotic, linguistic, psychological, sociological, pedagogical, and anthropological, that can be applied in the exploration of representational and communicative phenomena (Bezemer & Jewitt, 2010). Although the term has garnered much scholarly attention, multimodality is simply an inherent feature of all aspects of our lives throughout human evolution (Matthiessen, 2007). Through known history, humans have composed and communicated through multimodal artifacts—from Quipu talking knots to online infographic generators. Van Leeuwen (2005) suggests that the logic of a multimodal artifact is that in which the modes work together like instruments in an orchestra—simultaneously effecting meaning yet distinct (see also Unsworth, 2008a, 2008b). In a multimodal argument in comic form, Sousanis (2015) eloquently describes the "mutually affecting relationships" (p. 65) between linguistic and visual modes as a dance between modes for both the reader (as he or she interprets) and the writer (as he or she composes). Considering the history of media creation from analog film and television to the widespread digitization of media creation with multipurpose devices, Kalantzis and Cope (2015) argue that digitization has brought on a tighter knitting of text with other modes in new media. They explain that text and other modes

> functionally depend on each other. They form a grammatical and structural unity: the comment that makes no sense without the image; the caption that points to criterial features in the image; the textual metadata that makes an image discoverable and links the preceding image to the next.
>
> (p. 377)

Although multimodality is not new to meaning-making processes, technological advances have incited new strategies and forms of multimodal production and distribution (Lankshear & Knobel, 2011). With new and evolving technologies on mobile, multipurpose digital devices, multiple modes of knowledge representation and communication can be produced, shared widely, and remixed while people are physically on the move (Leander & Vasudevan, 2009). Digital-born media are more often than not multimodal, and screens are awash with multimodal media created and consumed by the writer-readers of the Internet (Lessig, 2008; Smith & Hull, 2013; Tierney & Pearson, 1983). Kress (2003) has suggested that digital technologies have made multimodal composition not only easy but also "usual" and "natural" (p. 5). Multimodal composition and communication have become inherent in the discourse of e-learning ecologies; wherein multimodal aspects of messages are no longer merely a decorative or juxtaposed accouterment to a central print text (Bezemer & Kress, 2008).

The potentials made available in the digitization of multimodal communication for learning, instructional design, and assessment have led many to express interest in fulfilling the promises of digital multimodality. In higher education, several calls have been made to expand the acceptable forms of thesis and dissertation work to include digital and multimodal representations of knowledge and findings (Andrews et al., 2012; Dalgleish & Powell, 2015). In statements regarding K–12 education, similar calls have been made for extending the definition of literacy to underscore the need for youth to gain experience with the digital tools for composing and reading multimodally in collaborative and cross-cultural problem solving (e.g., International Reading Association, 2012; National Council of Teachers of English, 2003, 2005, 2013).

Along with affordances and possibilities, evolving digital interfaces and new media elicit new demands, roles, and relations for learners in e-learning ecologies. Multimodal reading pathways are not fixed in online spaces, as readers follow their own textual pathways across sites, modes, media, and evolving genres and forms (Coiro & Dobler, 2007; Domingo, Jewitt, & Kress, 2015). Researching the multimodal communicative practices of youth on an educational social network, Hull, Stornaiuolo, and Sterponi (2013) suggested that such changes require a form of nimbleness in reading: "These texts require of those who would communicate effectively the flexible capacity to make meaning across an increasingly complex range of textual forms that integrate multiple semiotic modalities" (p. 1208). Indeed, as Lemke (1998) describes, "Meanings in multimedia are not fixed and additive (the word meaning plus the picture meaning), but multiplicative (word meaning modified by image context, image meaning modified by textual context), making a whole far greater than the simple sum of its parts" (p. 312). Further, as digital, multimodal textual forms evolve, the capacity for multimodal interaction between authors and readers, and among geographically and culturally distant co-readers, has recast and developed new social roles and relations among the writer-readers of the Internet (Andrews & Smith, 2011; Lunsford & Ede, 2009). Such interactions in e-learning ecologies invite learners to consider newly accented ethical stances and dispositions for reading and writing, such as "hospitable" interpretation and reflexive self-presentation (Hull & Stornaiuolo, 2010; Smith & Hull, 2013).

This chapter examines the particular affordances and demands of multimodality for learning in e-learning ecologies. Drawing from international studies and using examples of current, evolving technologies, we consider implications that multimodality has for learners and instructors alike in new learning ecologies. Specifically, the chapter will outline promising possibilities in regard to (1) reading and composing multimodal texts in the processes of learning across disciplines and (2) designing for instruction and assessment that enables student agency throughout ongoing multimodal learning processes.

Multimodality in the Processes of Learning

In the digitization of multimodality, a new welcoming orientation toward learning is emerging—one that is experimental, flexible, and connected. Scholars in the Modern Language Association (Davis et al., 2015), for instance, are in the midst of creating a "curated collection of downloadable, reusable, and remixable pedagogical artifacts" composed using the open repository and code-sharing platform GitHub. In this growing, multimodal, collaborative "text-in-the-making," scholars have identified a series of pedagogical keywords fit for contemporary processes of learning and characteristic of the changing emphases that e-learning ecologies afford the processes of learning. These words include *remix, play, collaboration,* and *failure.* These keywords and the open, collaborative means used to create the collection indicate a much broader dispositional turn among educators and leading organizations toward a renewed recognition that learning entails a process of attempts, misunderstandings, and reformulations.

Learners' processes of coming-to-know are punctuated with *representations* of their present, contingent understandings. These learning processes are never quite finished, even when a representation of their current understanding may be. Prior and Hengst (2010) encouraged educators to consider the chains of meaning that are "drawn from a history of sign use, tuned to present interaction, and oriented to future responses and acts" (p. 7) as individuals learn while designing with the texts, tools, and patterns available to the composer (New London Group, 1996). Indeed, the processes and trajectories of coming-to-know are rich with multimodal media—those that are read and viewed as well as those that are designed and composed (Halverson, 2012). These processes may begin with a deceptively simple multimodal sequence of a child muttering the main points of a reading to himself or herself while gesturing a count on his or her fingers and can include rich and layered multimodal representations that are found in classroom blogs and podcasts.

In e-learning ecologies, texts, talk, and media evolve from situation to situation, move online and off, and intersect in various modes of representation. Learning opportunities can be designed intentionally to support such iterations of composing and interpreting print, nonprint, digital, and mixed representation artifacts and performances in what Newfield (2014) calls transmodal moments. By foregrounding modes in addition to written text in learning artifacts, instructors are able to support students in meaning-making processes within and *beyond* their shared time as a class. Selfe (2009) argued that the processes of composing with audio and paying attention to aurality engage teachers and students alike in opportunities to "realize that different compositional modalities carry with them different possibilities for representing multiple and shifting patterns of identity, additional potential for expression and resistance, expanded ways of engaging with the world" (p. 645). In a study of youths' learning in one after-school program, Pacheco and Velez (2009) noted that the experience of creating multilayered digital maps, embedded with images and geospatial markers using GIS technologies, "can help students theorize from multiple perspectives about the role that space and spatial relationships play in their immediate lives, local communities, and beyond" (p. 294). Such intentionally designed representational traversals across modes, media, and technologies provide learners consistent scaffolded support along their learning pathways beyond a classroom space.

The modalities of a representation are also tightly intertwined with the affordances of the materials and devices used to make and carry expression. Paper and pen, the materials of traditional classroom spaces, are a good fit for printed text, and the traditional practices of copying notes and reproducing charts on a study sheet are apt for the limitations of those materials. In e-learning ecologies, the digital devices with which learners interact are oriented toward viewing, composing, and revising multiple aspects of a multimodal artifact (Jewitt, 2006). An image, for instance, can be uploaded, remixed, or composed on a screen, and with a variety of free apps and other software options, there is a near limitless range of manipulations from visual effects (colors, layers, inversions) to animations that can be applied with a tap on a screen. In e-learning ecologies, multimodal mediation and subsequent remediation not only become feasible but also are well suited to learning as a process of coming-to-know in ways not seen a decade ago. These new ways of multimodally representing and communicating have shifted how we engage in our workplaces and in academic disciplines of study. No longer are the staples of traditional schooling, such as copying notes and reproducing charts on study sheets, sufficient for the new norms of knowledge making in the disciplines and in their industries. In this section, we will first explore multimodality as a mediator in the processes of learning before turning to the demands and shifts in the multimodality of disciplines of study.

Synesthesia in the Processes of Learning

Rather than mere reproductions of knowledge, Kalantzis and Cope (2012) argue that multimodal expressions are vehicles for active knowledge construction (see Chapter 3 in this volume). They suggest a term borrowed from cognitive psychology, *synesthesia,* to describe this learning process (see also Kress, 1997). Synesthesia indicates when sensory inputs (like a smell or a sound) contribute to sensation in a different sense (like a taste or an image). They argue that in reading and writing *across* modes, the learner experiences synesthesia, a kind of meaning making germane to the human body. In studying learning in a second language, Nelson (2006) argued that "synaesthetically derived meaning may be a natural part of the process of creating multimodal texts" (p. 56). In everyday interactions, *monomodal* representations are rare. We may attend to one mode or one mode may be foregrounded (as is the case with written text in typical education practices), but modes are essentially intertwined: an image is accompanied by gesture, which is paired with word; a text annotated with doodles is read aloud. Kalantzis and Cope suggest that as learners represent meaning in one mode or combinations of modes (such as writing and drawing marginalia) and then remediate their understandings with another combination of modes (such as in a reflective blog post with images and video clips curated from Internet searches) learners (re)experience the "known," and new meaning is birthed. Focusing on different aspects of this phenomenon (with accompanying terms: transmediation [Semali, 2002; Suhor, 1984], resemiotization [Iedema, 2003], transmodal remaking [Mavers, 2011], transmodal moments [Newfield, 2014]), many other educational scholars emphasize the "generative power" (Siegel, 1995, p. 455) of intentionally working across modes in the pursuit of learning.

Studying the learning processes of youth who were taking a traditional philosophy course on ethics, a composition course, and participating in an international e-learning social network, Smith and Hull (2013) traced the remaking processes of two students' conceptual development across modalities and media. One young man, Tyson, was struggling to find connection with the core text, a traditional print book, in a course on ethics in the modern era. In class discussions, he rarely spoke. In the composition course, he busied himself making a short video about his "money problems" to post on the course's international social network. The video initially consisted of a series of images of stacks of money and material goods like expensive shoes. Through processes of reading articles and other print text, remixing videos made by international peers, composing images, sequencing these together using the core text's organization, and layering carefully selected and timed music, the short video about his money problems eventually became a film that analyzed human "struggle" for basic rights as defined by the course's core text—food, shelter, health, and education. The traversals of his understanding of the core text and what he meant in his processes of video production developed through transmodality—of working across modes of expression and communication.

Tyson's learning processes were also heavily influenced by the affordances of the e-learning ecology in which he was working. He was not only able to manipulate images in intentional ways with particular software but also to access the multimodal representations and interact with peers geographically and culturally far distant. The first major shift in his processes of coming-to-know the content of his course readings was viewing a video composed and posted by a 14-year-old girl living in India who had sequenced images of her daily routine, which included her work as a maid and her kitchen in which they used an open fire for cooking. She paired these images with a voice-over in which she referenced her father's alcohol abuse. Tyson's emotional response to the images and voice-over prompted a conceptual shift in the video he was making, and in the end, he remixed portions of her video into his. He later posted the video inviting her response and invited the author of the core text to respond as well. Smith and Hull (2013) conclude, "Their learning was mediated by on- and offline iterations of integrated reading, writing, designing, and discussing. . . . [C]ritical digital authorship was instrumental to comprehending traditional print texts, as well as reading their social network and interpreting distant youths' artifacts" (p. 79).

Similar findings regarding increased content understanding when students are engaged in multimodal reading and writing have been reported in studies across grade ranges. Wemmer and Drew (as referenced in Stein, 2008) reported that after instructors of a medical course for audiology specialists introduced a series of digitally mediated, print, and embodied opportunities to study ear pathology, external examiners found that students demonstrated a better understanding of procedures in application. Studying the learning outcomes across a school year during which a teacher increased opportunities for ninth-grade students to engage in multimodal reading and writing across a range of subjects, Bailey (2012) reported improved vocabulary usage, researching strategies, and content comprehension, claiming that use of each mode, whether sound, image, or word, prompted "a cognitive response—thinking, searching and creating" (p. 55) in other modes. The teacher and researcher also noted changes in the students' academic identities, from regarding learning as a passive activity to considering themselves as scholars and potential producers of knowledge (for more on active knowledge making, see Chapter 3 in this volume). One young man, Max, reported, "Now we have seen so many different ways to understand reading. This class has opened up my eyes" (p. 60). Contemporary media and technologies make multimodal traversals possible, easy, and natural (Kress, 2003); however, intentionally designed multimodal learning sequences like those reported in this chapter are still rare in traditional schooling settings. If instructors in e-learning ecologies merely replicate the typical practices of traditional schooling (as is often the case in lecture-to-quiz MOOC formats), the potentials of synesthesia in learning processes will remain untapped.

Multimodality in the Study of Subjects

Ways of knowing, doing, and evaluating knowledge vary by academic discipline and industry. Further, the ways a person reads or writes are integral to understanding and communicating the disciplinary content they are learning (Moje, 2008; Zygouris-Coe, 2012). With this understanding, interest in the specialized reading and writing demands of differing disciplines has increased in recent decades (O'Brien, Moje, & Stewart, 2001). Standards and frameworks across academic disciplines in K–12 education, such as Next Generation Science Standards (NGSS Lead States, 2013) and the College, Career, and Civic Life (C3) Framework for Social Studies State Standards (National Council for Social Studies, 2013), have incorporated explicit mention of the literacy demands of these subject areas. The Common Core State Standards Initiative includes standards regarding some of the multimodal facets of some of these disciplines, such as: "translate quantitative or technical information expressed in words in a text into visual form (e.g., a table or chart)" and "translate information expressed visually or mathematically (e.g., in an equation) into words" (CCSS.ELALITERACY.RST.9–10.7). Each of these standards involves specialized disciplinary knowledge, multimodal composing skill, and practice working across modes and disciplines.

In order to ensure that youth have such disciplinary practice, Wilson (2011) has suggested that teachers become more aware of the predominant ways modes are used in the subject areas they teach. This is a critical first step, she argues, for providing students opportunities to develop meta-awareness and language about ways modes are used differently across disciplines of study. Math, for example, is one of the most obviously multimodal subjects because the primary semiotic systems of mathematics are numeric and symbolic and involve a variety of multimodal text types and materials, such as graphs, physical models, sketches, rulers, and so on. These modes serve particular disciplinary purposes and imply particular practices that are learned along with the mathematical content, such as an orientation toward precision, and standardized meaning and orders of operation. In the processes of learning math or any other subject, Wilson suggests:

> As students read and write texts while attending to their affordances, they can use the concept of affordances to identify why some modes are apt (or inept) conveyors of discipline-specific content, and they can themselves reflectively design representations that most fully enable them to convey desired meanings.
>
> (p. 441)

In a similar study focused on the professional development in educational technology for content area teachers, McVee, Bailey, and Shanahan (2012) found that teachers' awareness of disciplinary multimodal features increased when they were engaged in composing multimodal texts with digital technologies. The same was not found when teachers were focused merely on using a new piece of technology in their disciplinary teaching. For teachers and students alike, it seems that engaging in multimodal sequences of interpretation and composition are important for increasing their metacognitive awareness of the disciplinary uses of modes to represent and communicate knowledge (for more on metacognition, see Chapter 7 in this volume). Professional development efforts, such as the National Writing Project's Connected Learning MOOC, an online learning opportunity focused on engaging educators in making and remixing multimodal artifacts with emerging technology (see Smith et al., 2016), are critical to support.

With the turn to digitization, multimodal aspects of disciplines are amplified, and this holds great potential for learning in the disciplines. For instance, in the science arena, visual displays and images are abundant and serve the purpose of illuminating otherwise invisible processes, such as cell mitosis or evolution, and illustrating variants of scale of natural world phenomena, such as the levels of a rain forest. From videos to interactive models and diagrams, vast repertoires of dynamic images have not only become accessible to instructors but also learners and instructors alike can search, compare, and manipulate multiple free resources. Interactive tools, such as those on Wolfram | Alpha, allow users to interact with visualizations—varying the inputs of basic equations and databases to test changes such manipulations make. These interactives are available in several science categories, such as earth science, chemistry, and life sciences, as well as categories for socioeconomics, music, mathematics, and more. In these ways, disciplinary concepts are digitally displayed in word, image, and numeric expression, and students of various disciplines can interact across these modes in their processes of learning content.

A team at the University of Illinois at Urbana–Champaign is currently researching the role of sketching, and collaborative sketching mediated by technologies, in the processes of engineering and engineering learning. Sketching, and further, collaborative sketches using evolving technologies, argues Professor Emma Mercier, are central mediators in the workflows of engineers, but these multimodal representations are rarely attended to in collegiate study. This current work with undergraduate engineering students is built on previous research (Mercier & Higgins, 2014) that explored how large multi-touch tables were used by groups of fifth-grade students as a way to visually represent their collaborative understandings during a series of problem-solving tasks. Without prompting, youth used the visual and spatial capabilities of the multi-touch tables, such as resizing pieces of evidence and arranging data spatially, to show relationships and to facilitate the collaborative problem-solving and learning processes. The authors concluded that, particularly in collaborative settings, having digital tools that facilitated collaborative viewing and interaction with spatial, visual, and linguistic modes were central to effective problem solving.

Further, the disciplines themselves are seeing minor to major shifts in the ways they are practiced in this digital era. For example, language arts and literature studies have a strong history of emphasizing individual ideation and creation. In the study of literary texts, the author of texts, and the interpretation of the author's perspectives and intentions, their individual styles and patterns of structure hold a place of importance. As the discipline moves to online spaces, authors of texts are further highlighted in interactive, multimodal form—in avatars, podcasts, links to profile pages—heightening the ways authors are individuated and increasing the means readers must contend with to interpret the literary text. With the web-based application and extension Hypothes.is (https://hypothes.is/), readers can multimodally annotate texts anywhere on the Internet. These multimodal annotations can be responded to, contested, upvoted, curated, shared via social media, and so on. Through these processes, annotators not only create a discussion community but also become coauthors of a newly layered text.

These interactive capabilities are part of a wider range of changes in ways author and audience relate and the roles they play in online interaction (Lessig, 2008). In her work on the differing semiotic resources adult students use in e-learning environments utilizing online role-playing in the learning processes, Doerr-Stevens (2011) found that adults crafted fictional online personas that allowed them to have particular interactions that differed from those made offline. Similar affordances were found in Kirkland (2009) where social positionings offline were mitigated by carefully crafted fictional avatars and personas in online virtual spaces. Space and place, and humans' relations to those places, are becoming units of analysis in humanities courses in which students are using GPS and online mapping tools to crowdsource the locations of historical primary and secondary sources, along with fictional events and tales, on shared maps (e.g., Kretzschmar, 2013). These forms of literary analysis are radically different from the traditional written text-only essays that were foundational for decades. The field is shifting, and educational practice must follow suit if it hopes to maintain relevance in a rapidly changing landscape of disciplinary multimodal, interactive composition.

Across disciplines, efforts must be made to mitigate the gap between traditional study in the disciplines and the demands of a new evolving digital global economy. Teachers and students of all ages need familiarity and experience with evolving communication technologies and subsequent transforming disciplinary practices for savvy engagement in a transforming communication landscape. This includes an increased knowledge and use of modes not typical in traditional schooling. As Miller and McVee (2012) argued, "Facility with design—the process of orchestrating representational modes and their interconnection—is vital for composing a text that can meet the demands of new and future multimodal environments" (p. 2).

Designing Instruction for Multimodal Meaning Making

New learning spaces ask instructors to consider—and reconsider—their stances toward teaching, learning, and technology; the ways they frame and support student learning; and the design processes they use to create learning opportunities with generative constraints. As teachers try out new tools, plan for multimodal instruction, determine the practices that scaffold students' agency, and engage in reflection, they participate in the facilitative and collaborative teaching roles that new learning environments invite. Indeed, the multimodal possibilities for designing and engaging in instruction have implications not only for how instruction plays out in new learning spaces but also for how they build student and teacher capacity for learning beyond their time together. This section discusses opportunities that new learning environments make possible and explores ways that instructors can design within these environments to facilitate ongoing multimodal knowledge making. To do so, we consider supportive stances for new learning, ways of constructing generative constraints within e-learning spaces, purposes of participatory assessment for learning, and how instructors can use multimodal tools for professional practices.

Supportive Stances for New Learning

Instructors' stances toward multimodal learning shape the experiences that they design for their students. Their beliefs about knowledge, students, multimodality, and technologies have important implications for the ways in which they invite students to construct meaning in their classes. The features of e-learning ecologies, which are increasingly collaborative, interactive, and multifaceted, support students in the social construction of knowledge, enabling instructors to better support and scaffold ongoing instruction. The following are four orientations that, within e-learning ecologies, enable instructors to engage with students as co-constructors of their learning.

Technologies as Vehicles for Learning Processes

Often, the word *technology* brings to mind digital (e.g., word processors, tablets, and wearables) and non-digital tools (e.g., hammers, fire, and scissors). Including tools, but not limited to them, we define technologies as inclusive of the practices and processes we use—individually and collectively—in order to accomplish a task. For example, the scientific method as a technology foregrounds tools like sketches, pencils, tables, notebooks, and debates—not to mention the myriad of technological devices that fill laboratories. The technologies used in a writing process might include the coordination of multiple technological tools like pens, paper, photographs, a writing conference, and PDF files. By recognizing technologies as both the tools we use and the processes by which we use them, we can think more expansively about learning as socially constructed. Instructors can position multiple technologies as vehicles for multimodal meaning making, opening up pathways for collaborative student learning processes.

When teachers consider technologies as both processes and tools, they can capitalize on multimodal practices of constructing knowledge. They can invite the ways in which students already make meaning with new digitally mediated social processes—collaborative, iterative, and in synchronous and asynchronous relations across modes and media. Positioning students as both knowledge producers and consumers has democratizing effects: no longer tied to the traditional architecture of schools—with one teacher talking and multiple students listening—students and teachers can leverage the affordances of new media for diverse collaborations (Morrell et al., 2013). Intentionally deploying these newly available technologies that democratize hierarchies of knowledge, teachers can position learners as "co-designers of knowledge, developing habits of mind in which they are comfortable members of knowledge-producing and knowledge-sharing communities" (Kalantzis & Cope, 2008, p. 40). In a meta-analysis of seven studies focused on shifts in instructional design as teachers took on digital multimodal composing in their planning and teaching, Miller and McVee (2012) concluded that when students *and* teachers "had opportunities to compose their understanding of curriculum with 'multimodal composing' they used images, gestures, sounds, music, movement to represent and communicate meaning—and that changed how they experienced school and learning" (p. xi). In addition to "making design elements explicit as meaning-making tools" (p. 136), Miller and McVee reported that essential to these results were peer-to-peer learning opportunities that were teacher and student co-constructed and that integrated knowledge from outside the classroom. A broader framing of technology recognizes—and celebrates—the ways in which teachers and students co-construct knowledge through processes and artifacts over time.

This stance on technologies provides an entry point to understanding learning as a series of structured opportunities where students compose and reflect multimodally. Initial assignments can invite students into the work of the class, asking them to create multimodal artifacts and participate in multi-modal disciplinary practices. In ongoing co-constructed assignments, students can continue to ask questions and reflect on their learning using the potentials of available digital tools. As this sequence of events builds on itself, students can represent and re-represent knowledge, accumulating a digital series of artifacts that they can use for ongoing reflection and learning (Olmanson et al., 2015). These iterative learning opportunities open up increasing opportunities for students' choice and agency, as the work within these assignments becomes increasingly complex. Because students have had meaningful opportunities for choice in earlier assignments, they are better prepared to make more and more sophisticated choices in later assignments, a process that builds—and draws on—their developing multimodal repertoire.

Teaching as Responding to Students

Learners, adept at communicating in multimodal forms of their own choosing, already engage in evolving social practices rarely invited into classrooms (Alvermann, 2008; Domingo, 2014; Vasudevan, DeJaynes, & Schmier, 2010). Their rich on/offline lives can be invited into e-learning spaces, where diverse experiences, practices, and perspectives can be integrated into instruction (Guzzetti, Elliot, & Welsch, 2010). Instructors, in their intentional use of the e-learning space, can make opportunities available for students to share their multimodal expertise in a variety of forms. To begin, instructors could use common social networking practices, such as introductory posts, profile pages, and discussion threads. As the course material becomes more complex, and the instructor and students more comfortable with using digital tools and practices in the e-learning environment, so can the ways in which students engage in public and disciplinary dialogue (e.g., through forums, video responses, or memes).

If instructors don't take the initiative to learn from and with their students' digitally mediated communicative practices, then challenges can arise. When teachers' expectations and cultural discourse practices are disconnected from those of their students, it can lead to misunderstandings and decreased opportunities for student participation (Cazden & Beck, 2008). Non-digital cultures, discourses, and communication patterns often shape online interaction in educational spaces (Gunawardena & LaPointe, 2007; Turner et al., 2014). As Banks (2011) argued, uncritical acceptance of common educational practices can exacerbate long-standing inequalities. Banks, in talking about African American rhetorical practices with various technologies, reminds us that in

> acts of writing, the social networks and cultural contexts in which they take place still involve systems of power, still reflect the relationships between individuals and groups within those systems, and still entail questions of what it means to be and how we come to see, hear, sense, and know the world with all of those technologies, power relations, social networks, and cultural contexts.
>
> (p. 154)

Similarly, online structures can affect who engages and how they engage with e-learning courses. In a study of online courses in higher education, Eddy and Hogan (2014) found that within "moderate-structured" courses, meaning courses that had increased the number of assignment options and student dialogue within class-time activities, all student populations performed better on exams than in the online courses patterned after more traditional course structures, with few assignments, limited feedback on those assignments, and little to no interaction during class time. Eddy and Hogan found, however, that the difference in the success of black and first-generation students in moderately structured courses versus more traditionally structured courses was above and beyond other populations—a finding that has important implications for addressing inequities in educational spaces. Thus, it is imperative for instructors to attend to the design of the course and the ways it asks students to engage in their learning. As always, instructors must reflect on their own communication patterns, preferences, and presentation of content and activities and evaluate these in light of the students they are teaching and the broadened range of communicative and compositional technologies available.

Teacher as Knowledgeable Guide Learning Alongside Students

With expertise in their disciplines, subject areas, and practices, instructors often feel pressure to also be experts in the evolving technological tools they use (be it the latest devices or the most recent platforms). However, when instructors embrace that they can't foresee every use and learn all the ins and outs of their evolving instructional tools, there is less pressure to be the "expert" (Franklin & Gibson, 2014). Instead, their role becomes one of a knowledgeable guide, someone who is familiar with the instructional tools, thoughtful about how these tools can influence students' learning experiences, and pedagogically responsive to students' use of the tools. As students encounter instructional platforms, they might use them in unexpected ways; as they create multimodal texts, they might interpret and compose multimodal artifacts outside the teacher's intentions. With the variation inherent in new learning ecologies, instructors' stances as knowledgeable guides focus their instructional goals on the learning process rather than on the minutia of a particular tool.

As knowledgeable guides of disciplinary demands, teachers are well positioned to model multimodal creation with constantly evolving digital tools. Hicks (2014) looked at one teacher's growth in using digital writing over three years and found that her digital writing practices—from creating wiki pages to composing a digital story with script, images, and music—affected both her own learning and the learning opportunities she provided her students. In addition, a teacher's degree of consistency in using digital platforms can influence instructional practices. Felix (2008) surveyed 168 teachers on how they used blogs in their classrooms over a two-year period, complementing this data with interviews of 12 teachers on perceptions of students' learning and analysis of teachers' blogs. He found that teachers who blog have their students blog more frequently, and that 89% of teachers indicated that blogging changed their methods as well as increased collaboration and peer interaction. Miller (2010) found that teachers whose use of digital video composing transformed their classroom practices co-constructed authentic purposes for assignments *with* their students and focused explicitly on multimodal design and critique of multimodal texts. As these examples highlight, teachers' time spent as learners provides new understandings of digital environments, a familiarity that encourages digital innovative classroom behavior (Thurlings, Evers, & Vermeulen, 2015).

Teaching as Enabling Autonomy and Agency

Traditional school-based assignments often establish the individual student as author, the teacher as sole audience, and the assignment boundaries as highly structured and often narrowly contextualized. In new learning ecologies, instructors can transform those inherited restrictions. Taking into account new possibilities for structure and flow in e-learning environments, they can reconsider the goals of the assignment, the production of the assignment with collaborative and material variations, and how the assignment is intended for and delivered to which audiences. In each of these potential hot spots for redesign, the instructor can also rethink when and how to engage students in these pedagogical decisions. Asking students to engage in deciding the process and/or outcome of the learning co-constructs the assignment in ways they could find meaningful, as these processes build their repertoire as a disciplinary composer as well as their agency in learning.

Inviting student voice and choice does not entail an anything-goes attitude. Instructors are key to helping students build rhetorical agency. As they scaffold ongoing connections between what students are doing and how they're doing it, teachers can emphasize the bridges between purposes and communicative strategies. Without this help, students can fail to see connections within and across contexts. Anson, Dannels, and St. Clair (2005) constructed a multimodal opportunity for students to deliver an oral presentation and provide a paired handout. Students who didn't see the relationship between the two modes of communication divided the purposes of each and didn't draw on the mutually informative potentials. This offline example has implications for online work as teachers develop assignments for digital presentations during which students need to be able to draw on the potentials in all of the communicative modes they deploy.

Shipka (2005) argues for an instructional stance that invites students' multimodal agency. In her pedagogy, students decide on the products, processes, technologies, and resources needed to accomplish them as well as the conditions under which the audience will receive their work. She argues that a "multimodal task-based framework not only requires that students work hard, but, related to this, *differently*, and it does so by foregrounding the complex processes associated with goal formation and attainment" (p. 290). Instead of isolating modes, Shipka's multimodal framework asks students to be thoughtful engineers of multipart rhetorical events, drawing on modes as they serve their needs for particular audiences. In online spaces, this flexibility and accountability to both product and process is especially important, as students have access to various emerging technologies, platforms, and devices with which they can create a broad range of learning artifacts.

Constructing Generative Constraints Within e-Learning Spaces

There are multiple entry points when designing instruction for new learning ecologies. Teachers might start planning with course content (e.g., cell biology, *Beloved*, or the civil rights movement), with their students and their experiences (e.g., students have an interest in collecting oral histories or will create a persuasive podcast as a final assessment), or even with the available classroom technologies (e.g., digital sticky-note walls or video-editing software). Whatever the instructors' starting place, their subsequent processes lead them to reflect on contextual factors as they make decisions about the roles that multimodality will play in students' learning experiences.

An instructor's instructional deliberation and decision making can be characterized as a process of selecting generative constraints for classroom experiences. Generative constraints are the resources that an instructor orchestrates to guide students' experiences and that result in creative and fruitful demonstrations of learning. They provide just enough organization for students to elicit individual and collective meaning making but not so much as to stifle or prescribe specific outcomes (c.f. Davis, Sumara, & Luce-Kapler, 2008). Examples of constraints might include the boundaries laid out in an assignment, instructions like "work with a partner from a different country," or affordances of digital tools such as a screen-recording feature—all of which can be used purposefully to generate intellectual and creative freedom.

Instructors select and develop generative constraints over their planning process and, as various possibilities arise and different conditions emerge during the course, these constraints also evolve. By designing generative constraints that are flexible across time, instructors can support student agency through a series of learning opportunities that increasingly rely on learners to make meaningful disciplinary decisions. These choices shape students' multimodal artifacts and practices (e.g., remixing a video lecture from a previous week that leads to creating a supplementary lecture for a future week, or remediating the argument of an article into an infographic that leads to remediating a disciplinary theory as a transmedia experience). Thus, instructors design learning activities that provide just enough support to enable active knowledge making, create meaningful spaces for reflection, and respond to how students make intentional choices within assignments—all the while trusting in and relying on students' own learning prowess.

How do instructors develop flexible generative constraints for new learning spaces? To start, instructors might take stock of predetermined influences, goals, and opportunities of the instructional situation, ranging from the course objectives to the number of students in the class. In an e-learning context, this may entail explicating how the course fits into current trends in its disciplinary field. As they plan, instructors foreground intellectual purposes like active knowledge making, authentic disciplinary inquiry, and ways students might find personal and community value in their work. To model authentic inquiry within disciplines, instructors might bring in multimodal disciplinary artifacts, such as a flowchart of disease transmission in health or a podcast on prosody in linguistics, to engage in learning processes beyond strictly print texts. Instructors also think about intentional sequences of learning experiences and how these integrate with opportunities for assessment. They can take advantage of possibilities for students to create digital multimodal artifacts within e-learning environments, where publishing opportunities are amplified, and ask for student reflection on the choices they made.

Instructors also plan for the nuts and bolts like course logistics, the learning environment, and the things they need to do that students don't or cannot do. An example of this might be exploring an online platform and determining how it enables multiple configurations for student collaboration or how the environment is inclusive in the ways that students access and engage within the digital space. These decisions are also made as the course evolves, as teachers support learning as an iterative process over time. Mayes and de Freitas (2007) argue that there is an often unrecognized "long tradition of describing learning as a cycle through stages" that could, if recognized, position "the e-learning designer to consider what kind of technology is most effective at what stage of learning" (p. 21). In considering these—and other—instructional factors, teachers determine what will serve as generative constraints within the e-learning ecology.

With all of these entry points to planning for generative constraints, it might be useful to focus on three underpinnings of multimodal learning in e-learning ecologies. In the process of asking questions about their contexts, instructors can use them as lenses to develop instruction.

- *Composing and reflecting.* What are opportunities for student multimodal making and metacognition? What text types are students composing within which disciplines? Asking questions like these helps teachers determine the role of multimodality and active knowledge making in individual and collective assignments. They might ask: What multimodal resources do students have available for their assignments (Ranker, 2012)? How will students negotiate and select multimodal choices available to them (Shipka, 2006)? How can students leverage the networked capabilities of digital writing (Hart-Davidson et al., 2005)?
- *Sequence of experiences.* What are the learning experiences that build on one another and increase learners' autonomy and agency in the learning process? Constructing an intentional sequence of experiences helps students and teachers iterate with student-produced multimodal content knowledge and skills. What are the smaller multimodal assignments that build toward complex and independent learning (Benko, 2012)? How can students select from previous experiences to represent their learning multimodally (Jocius, 2013)?
- *Environment.* What are the characteristics of the e-learning environment, and what practices do its features enable? Which modes does the environment facilitate, which does it restrict, and how could those features be pedagogically useful? A digital environment's space, and the movement enabled within that space, shape how students complete assignments and how they collaborate with their peers. What does the design of the space make available through its features and its visual, multimodal rhetoric (Wysocki, 2004)? What are the potential portals for various types of multimodal activities (Shearer, 2007)? How does the space support the dynamism of these roles and relationships over time (Gee, 2005)?

These are only three areas to explore when creating generative constraints, but they can inform the developing instructional design in important ways. As instructors consider these and similar provocations, they are inspired to consider and reconsider related aspects of instruction, and through this mutually informing process (visualized in Figure 4.1), an instructional approach attuned to generative constraints emerges. In this sense, these areas themselves are not generative—what instructors determine as the shape, structure, and scope of what students do opens up opportunities for meaningful choice and trajectories of agency.

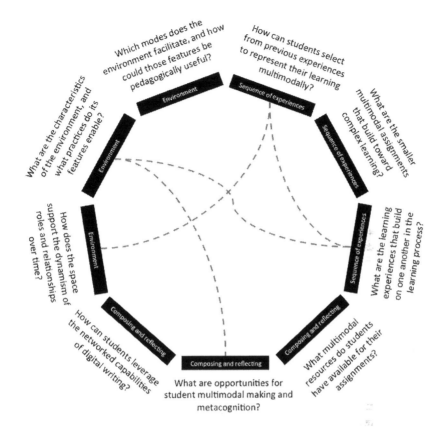

Figure 4.1 Visual representation of the dynamic instructional design process guided by mutually informing entry points

Participatory Multimodal Assessment

As discussed, e-learning ecologies bring new possibilities for the ways learners may be asked to represent their learning and share in negotiating their learning pathways. The old media demands of creation and distribution, such as codes to a copy machine in the faculty room and physical in-boxes on teachers' desks, necessitated segmentation and individuation of assignments, assessments, and feedback. With new media in e-learning ecologies, no longer must the teacher be positioned as a gatekeeper of assignments and assessment, but rather, the teacher can act as an orchestrator of opportunities for multimodal composition, collaborative curation, shared assessment, and reflection (Littleton, Scanlon, & Sharples, 2012).

Taking advantage of the affordances of digital learning spaces, teachers can design recursive sequences of activities in which learners are partners as they materialize their understandings in multimodal forms, construct their learning experiences, and reconfigure their understandings through evaluation, feedback, and reflection (International Reading Association, 2013). For these radical shifts to happen, teachers and students alike must think about representation and assessment more broadly than traditional notions avail. As Curwood (2012) suggests, this involves

> shifting away from our assessment frameworks that were effective with print text in a theoretic culture in order to critically consider what literacy skills, rhetorical devices, social interaction, and meaning-making processes that we value in our present day virtual culture.
>
> (p. 236)

In this section, we reimagine the potential of thinking broadly about digital multimodality with two tried-and-true building blocks of assessment: the rubric and the portfolio.

Rubrics

Rubrics afford lenses to articulating student learning. Rubrics can guide learners throughout making and composing processes when they are provided or can be co-constructed at the onset of a learning sequence and referred to as learners compose. Particularly as disciplinary fields continue to shift their expectations for multimodal knowledge representation, assessing multimodal representations along learning pathways is critical to gauge growing understanding of disciplinary practices. In typical educational practice, however, rubrics are often applied to a single, final product as a definitive closure of a project. In attending to longer swaths of learners' digitally mediated learning processes, we can take up expanded notions regarding what we ask of the multimodal learning artifacts that punctuate learning processes, not to mention what we consider as artifacts of learning and how we collect them.

Educators and researchers focused on elementary-aged youth (e.g., Shanahan, 2012) through higher education and professional life (e.g., MLA Committee on Information Technology, 2012) have curated new questions and criteria for multimodal artifacts regarding the communicative potential of various modes, their limitations, and how they are used in concert when composing digital multimodal texts. Foregrounding multimodal practices, instead of only the learning artifact, recognizes the participatory cultural shifts (Jenkins, et al., 2009) occurring across disciplines. For instance, because collaborative interactions lead to a finished form, especially in e-learning ecologies where interactive audiences shape multimodal artifacts, Andrews and Smith (2011) suggested that, in addition to the substance and composition of multimodal representations, the collaborative interactions themselves offer sites for potential assessment and learning. They further argue that the practices and functionality of new media require of contemporary composers to consider the ways they are framing their compositions as ready for new media's distribution patterns, flexibility of forms, and changing, emergent genres (see also Andrews, 2011). The following questions are derived from these various sources and bring up new potential criteria to consider as instructors and learners review multimodal representations of learning.

- *Representation.* How are students using the medium's affordances and the communicative possibilities of various modes to establish a relationship *with* audience(s)? If remediating messages by changing modes and/or situation, how are students making decisive changes depending on the resources, audience, and disciplinary demands?
- *Audiences.* With whom are students engaging in composing collaboratively? From whom are they giving, receiving, and accepting feedback? What is the nature of those interactions? What rationale(s) do students give for how they addressed audience(s)—intended and potential?
- *Framing.* How do students use product formats for effective and clear communication? What existing genres (disciplinary and otherwise) are students drawing from and adjusting to to meet the needs of audiences and communities? Can students articulate their choices in shaping and positioning (posting) their writing in particular online spaces and communities? How do they leverage the affordances of those particular spaces and communities?

Shifting away from print-centric assessments and toward multimodal, iterative learning tasks generates new approaches and practicalities to assess with rubrics. Using online resources from collections such as Jenn Borgioli's quality rubrics wiki (available at http://qualityrubrics.pbworks.com/w/page/1067879/Resources), Jerry Steingarten's rubrics page (available at http://cybraryman.com/rubrics.html), or the Buck Institute's resource collection (available at http://bie.org/objects/cat/rubrics), teachers and students can share in the use and evolution of rubrics that embrace the complexity inherent in learning processes. This complexity, materialized in what a learning artifact is trying to say *and* how it is saying it, might not be recognized by traditional content-based rubrics. For example, a student's video on the histories of gun violence in the United States might be watched by thousands but score low on a rubric looking for a clear thesis statement and clearly organized paragraphs. Instead, this instructor might offer blank rows within a common rubric in a collaboratively and synchronously editable document, such as a Google Doc. Here the student might articulate criteria that draw attention to the ways in which his or her video made its argument by leveraging voice-over, images, and sequence within the screencast.

Applications for workflow management, such as Trello, and a range of interactive, multimodal time lines, such as Timeglider and TimeRime, can help learners track their collaborative processes by hyperlinking to the range of multimodal representations of learning and collaboration that lead up to final products. In the previous example of a video project, this could include the storyboards, rough cuts with audience feedback, and process logs. Rubrics could then be used with and informed by these processes and the artifacts that punctuate them. This rich synthesis of time, process, audience, and intention positions the rubric not only as a dialogue about a contextual learning artifact but also as a functional splash page of associated invention.

Understanding the complex choices that students make shouldn't be a guessing game for instructors. Asking students to reflect on and justify what they have done can be a powerful way to acknowledge their intentional design choices (Shipka, 2005). Arola, Sheppard, and Ball (2015) ask their college-aged students to articulate their meta-awareness as written rationales, class presentations, and formal cover letters. Other instructors might ask for a recorded rationale—either audio or video—at various scales (fine grained for one assignment or more broadly across multiple artifacts) as well as synthesize learning that has happened over time. For instance, an instructor may prompt: "How has your multimodal meaning making become more sophisticated over our time together?" or "Choose a thread of inquiry you have followed and explain how your work—using your multimodal artifacts and processes—relates to disciplinary conversations." As learners become partners in assessing their own multimodal representations, the ways in which they participate in disciplinary practices can be supported by increasingly contextual and collaboratively written rubric criteria. Such reflective and dialogic assessment would position assessment as a learning opportunity for student and teacher alike, facilitating what Boud (2000) calls sustainable assessment or assessments that "meet the specific and immediate goals of a course, as well as establishing a basis for students to undertake their own assessment activities in the future" (p. 151).

Portfolios

As students represent learning over time, portfolios can be vehicles for students to purposefully collect, reflect, and become partners in assessing their digital multimodal work (Brookhart, 2008). However, to support learning processes and take advantage of the networked, multimodal capacities of the digital spaces, portfolios would need to be reimagined and refigured to address several of the aspects identified by Andrews and Smith (2011):

1. portfolios are generally limited to final written products—leaving processes, practices, dispositions and skills unaccounted for;
2. portfolios are often either teacher selected or student selected—either way the selection process results in a loss of the necessary ecological snapshot;
3. the reflective responses that accompany some portfolios are a start, but they are not sufficient to account for the social, cultural, instructional and contextual factors that enable and constrain development.

(pp. 170–171)

We add to this list three additional shifts that could be addressed by leveraging the potentials of new learning ecologies: (1) collections of artifacts can be conducted over longer times with a wider range of multimodal representations; (2) production and review of portfolios can involve communal curation and interactive assessment; and (3) emerging technologies can afford new ways of encountering and interpreting portfolios.

Learning and reflection take place over time and through a range of multimodal artifacts. Collecting evidence of learning in this way can be a form of building evidence of disciplinary expertise. In some vocational programs, learners use portfolios to collect written case reports, professional CVs, logbooks, or other specific multimodal artifacts, many of which are increasingly being digitized and stored online (Ellaway, 2007). Continuing collection over time can reveal learning patterns and development of skills and knowledge. As instructors support this consistent practice, they can target key points in the year for student reflection and metacognition. In a study taking place at the end of the school year, Kissel, Putman, and Stover (2014) observed fourth-grade students who selected pieces of work from throughout the year and reflected on their growth as writers. In addition to digital work, they took pictures of handwritten and hand-sketched work and uploaded them to their portfolios. The electronic nature of the portfolio supported a range of multimodal artifacts and became an important vehicle for how students shared their work with one another. In selecting, reflecting, and connecting with one another, students were able to shift from skill driven "best work" to orienting toward a fuller audience that helped explain their growth.

Portfolios, as communal, interactive learning spaces, offer students and teachers places to both collect ongoing work and curate that work for various purposes, including their ongoing inquiry (Hicks et al., 2007). Using a digital portfolio, students might collect written drafts, pictures of sketches, audio of think-alouds, and screencasts where they prototype an idea and include what they are stuck on. With applications such as Videonot.es or Vialogues, students could then take video-synchronized notes and return them to the original author for review. Students might curate their collected multimodal artifacts for a variety of purposes and audiences: the multimodal artifacts that show the most growth for a conference with a group of peers, pieces that would synthesize into an infographic on their topics for a final project, or a transmedia argument about a contemporary social issue. Groups might use a shared portfolio to collect and curate multimodal artifacts as an evolving repository for collaborative tasks. Collection and curation practices are supported with digital media, as are ongoing check-ins by the instructor, who is able to asynchronously comment on stages of a group's progress or add resources for a particular student.

As teachers keep their own portfolios alongside their students, they too can curate collections that serve multiple purposes (including for department presentations, future classes, and personal growth). In working with one first-grade teacher who curated a digital professional portfolio—using tools such as

Word, HyperCard, and HyperStudio—while her students created their own academic ones, Kieffer, Hale, and Templeton (1998) noted that the collection and curation practices helped her become more reflective about the choices she was making as a teacher. This teacher's purposes for portfolios, from collecting and creating artifacts to inform her teaching to reflecting on ways of knowing about herself and her students, indicates the potential collecting and curating various multimodal artifacts over time has for powerful multifaceted professional practice.

Facilitated by evolving technologies, instructors and students have multiple ways of encountering and interpreting digital portfolios. In considering how instructors engage with digital portfolios, Yancey, McElroy, and Powers (2013) highlighted that assessment with digital portfolios includes thoughtful attention to how they are navigated, read, and visualized. From the metadata collected in learning analytics (cf. Cope & Kalantzis, 2015) to visualization software, evolving technologies allow for analysis of learning at various scales and time spans. To take up the affordances of interactive, collaborative visualizations at various scales, Andrews and Smith (2011) suggested the development of *multiples* as derived from medical charts (Tufte, 1997) as a hyperlinked one-glance splash page for digital portfolios. This splash page (see Figure 4.2) would consist of hyperlinked thumbnails (e.g., numerous and varied multimodal products, prompts, contextual artifacts, and other indicators of learning) that are collaboratively gathered and color-coded according to their salient disciplinary and composition practices identified locally through "deep viewing" (Penrod, 2010). Through such knowledge representations and

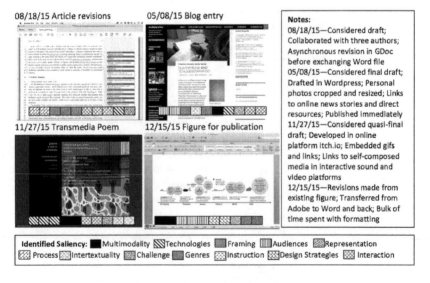

Figure 4.2 Portfolio 2.0 splash page mock-up patterned after Andrews and Smith (2011)

multimodal practices, learners and their instructors become partners as they interactively and responsively collect, curate, and view growth in understanding, in disciplinary practices and skills, and in experiences.

Conclusion

There are several avenues that could be taken to capitalize on the affordances of the multimodality of e-learning ecologies. This chapter introduced just a few of the directions that reimagine the educational domain in radically multimodal ways. We reviewed the functional and generative role that multimodal representations play in the processes of learning, suggesting that dispositions toward experimentation, flexibility, and connection making are foregrounded in the making and sharing of such representations. Learners' concept building is facilitated and new understandings arise as they compose and consume across modalities with digital tools and within digitally networked spaces. Further, the multimodality of disciplines—both the dominant modes of communication and the ways modes are used to represent and communicate knowledge across varied disciplines of study—are knowable and can be put to use in the learning processes. This requires attentiveness to the changing landscape of multimodal composing and attendant practices.

Designing instruction within and for new e-learning spaces to support multimodal learning processes involves negotiating a complex set of practices, technologies, and resources. The new roles demanded of instructors necessitate shifts in teachers' dispositions, attention to learning artifacts and processes, and stances toward knowledge, students, multimodal texts, and technologies. As they explore ever-developing digital environments, instructors' own learning experiences inform how they design learning experiences with multimodal composing and reflecting. The extensive work of engaging as an ongoing learner has implications for teachers' roles as assessors, especially as they invite meaningful student participation into a realm traditionally controlled solely by the teacher. Instructors can further leverage multimodal digital tools for their professional practice. When instructors use digital tools, possibilities emerge for reflecting on their own routines, archiving student work, and remixing instruction for future use. As tools and practices co-evolve, instructors will have even more resources as their disposal to leverage multimodality in their teaching and as part of their professional practice. Such shifts in the environments, foci, and practices of learners and their teachers hold great promise for multimodal practices that enrich the experience of learning and teaching in e-learning ecologies.

References

Alvermann, D. E. (2008). Why bother theorizing adolescents' online literacies for classroom practice and research? *Journal of Adolescent & Adult Literacy, 52*, 8–19. http://doi.org/10.1598/JAAL.52.1.2

Andrews, R. (2011). *Re-framing literacy: Teaching and learning English and the language arts.* New York: Routledge.

Andrews, R., Borg, E., Boyd Davis, S., Domingo, M., & England, J. (Eds.). (2012). *The Sage handbook of digital dissertations and theses.* London: Sage.

Andrews, R., & Smith, A. (2011). *Developing writers: Teaching and learning in the digital age.* London: Open University Press.

Anson, C. M., Dannels, D. P., & St. Clair, K. (2005). Teaching and learning a multimodal genre in a psychology course. In A. J. Herrington & C. Moran (Eds.), *Genre across the curriculum* (pp. 171–195). Logan: Utah State University Press.

Arola, K., Sheppard, J., & Ball, C. E. (2015, June 25). Strategies for assessing multimodal projects Kristin Arola, Jennifer Sheppard, and Cheryl E. Ball [Video file]. Retrieved from https://www.youtube.com/watch?v=wwj79Vkzf_c

Bailey, N. (2012). The importance of a new literacies stance in teaching English language arts. In S. M. Miller & M. B. McVee (Eds.), *Multimodal composing in classrooms: Learning & teaching for the digital world* (pp. 44–62). New York: Routledge.

Banks, A. (2011). *Digital griots: African American rhetoric in a multimedia age.* Carbondale: Southern Illinois University Press.

Benko, S. L. (2012). Scaffolding: An ongoing process to support adolescent writing development. *Journal of Adolescent & Adult Literacy, 56,* 291–300. http://doi.org/10.1002/JAAL.00142

Bezemer, J., & Jewitt, C. (2010). Multimodal analysis: Key issues. In L. Litosseliti (Ed.), *Research methods in linguistics* (pp. 180–197). London: Continuum.

Bezemer, J., & Kress, G. (2008). Writing in multimodal texts: A social semiotic account of designs for learning. *Written Communication, 25,* 166–195. http://doi.org/10.1177/0741088307313177

Boud, D. (2000). Sustainable assessment: Rethinking assessment for the learning society. *Studies in Continuing Education, 22*(2), 151–167.

Brookhart, S. (2008). Portfolio assessment. In T. L. Good (Ed.), *21st century education: A reference handbook* (Vol. 1, pp. 443–450). Thousand Oaks, CA: Sage.

Cazden, C., & Beck, S. W. (2008). Classroom discourse. In A. C. Graesser, M. A. Gernsbacher, & S. R. Goldman (Eds.), *Handbook of discourse processes* (pp. 165–198). Mahwah, NJ: Lawrence Erlbaum.

Coiro, J., & Dobler, E. (2007). Exploring the online comprehension strategies used by sixth-grade skilled readers to search for and locate information on the Internet. *Reading Research Quarterly, 42,* 214–257.

Cope, B., & Kalantzis, M. (2015). Sources of evidence-of-learning: Learning and assessment in the era of big data. *Open Review of Educational Research, 2*(1), 194–217. doi:10.1080/23265507.2015.1074869

Curwood, J. S. (2012). Cultural shifts, multimodal representations, and assessment practices: A case study. *e-Learning and Digital Media, 9,* 232. http://doi.org/10.2304/elea.2012.9.2.232

Dalgleish, M., & Powell, D. (2015). Beyond the dissertation as proto-monograph: Examples and reflections. *#alt-academy: A media commons project.* Retrieved from http://mediacommons.futureofthebook.org/alt-ac/cluster/beyond-dissertation-1

Davis, B., Sumara, D., & Luce-Kapler, R. (2008). *Engaging minds: Changing teaching in complex times* (2nd ed.). New York: Routledge.

Davis, R., Gold, M., Harris, K., & Sayers, J. (2015, October 12). Digital pedagogy in the humanities: Concepts, models, and experiments. *GitHub.* Retrieved from https://github.com/curateteaching/digitalpedagogy/blob/master/announcement.md

Doerr-Stevens, C. (2011). Building fictional ethos: Analyzing the rhetorical strategies of persona design for online role-play. *E-Learning & Digital Media*, 8, 327–342.

Domingo, M. (2014). Migrating literacies: Multimodal texts and digitally enabled text making. *Text & Talk*, 34, 261–282. http://doi.org/10.1515/text-2014-0002

Domingo, M., Jewitt, C., & Kress, G. (2015). Multimodal social semiotics: Writing in online contexts. In J. Rowsell & K. Pahl (Eds.), *The Routledge handbook of literacy studies* (pp. 251–266). London: Routledge.

Eddy, S. L., & Hogan, K. A. (2014). Getting under the hood: How and for whom does increasing course structure work? *Cell Biology Education*, 13, 453–468. http://doi.org/10.1187/cbe.14-03-0050

Ellaway, R. (2007). Discipline-based designs for learning: The example of professional and vocational education. In H. Beetham & R. Sharpe (Eds.), *Rethinking pedagogy for a digital age* (pp. 153–165). London: Routledge.

Felix, J. P. (2008). Edublogging: Instruction for the digital age learner. *Talking Points*, 19, 14–21.

Franklin, K. R., & Gibson, K. (2014). Translating traditional writing process tools to digital ones: Integrating digital writing in K-12 classrooms. In R. S. Anderson & C. Mims (Eds.), *Handbook of research on digital tools for writing instruction in K–12 settings* (pp. 386–400). Hershey, PA: IGI Global.

Gee, J. P. (2005). Semiotic social spaces and affinity spaces. In D. Barton & K. Tusting (Eds.), *Beyond communities of practice language power and social context* (pp. 214–232). New York: Cambridge University Press.

Gunawardena, C. N., & LaPointe, D. (2007). Cultural dynamics of online learning. In M. G. Moore (Ed.), *Handbook of distance education* (pp. 593–607). Mahwah, NJ: Lawrence Erlbaum.

Guzzetti, B., Elliot, K., & Welsch, D. (2010). *DIY media in the classroom: New literacies across content areas*. New York: Teachers College Press.

Halverson, E. R. (2012). Digital art making as a representational process. *Journal of the Learning Sciences*, 22(1), 412–419.

Hart-Davidson, B., Cushman, E., Grabill, J., DeVoss, D., & Porter, J. (2005). Why teach digital writing? *Kairos*, 10(1). Retrieved from http://kairos.technorhetoric.net/10.1/coverweb/wide/introduction.html

Hicks, T. (2014). Adding the "digital layer": Examining one teacher's growth as a digital writer through an NWP Summer Institute and beyond. In K. E. Pytash & R. E. Ferdig (Eds.), *Exploring technology for writing and writing instruction* (pp. 345–357). Hershey, PA: IGI Global.

Hicks, T., Russo, A., Autrey, T., Gardner, R., Kabodian, A., & Edington, C. (2007). Rethinking the purposes and processes for designing digital portfolios. *Journal of Adolescent & Adult Literacy*, 50, 450–458. http://doi.org/10.1598/JAAL.50.6.3

Hull, G. A., & Stornaiuolo, A. (2010). Literate arts in a global world: Reframing social networking as cosmopolitan practice. *Journal of Adolescent and Adult Literacy*, 54(2), 84–96.

Hull, G. A., Stornaiuolo, A., & Sterponi, L. (2013). Imagined readers and hospitable texts: Global youth connect online. In D. Alvermann, N. Unrau, & R. Ruddell (Eds.), *Theoretical models and processes of reading* (6th ed., pp. 1208–1240). Newark, DE: International Reading Association.

Iedema, R. (2003). Multimodality, resemiotization: Extending the analysis of discourse as multi-semiotic practice. *Visual Communication*, 2(1), 29–57.

International Reading Association. (2012). *Adolescent literacy: A position statement of the International Reading Association*. Newark, DE: Author.

International Reading Association. (2013). *Formative assessment: A position statement of the International Reading Association*. Newark, DE: Author.

Jenkins, H., Purushotma, R., Clinton, K., Weigel, M., & Robison, A. (2009). Confronting the challenges of participatory culture: Media education for the 21st century. Building the field of digital media and learning. Cambridge, MA: MIT Press.

Jewitt, C. (2005). Multimodality, "reading," and "writing" for the 21st century. *Discourse: Studies in the Cultural Politics of Education*, 26, 315–331. http://doi.org/10.1080/01596300500200011

Jewitt, C. (2006). *Technology, literacy and learning: A multimodal approach*. London: Routledge.

Jewitt, C. (2013). Multimodal methods for researching digital technologies. In S. Price, C. Jewitt, & B. Brown (Eds.), *The Sage handbook of digital technology research* (pp. 250–266). London: Sage.

Jocius, R. (2013). Exploring adolescents' multimodal responses to *The Kite Runner*: Understanding how students use digital media for academic purposes. *The Journal of Media Literacy Education*, 5, 310–325. http://digitalcommons.uri.edu/jmle/vol5/iss1/4/

Kalantzis, M., & Cope, B. (2008). *New learning: Elements of a science of education*. Cambridge: Cambridge University Press.

Kalantzis, M., & Cope, B. (2012). *Literacies*. Cambridge: Cambridge University Press.

Kalantzis, M., & Cope, B. (2015). Regimes of literacy. In M. Hamilton, R. Hayden, K. Hibbert, & R. Stoke (Eds.) *Negotiating spaces for literacy learning: Multimodality and governmentality* (pp. 15–24). London: Bloomsbury.

Kieffer, R., Hale, M. E., & Templeton, A. (1998). Electronic literacy portfolios: Technology transformations in a first-grade classroom. In D. Reinking, M. McKenna, L. Labbo, & R. Kieffer (Eds.), *Handbook of literacy and technology* (pp. 145–163). Mahwah, NJ: Lawrence Erlbaum.

Kirkland, D. (2009). Researching and teaching English in the digital dimension. *Research in the Teaching of English*, 44, 8–22.

Kissel, B., Putman, S. M., & Stover, K. (2014). Using digital portfolios to enhance students' capacity for communication about learning. In K. E. Pytash & R. E. Ferdig (Eds.), *Exploring technology for writing and writing instruction* (pp. 37–53). Hershey, PA: IGI Global.

Kress, G. (1997). *Before writing*. London: Routledge.

Kress, G. (2003). *Literacy in the new media age*. London: Routledge.

Kress, G., & van Leeuwen, T. (2001). *Multimodal discourse: The modes and media of contemporary communication*. London: Arnold.

Kretzschmar, W. (2013). GIS for language and literary study. In K. M. Price & G. R. Siemens (Eds.), *Literary studies in the digital age: An evolving anthology*. New York: Modern Language Association. doi:10.1632/lsda.2013.0

Lankshear, C., & Knobel, M. (2011). *New literacies: Everyday practices and social learning*. New York: Open University Press.

Leander, K. M., & Vasudevan, L. (2009). Multimodality and mobile culture. In C. Jewitt (Ed.), *The Routledge handbook of multimodal analysis* (pp. 127–139). London: Routledge.

Lemke, J. L. (1998). Metamedia literacy: Transforming meanings and media. In D. Reinking, L. Labbo, M. McKenna, & R. Kiefer (Eds.), *Handbook of literacy and technology: Transformations in a post-typographic world* (pp. 312–333). Mahwah, NJ: Lawrence Erlbaum.

Lessig, L. (2008). *Remix: Making art and commerce thrive in the hybrid economy*. New York: Penguin.

Littleton, K., Scanlon, E., & Sharples, M. (2012). *Orchestrating inquiry learning*. New York: Routledge.

Lunsford, A., & Ede, L. (2009). Among the audience: On audience in an age of new literacies. In M. Weiser, B. Fehler, & A. Gonzalez (Eds.), *Engaging audience: Writing in an age of new literacies* (pp. 42–73). Urbana, IL: NCTE.

Matthiessen, C.M.I.M. (2007). The "architecture" of language according to systemic functional theory: Developments since the 1970. In R. Hasan, C.M.I.M. Matthiessen, & J. Webster (Eds.), *Continuing discourse on language* (Vol. 2, pp. 505–561). London: Equinox.

Mavers, D. (2011). *Children's drawing and writing: The remarkable in the unremarkable*. New York: Routledge.

Mayes, T., & de Freitas, S. (2007). Learning and e-learning. In H. Beetham & R. Sharpe (Eds.), *Rethinking pedagogy for a digital age* (pp. 12–25). London: Routledge.

McVee, M., Bailey, N., & Shanahan, L. (2012). The (artful) deception of technology integration and the move toward a new literacies mindset. In S. M. Miller & M. B. McVee (Eds.), *Multimodal composing in classrooms: Learning & teaching for the digital world* (pp. 13–31). New York: Routledge.

Mercier, E., & Higgins, S. (2014). Creating joint representations of collaborative problem solving with multi-touch technology. *Journal of Computer Assisted Learning, 30,* 497–510. doi:10.1111/jcal.12052

Miller, S. M. (2010). Reframing multimodal composing for student learning: Lessons on purpose from the Buffalo DV project. *Contemporary Issues in Technology and Teacher Education, 10.* Retrieved from http://www.citejournal.org/volume-10/issue-2-10/english-language-arts/reframing-multimodal-composing-for-student-learning-lessons-on-purpose-from-the-buffalo-dv-project/

Miller, S. M., & McVee, M. (2012). *Multimodal composing in classrooms*. New York: Routledge.

MLA Committee on Information Technology. (2012). *Guidelines for evaluating work in digital humanities and digital media*. New York: Modern Language Association.

Moje, E. (2008). Foregrounding disciplines in secondary literacy teaching and learning: A call for change. *Journal of Adolescent & Adult Literacy, 52,* 96–107.

Morrell, E., Dueñas, R., Garcia, V., & López, J. (2013). *Critical media pedagogy*. New York: Teachers College Press.

National Council for Social Studies. (2013). *College, career, and civic life (C3) framework for social studies state standards: Guidance for enhancing the rigor of K–12 civics, economics, geography, and history*. Silver Spring, MD: Author.

National Council of Teachers of English. (2003). *Resolution on composing with nonprint media*. Urbana, IL: Author.

National Council of Teachers of English. (2005). *Position statement on multimodal literacies*. Urbana, IL: Author.

National Council of Teachers of English. (2013). *The NCTE definition of 21st century literacies*. Urbana, IL: Author.

Nelson, M. (2006). Mode, meaning, and synaesthesia in multimedia L2 writing. *Language Learning & Technology, 10,* 56–76.

Newfield, D. (2014). Transformation, transduction and the transmodal moment. In C. Jewitt (Ed.), *The Routledge handbook of multimodal analysis* (2nd ed., pp. 100–113). Abingdon, UK: Routledge.

New London Group. (1996). A pedagogy of multiliteracies: Designing social futures. *Harvard Educational Review, 66,* 60–92.

NGSS Lead States. (2013). *Next generation science standards: For states, by states.* Washington, DC: National Academies Press.

O'Brien, D. G., Moje, E. B., & Stewart, R. A. (2001). Exploring the contexts of secondary literacy: Literacy in people's everyday school lives. In E. B. Moje & D. G. O'Brien (Eds.), *Constructions of literacy: Studies of literacy teaching and learning in secondary classrooms and schools* (pp. 27–48). Mahwah, NJ: Lawrence Erlbaum.

Olmanson, J., Kennett, K., Magnifico, A., McCarthey, S., Searsmith, D., Cope, B., & Kalantzis, M. (2015). Visualizing revision: Leveraging student-generated between-draft diagramming data in support of academic writing development. *Technology, Knowledge, & Learning, 21*(1), 99–123.

Pacheco, D., & Velez, V. N. (2009). Maps, mapmaking, and a critical pedagogy: Exploring GIS and maps as a teaching tool for social change. *Seattle Journal of Social Justice, 8,* 273–302.

Penrod, D. (2010). *Composition in convergence: The impact of new media on writing assessment.* Mahwah, NJ: Lawrence Erlbaum.

Prior, P., & Hengst, J. (2010). Introduction. In P. Prior & J. Hengst (Eds.), *Exploring semiotic remediation as discourse practice* (pp. 1–23). New York: Palgrave MacMillan.

Ranker, J. (2012). Young students' uses of visual composing resources in literacy classroom contexts: A cross-case analysis. *Visual Communication, 11,* 461–483. http://doi.org/10.1177/1470357212454093

Scollon, R. (2001). *Mediated discourse: The nexus of practice.* New York: Routledge.

Selfe, C. L. (2009). The movement of air, the breath of meaning: Aurality and multimodal composing. *College Composition and Communication, 60,* 616–663.

Semali, L. M. (2002). *Transmediation in the classroom: A semiotics-based media literacy framework.* New York: Peter Lang.

Shanahan, L. E. (2012). Lessons in multimodal composition from a fifth-grade classroom. In S. M. Miller & M. B. McVee (Eds.), *Multimodal composing in classrooms: Learning & teaching for the digital world* (pp. 97–113). New York: Routledge.

Shearer, R. (2007). Instructional design and the technologies: An overview. In M. G. Moore (Ed.), *Handbook of distance education* (2nd ed., pp. 219–232). Mahwah, NJ: Lawrence Erlbaum.

Shipka, J. (2005). A multimodal task-based framework for composing. *College Composition and Communication, 57,* 277–306.

Shipka, J. (2006). Sound engineering: Toward a theory of multimodal soundness. *Computers and composition, 23,* 355–373. http://doi.org/10.1016/j.compcom.2006.05.003

Siegel, M. (1995). More than words: The generative power of transmediation for learning. *Canadian Journal of Education, 20*(4), 455–475.

Silverstone, R. (2007). *Media and morality: On the rise of the mediapolis.* Malden, MA: Polity.

Smith, A., & Hull, G. (2013). Critical literacies and social media: Fostering ethical engagement with global youth. In J. Ávila & J. Zacher Pandya (Eds.), *Critical digital literacies as social praxis: Intersections and challenges* (pp. 63–84). New York: Peter Lang.

Smith, A., West-Puckett, S., Cantrill, C., & Zamora, M. (2016). Remix as professional learning: Educators' iterative literacy practice in CLMOOC. *Education Sciences, 6*(12), 1–19. doi:10.3390/educsci6010012

Sousanis, N. (2015). *Unflattening.* Cambridge, MA: Harvard University Press.

Stein, P. (2008). Multimodal instructional practices. In J. Coiro, M. Knobel, C. Lankshear, & D. J. Leu (Eds.), *Handbook of research in new literacies* (pp. 871–898). Mahwah, NJ: Lawrence Erlbaum.

Suhor, C. (1984). Towards a semiotics-based curriculum. *Journal of Curriculum Studies, 16*(3), 247–257.

Thurlings, M., Evers, A. T., & Vermeulen, M. (2015). Toward a model of explaining teachers' innovative behavior: A literature review. *Review of Educational Research, 85*, 430–471.

Tierney, R. J., & Pearson, P. D. (1983). Toward a composing model of reading. *Language Arts, 60*, 568–580.

Tufte, E. (1997). *Visual explanations: Images and quantities, evidence and narrative.* Cheshire, CT: Graphics Press.

Turner, K. H., Abrams, S. S., Katic, E., & Donovan, M. J. (2014). Demystifying digitalk: The what and why of the language teens use in digital writing. *Journal of Literacy Research, 46*, 157–193. http://doi.org/10.1177/1086296X14534061

Unsworth, L. (2008a). Multiliteracies and metalanguage: Describing image/text relations as a resource for negotiating multimodal texts. In J. Corio, M. Knobel, C. Lankshear, & D. J. Leu (Eds.), *Handbook of research on new literacies* (pp. 377–405). New York: Routledge.

Unsworth, L. (2008b). Explicating inter-modal meaning-making in media and literary texts: Towards a metalanguage of image/language relations. In A. Burn & C. Durrant (Eds.), *Media teaching: Language, audience and production* (pp. 48–78). Kent Town, South Australia: Wakefield Press.

van Leeuwen, T. (2005). *Introducing social semiotics.* London: Routledge.

Vasudevan, L., DeJaynes, T. A., & Schmier, S. (2010). Multimodal pedagogies: Playing, teaching and learning with adolescents' digital literacies. In D. E. Alvermann (Ed.), *Adolescents' online literacies: Connecting classrooms, digital media, and popular culture* (pp. 5–25). New York: Peter Lang.

Wilson, A. (2011). A social semiotics framework for conceptualizing content area literacies. *Journal of Adolescent & Adult Literacy, 54*, 435–444.

Wysocki, A. F. (2004). The multiple media of texts: How onscreen and paper texts incorporate words, images, and other media. In C. Bazerman & P. Prior (Eds.), *What writing does and how it does it* (pp. 123–163). Mahwah, NJ: Lawrence Erlbaum.

Yancey, K. B., McElroy, S. J., & Powers, E. (2013). Composing, networks, and electronic portfolios: Notes toward a theory of assessing eportfolios. In H. A. McKee & D. N. DeVoss (Eds.), *Digital writing assessment & evaluation* (pp. 1–32). Logan, UT: Computers and Composition Digital Press/Utah State University Press.

Zygouris-Coe, V. (2012). Disciplinary literacy and the Common Core State Standards. *Topics in Language Disorders, 32*, 35–50.

5   Recursive Feedback

Evaluative Dimensions of e-Learning

Anna Smith, Sarah McCarthey,
and Alecia Magnifico

Systems of Feedback in New Media and Their Promise for Educational Spaces

From Fitbit bracelets that visualize real-time physical activity to GPS-powered phones that reroute driving plans on the fly, systems of feedback in new media are pervasive—in the design of new media and in its use, particularly in the ways social interaction is evaluated and guided. In an era Jenkins et al. (2009) characterized as a digitally mediated participatory culture, emerging communication practices have created opportunities for new and varied associations and relationships among learners. Key features of this era include reading spaces that are also writing spaces—a conflation of more than just modes of communication but a reorientation toward notions of knowledge generation and ownership. Rarely do online artifacts, as representations of knowledge—a blog post, a GPS map of a jogging route, a video on YouTube—stand still and unchanged when "read"; they are more often than not voted and commented on, sent off to new locations, hacked, remixed, and repurposed (cf. Lessig, 2008; Smith et al., 2016). Even simple machine-mediated actions made in response to posted content, such as upvoting in Reddit and retweets that take off in Twitter, affect the further distribution and future interpretations of messages. The dialogic nature of representations of knowledge in theory becomes practically manifest in the workings of many everyday technology interfaces and the social practices that are produced with their use (Ito, 2005; Leander & Vasudevan, 2009; Ling & Campbell, 2009).

Feedback among users and devices in these systems is also oftentimes recursive; recursive feedback is built into programming of devices and platforms in such a way that the messages, and even the lines of communication, are fed back on themselves, enabling further reflection and iterative potential. Within new learning ecologies, the pervasiveness of and potential for recursive feedback hold great promise for learning and instructional design. For example, Lammers, Magnifico, and Curwood (2014) described the role of e-learning platform-mediated recursive feedback in the case of Darrell and his seventh-grade classmates. Using an e-learning environment, *Scholar*, these students discussed writing and reviewing as intertwined processes that fed back into each other as they wrote multiple drafts of narrative stories. While composing his story, Darrell revised in response to several requests for more information; for example, he added setting details when a classmate noted that she couldn't easily imagine where his story was taking place. While completing these revisions, he also provided feedback to his peers on their compositions, and the reviews Darrell wrote featured questions about classmates' setting details. In a post-writing focus group, Darrell noted the connections between receiving and providing feedback: "when you see how this person's reviewing your story, that also gives you a starting point on what to look out for in someone else's story" (p. 197). Although students had initially complained about having to perform reviews (because reviewing others' stories presented a whole new kind of work in their classroom writing), Darrell and his classmates ultimately described reviewing as an iterative, recursive "circle of help" (p. 196) that taught them more about their stories, their classmates as coauthors, and their understanding of reviewing itself.

Such formative feedback is a critical feature of learning, as learners strive to understand a new discipline's practices, to master concepts, and to create effective performances. In this chapter, we explore the promise of recursive feedback for learning and instructional design in e-learning ecologies. In the first section of this chapter, we argue that multimodal composition—an activity that deepens learning and engages learners in disciplinary practices through iterative processes of knowledge making and remaking—is the primary mode of new media. When feedback is pervasive in the design of an e-learning environment, evaluations of learning and interventions can be foregrounded throughout these processes of learning rather than serving as merely monitoring or assessing functions after artifacts of learning are complete. Further, in e-learning environments, interactions with knowledgeable others beyond the instructor, including peers and outside experts, can be made readily available. Such designs and use can disrupt the top-down, one-way structures that have characterized formal teaching and learning for centuries. The collaborative and cooperative learning relations among instructors and students produced in these interactions are a move toward more equitable power relations in a classroom space. Finally, machine mechanisms make analytics on usage, interaction, and composition available to learners and their instructors in real time. As such, new media have the potential to foreground formative assessment via a broadened range of assessment modes, including commentary, annotations, rankings, survey systems, and interaction analytics.

In the second part of this chapter, we share cases revealing how teachers and students have responded to opportunities for recursive feedback. We examine data from several educational settings each using the e-learning environment *Scholar* (available at cgscholar.com), which is a collaborative writing tool intentionally designed to enable the generative feedback and revision cycles discussed here. In our analyses, we have identified four initiators of recursion in the design and use of the *Scholar* platform: feedback, reflection, dialogue, and democratizing relations. We have found that teachers' attempts at incorporating these elements to instigate recursive feedback show potential for disrupting the top-down, teacher-led nature of many traditional educational practices.

Composition-Mediated Learning

Writing—as a means to communicate, to demonstrate learning, to provide feedback, to try on new ideas, and to engage in revision—plays a central role in new media (Brandt, 2015). Thus, in new learning ecologies, writing—often multimodal writing—is the predominant means of interaction and engagement in learning processes. Across disciplines, researchers have pointed to writing as an activity that deepens learning by helping learners clarify their thoughts (NCTM, 2000) and improve their disciplinary-specific reasoning and problem solving (Pugalee, 2005). Calkins, Ehrenworth, and Lehman (2012) suggest that active engagement with writing processes and feedback helps students to understand how others in their field evaluate their work. For students of all ages to see themselves as writers engaging in a discipline, they need readers—peers and instructors who offer authentic responses to their drafts. Engagements in e-learning ecologies can afford this possibility.

New ecologies bring writing to the forefront of learning, especially in classrooms where, historically, reading has been more central to learning and instruction. As Yagelski (2012) puts it, school writing has not been seen as a meaningful social practice, much less one that is central to understanding and meaning making. Rather, "it is a procedure—and usually a tedious one at that" (p. 189). Witte (2013) has documented similar tendencies in a pre-participation survey of National Writing Project teachers, showing that only 30% spent more than two hours per month on "revision discussions and writing time" (p. 41). Combined with typical K–12 classroom foci on evaluation and writing conventions, this aversion to teaching revision practices often leads students to copyedit rather than to revise their work (Beach & Friedrich, 2006). Both in face-to-face instructional environments (e.g., Beason, 1993; Simmons, 2003) and in online environments (e.g., Cho & MacArthur, 2010), studies have found that students are generally unlikely to engage in significant revision of their texts.

In other words, true reworking of ideas through composing processes is rare in typical classroom practice. Students make few revisions that alter a piece's ideas or meanings (e.g., reworking a thesis statement), even while they make many word-level revisions (e.g., correcting writing conventions) and local revisions (e.g., adding examples). A 2002 National Assessment of Educational Progress survey embedded within the writing assessment revealed that "mak[ing] changes to fix mistakes" was, by far, the most-cited revision strategy among both eighth and twelfth graders (Applebee & Langer, 2006, p. 24).

Thus, a radical shift in the status and attention to writing and revision is needed as we move to more hybrid learning spaces where the locus of teaching and learning is mediated by writing, feedback, and revision.

These trends in the status of writing in typical classrooms stand in contrast to decades of research regarding effective writing pedagogies from teachers such as Nancie Atwell (2014), Lucy Calkins (1994), Donald Graves (1983), Penny Kittle (2008), and Donald Murray (2004). These educators have argued for the value of teaching writing processes in classroom workshops where students receive iterative feedback from their peers and teachers. While the foci of their inquiry, students' grade levels, and details of their methods differ, all of these teacher-researchers value student topic choice, ongoing formative feedback and revision, peer and/or teacher collaboration, writing for varying audiences and purposes, reading model texts, and teaching skills as students need them (often through mini-lessons). Typical school schedules and short class periods, though, can make it difficult for teachers to provide this kind of choice, feedback, and attention to individual writers and written pieces. e-Learning ecologies offer the opportunity to transform classrooms by preserving chains of drafts and allowing feedback processes to occur outside of face-to-face learning time. As such, effective uses of these systems can allow teachers to more effectively focus on the formative feedback and collaborative aspects of teaching writing in their disciplines.

Intentionally Designed Feedback Systems to Support Processes of Learning

e-Learning environments can be intentionally designed to take advantage of the iterative sequences that composition affords. What distinguishes e-learning spaces from the open web are the scaffolds that can be put into place to encourage meaningful feedback throughout reading and composition processes. Key features of environments that can scaffold written learning tasks include:

1. Suggestion frameworks, such as review criteria and/or coded annotations, that guide learners to attend to particular aspects of learning artifacts;
2. Versioning, which supports the temporal progression through composing processes with structured pauses for feedback and comparative reflection (e.g., initial draft, draft with feedback, version post-feedback);
3. Unstructured interactional space for open discussion of classroom happenings or artifacts, source materials, written drafts, teacher guidance, and/or classmates' contributions.

The balance of these three features seems especially important. Systems that primarily provide space for teachers to post rubrics and track drafts (items 1 and 2) can support the management of student workflow toward academic goals. At the same time, Wilson (2006) and others have warned that tightly constrained assignment, suggestion, and assessment structures can restrict student writing and teacher response (cf. Magnifico, Woodard, & McCarthey, 2014; Newkirk, 2014). Features such as annotation or discussion spaces that allow members to provide less structured feedback and react as *readers*, not just as *assessors* (item 3), can be very important. They can allow for negotiation of topic, genre, and assignment demands and make room for multiple approaches to or ideas about particular pieces of classroom writing.

In the cross-curricular writing and portfolio system built by teachers at the Science Leadership Academy in Philadelphia, for instance, the interface was intentionally designed to provide students with feedback on their progress via images of their own work. Teacher-designer Larissa Pahomov (Garcia, 2014) explained:

> This online portfolio system keeps students tuned in to their own academic growth by design. Every part of their writing process is preserved, and students are naturally encouraged to revisit past work. They literally have to scroll past it before composing something new.
>
> (p. 45)

Students are encouraged to stretch their learning goals across artifacts, those in draft form and those revised, as teachers and students take the long view on assessment and feedback. Such thoughtful design responds to the critique from Andrews and Smith (2011) that the digitization of portfolios had left much to be desired, arguing that portfolios no longer needed to serve merely a record-keeping function: "Portfolios need their own Web 2.0 revolution. With Portfolio 2.0 . . . the whole community—students, teachers, parents and other stakeholders—could be in constant communication and exchange" (p. 172).

Many emerging technologies and collaborative writing spaces (e.g., blogs, wikis, Google Docs) do function as spaces for writing, collaboration, and dissemination, but they are not designed for recursive feedback and formative assessment. In participatory online spaces that archive participants' work and feedback over time, substantial formative feedback and constructive criticism are rare, even though writers often overstate the constructive quality of the feedback they receive, suggesting that benefits may result from even relatively thin praise (Lundstrom & Baker, 2009; Padgett & Curwood, 2015). In research on the typical feedback practices in online fan-fiction communities, for instance, Magnifico, Curwood, and Lammers (2015) found that, although it is possible for fan-fiction authors and readers to have extended interactions, most people read stories, provide quick evaluative reviews (e.g., "great work!"), and move on (cf. Fields, Giang, & Kafai, 2013). This is similar to what Gee and Hayes (2011) call the "intimate strangers" (p. 35) that characterize the one-pass feedback relationships on the Internet. In order to exploit the potential of extended feedback cycles and peer feedback relationships in e-learning environments, these trends of social interaction must be intentionally included in instructional and/or interface design.

As learners engage with one another in intentionally designed e-learning environments, they can receive feedback on several aspects of their experiences that support their learning, such as the content, form, tool, pace of production, audience reach, and social norms of the learning community. In a study focused on the multimodal exchanges of youth with international peers within an education-focused social network, Hull and Stornaiuolo (2010) shared one particular interaction that typified the conversations they witnessed. Monica, a teenager based in a school in California, posted an avatar of a favorite anime character to which Rahim, a young man in Norway, commented in a derisive way, putting her down for her interest in anime. Monica immediately responded that he was wrong. Later, after he did not respond in turn, she sent another message—this time a personal invitation to correspond across the global sites as part of a project instigated at her school. In the invitation, Monica asked a series of questions about Rahim's interests and ended with a note about their previous exchange:

> She explained that she respects his criticism but reminded him to say it "in a nicer way" so that she could hear it better. She ended with a courteous gesture, thanking him for his opinion and complimenting him on his photo. Monica thus attempted to listen and indeed hear Rahim, and she encouraged him (through her thoughtful questions and carefully placed praise) to listen to and hear her as well. Indeed, he did hear her, later prefacing his thoughtful answers to her questions with an apology: "SRY for not saying it in a nice way xD." It is in this moment of peer-to-peer socialization into respectful communicative norms, socialization supported by classroom activities that foregrounded such reflective moves, that we might understand how listening to others can be an essential capacity for communication in the 21st century.
>
> (Hull & Stornaiuolo, 2010, pp. 93–94)

Rahim's feedback was not a single missive to Monica that she could take or leave once she had finalized her avatar. Rather, the function of a threaded conversation afforded Monica an opportunity to reply within the same stream of messages. Later, using another means of interaction—a post on his wall—Monica sent an additional piece of feedback regarding their interaction, along with a new invitation to correspond. Because these electronic tools were available, this interaction became dialogic and recursive—that is, through Rahim and Monica's multiple extended exchanges, they negotiated the nature of feedback itself. In comparison to typical dynamics in educational spaces, these exchanges were also democratizing; through rounds of exchange, the participants themselves worked to shape coherent social norms for interaction across widely disparate educational experiences, separated by geography, cultural expectations, and primary language. The traditional power hierarchies of educational spaces were flattened. Instead of a single adult teacher or mentor enforcing a version of good behavior, the youth, as learning partners, worked out productive interactional behaviors that would facilitate their learning.

Access to Peer Review and Feedback

Because new media increases the availability of recursive feedback, Kalantzis and Cope (2015) called for the distribution of assessment and feedback responsibilities across communities of learners. For large-scale, e-learning courses, such as MOOCs and cMOOCs, this distributed responsibility becomes a necessity, as it is impossible for a single instructor to provide feedback to thousands of participants. Fortuitously, researchers have found that the mean of two or more peers' assessments were remarkably close to the score of an expert rater (Cope et al., 2013; Piech et al., 2013; Schunn, Godley, & DeMartino, 2016). Beyond a practical solution for courses, distributing assessment and feedback activities across the participants, or crowdsourcing (Surowiecki, 2004), provides transparency to the processes of assessment that is often lacking in traditional educational spaces. In addition, when assessment and feedback are distributed across learners and teachers, distinct and varied perspectives become available to inform the learner.

It has been well established that peers' assessments and feedback matter a great deal to learners. In schools, access to feedback has been shown to be more predictive of improved test scores than prior cognitive ability, socioeconomic background, and reduced class size (Hattie & Timperley, 2007). In a synthesis of research from a team with the Digital Media Learning Hub, Ito et al. (2013) presented a framework, Connected Learning, to address needs for learners to thrive in an era when forms of information and social connection are abundant. Central to that report was the finding that effective learning was peer supported, indicating that learners should be "contributing, sharing and giving feedback in inclusive social experience" (p. 12). When elementary school teacher Christopher Working (Garcia, 2014) took up this framework and integrated student blogging into the learning processes in his classroom, he quickly found that students were especially attentive to the feedback they received from their peers, making changes to their understandings and writing based on their comment threads. He explained how the children found ways to let their peers know that they were addressing the feedback they had been given:

> Evidence began to surface that showed students were making direct changes and improvement in their writing based solely upon peer suggestions. A peer would ask a question in the comments, and students would use color to indicate revisions based upon the comment.
>
> (p. 14)

In a study focused on the learning processes of a group of Norwegian high school students working in a media lab, Nygard (2012) indicated that students were motivated to improve their composed artifacts before sending them to the community for review. Through peer-review and feedback cycles, students were attuned to the methods, approaches, and perspectives their peers had used in their compositions, beyond those indicated by the instructor. They used their peers' learning artifacts as feedback and inspiration for their future work, revealing another kind of iteration and potential recursion (see also Hall, 2015; Lammers, Magnifico, & Curwood, 2014).

Learning from Machine and Machine-Mediated Feedback

In addition to the expanded reviewer base with whom learners can engage in feedback cycles, the types of feedback learners encounter in e-learning environments can similarly be broadened and diversified to include machine (e.g., progression rates) and machine-mediated (e.g., survey results) feedback. Machines bring a capacity to document learning processes at a previously impossible degree of detail. Bienkowski, Feng, and Means (2012) note that "educational data mining and learning analytics have the potential to make visible data that have heretofore gone unseen, unnoticed, and therefore unactionable" (p. xi). From clicks to keystrokes, the minutia of learning in e-learning environments can be recorded and fed back to the learner as informative and actionable feedback. For instructors, such machine feedback can provide a range of fine-grained information that can be used in reflexive and evidence-centered pedagogical design (Cope & Kalantzis, 2015a; Mislevy et al., 2012). Although still an emerging field, analytics of this type are helpful for students and instructors when the data are presented visually and/or as prompts for future action (e.g., Eagle et al., 2015; Scheffel et al., 2014; West, 2012). Along with developing these promising technological advances, researchers working in the emerging field of learning analytics, such as Dawson and Siemens (2014), provide cautionary notes that machine feedback by itself is not sufficient evidence of learning, arguing that "the complexity of a social process in learning cannot be adequately assessed through basic metrics such as logins, time online, and clicks" (p. 298). Thus, rather than evaluative and consequential, it is recommended that usage metrics be treated as just one source of formative feedback for the learner and instructor.

In addition to usage metric collection possibilities, machine capacities bring a wider range of data types that can inform instructors and learners, such as natural language processes and logs of interaction patterns. Further, computer-adaptive tests, affect meters, simulations, and semantic mapping tools have built-in feedback loops that involve these varied types of machine feedback as intrinsic components of their programming (e.g., Natriello, 2013; Waters, 2014). Machine-mediated feedback, such as commentary, annotations, rankings, and surveys, similarly provide recursive feedback loops as essential to their functions. Further, when review and feedback loops are managed digitally, reviews of learning artifacts can be synchronized, aggregated, and monitored with relative ease. In these ways, machine and machine-mediated feedback afford a collapse in the time frame among instruction, practice, varied forms of feedback, reflection, and adjustments, resulting in tightened recursive learning sequences. Learners can gain access to a variety of actionable feedback without waiting for individuated responses from a single instructor. Cope and Kalantzis (2015b) assert that robust feedback plans, which include machine, instructor, and peer-generated prospective and constructive input throughout learning processes, assist in foregrounding feedback in the educational experience. As a result, feedback can be shifted from its typical retrospective and judgmental role to one that is formative and instructional (Cope & Kalantzis, 2013).

A Close Look at One Online Writing Environment Across Studies

In the remainder of this chapter, we consider the ways teachers and students respond to opportunities for recursive feedback provided in the e-learning environment *Scholar* (available at cgscholar.com), intentionally designed to support cross-curricular, multimodal writing, community feedback, and revision cycles. Created as a bridge toward more democratized ecologies of academic writing and expression, *Scholar* has been used in elementary, middle, and high school, as well as with higher education institutions (Kline, Letofsky, & Woodard, 2013; Magnifico, McCarthey, & Kline, 2014; McCarthey et al., 2014). This section begins with an overview of the iteratively designed components of the *Scholar* platform. Then we draw from examples of teachers' pedagogies and students' developing writing practices as they use the platform. The examples highlighted in this chapter stem from a series of studies of teacher and student use and are chosen to demonstrate the potential for how teachers' use of *Scholar* can lead to recursive feedback in classroom spaces.

In our analyses, we have identified four initiators of recursion in the design and use of the *Scholar* platform: feedback, reflection, dialogue, and democratizing relations. Across the studies, we witnessed teachers and students initiating feedback through peer review and uptake of computer-mediated guidance in revision; students' reflections on their texts and plans for revision; dialogic sequences via annotation tools; and democratized negotiation of social norms in the environment. Instructors' attempts at incorporating these elements to instigate recursive feedback not only have drawn out students' ability to engage in drafting and revision processes in written assignments but also have opened up the discursive space in their classrooms to allow for a greater variety of student contributions and language use (Kline, Letofsky, & Woodard, 2013; Olmanson et al., 2015).

Scholar: An Online Writing Environment Designed for Recursive Feedback

Scholar was developed iteratively over several field-based trials. It currently consists of four components designed to broaden students' written communication: (1) Creator, a word processor where students compose, review, and annotate one another's multimodal compositions; (2) Publisher, a space where teachers design and manage projects with forms of peer review and rubrics with specific criteria; (3) Community, a networked space that provides access to classmates' profiles and a feed for interaction; and (4) Analytics, a tool that displays machine-enabled records of activities, projects, and assessment results.

Within Creator (see Chapter 1, Figure 1.12), once a student submits a draft, *Scholar* moves the draft through an (optionally) anonymous peer-review phase. The review tool displays an instructor-provided rubric alongside a peer's text and requires students to provide written feedback with a corresponding numeric evaluation for each criterion. The instructor and writer can also submit reviews in response to the piece and view the reviews that have come in. Beyond the rubric, an Annotation tool allows peer reviewers to highlight and comment on specific areas of a text. With this tool, peers can also prompt specific changes or additions using a drop-down bar. As peer reviews are completed and submitted, students are provided access to these responses and annotations in a sidebar. As they revise, they can toggle between reviews, rubrics, and annotations. The original author can also respond to each annotation directly, opening up potential for dialogic sequences about targeted areas of text. In Publisher, teachers design learning tasks and corresponding rubric criteria simultaneously and share these with students as the learning cycle begins. These criteria then provide guidance for students during their own composing processes as well as in reviewing peers' compositions.

Community was added in later iterations of *Scholar* to allow students and their teachers a space to make comments and correspond about their learning projects. In Community, *Scholar* combines aspects of social networking, including a profile page, thumbnails of colleagues or fellow students (here called peers), and an activity feed that shows recent status posts, responses, and notices of published written pieces. In this space, community members can engage in ongoing conversations via threaded replies that focus on aspects of their learning communities, reflections on personal learning pathways, and discussion of subject matter, including connections to current events. By encouraging students to be both creators and collaborators alongside their teachers through a free flow of information without specific criteria or guidance, it is designed to disrupt the traditional patterns of Initiation-Response-Evaluation that predominate in classrooms (Cazden, 2001).

Finally, the Analytics feature of *Scholar* automatically collects and stores data, including the number and length of each version the author has created linked to those drafts; the amount of change between each version; academic language level (vocabulary, syntax, etc.); average peer-review ratings; the number of reviews authored and their length; the number of annotations offered; and an overall score based on all of these variables. Teachers and learners alike can view this machine-produced feedback of learning progress in the Analytics tab. For teachers, these learning analytics can become formative feedback about the ways writing is mediating learning across their classes and can be used to make instructional decisions about the longer trajectories of learning they are guiding. As researchers, we also used this feature, along with interviews and observations, to analyze the learners' reviewing and revising processes over a series of studies from which the examples in this chapter are drawn.

Increased Access to and Uptake of Feedback Supports Iteration

One affordance of *Scholar* is that it provides access to peer review. While peer response has been encouraged since Graves's work in the 1970s (1983) and studied in the 1980s (Gere & Abbott, 1985), it has not been taken up as a common practice in secondary classrooms (Applebee & Langer, 2006, 2009; Witte, 2013). In our studies related to *Scholar* use in classrooms, we found that teachers increased the number of opportunities for peer-to-peer feedback as they began using the online platform. Peer review also afforded meta-awareness of composition strategies and revisions, and students employed these understandings in the feedback they composed for other students, demonstrating that cycles of feedback supported longer trajectories of learning (e.g., Lammers, Magnifico, & Curwood, 2014). Several teachers initiated use of peer review in conjunction with their use of the online platform. An eighth-grade teacher, Ms. Anderson, for example, felt empowered by the online tool and found that students were more willing to revise their writing in *Scholar* than offline, particularly when they received similar suggestions for revision by more than one peer reviewer (McCarthey et al., 2014). Students were able to see these similarities across reviews as they viewed side-by-side comparisons among text, rubric, review, and annotations in the online environment. For teachers who already had feedback cycles as a part of their learning practice in the classroom, the move to the e-learning environment was not an abrupt shift. In fact, students in Ms. Miller's college preparatory classes, who had previously engaged in offline peer review as a class, wrote longer, more explicit, and more directive review comments online than the youth in other classes (Magnifico, Woodard, & McCarthey, 2014).

Across studies, students have responded positively to engaging in the platform-mediated peer review process, even when the results of peer review indicated the need for extensive revision. Maddie, an eighth grader, described a long list of feedback she had received on a comparative essay. The feedback included compliments on her introduction and suggestions for rewriting her conclusion. When prompted to provide more about what changes she made based on this feedback, Maddie said, "They say you have a lot of good claims, but try to avoid run on sentences. So I went back and looked to see if I had any run on sentences. If I did, I fixed it. And then in evidence, 'You have no evidence to back them up. Try to give details or quotes in the story.' And that's when I put in [those specific details] and all that." Based on this peer-review experience, which Maddie explained, "helped me a lot," she requested more opportunities to give and receive feedback in the online environment. In this example, Maddie was able to articulate what feedback she found useful and how she incorporated it into her revised text. Such developing metacognitive awareness is a critical component in realizing the promise of iterative feedback.

In looking across feedback cycles facilitated in *Scholar,* we have found that students often directly draw from the review criteria provided by the instructor's rubric that are available for reference on the sidebar while students compose in Creator (see Chapter 1, Figures 1.17 and 1.18). In many cases, we have found that students refer to the same criteria they had attended to during their *own* composing processes when reviewing *others'* works (Lammers, Magnifico, & Curwood, 2014; McCarthey et al., 2013). When students make these kinds of iterative and varied uses of descriptive criteria, the criteria themselves can become instructional and formative. Like Darrell, the young man whose recursive feedback experience began this chapter, we have seen a common practice of students offering suggestions for meeting criteria with strategies they found that worked in their texts. Wiliam and Thompson (2006) have reported that

> research shows that the people providing the feedback benefit just as much as the recipient, because they are forced to internalize [the] learning intentions and success criteria in the context of someone else's work, which is less emotionally charged than one's own.
>
> (p. 56)

For example, students in Ms. Anderson's eighth-grade class were asked to write "an argumentative essay taking a stance on whether or not a mythical creature, legend, or phenomenon is real or just a hoax." In giving feedback to another student in response to the rubric criterion for essay organization, Kim wrote,[1] "You arranged your paragraphs very impressively. Add more sentences of support per paragraph." In response to the thesis she wrote, "You introduced your three main supports greatly! Revise using your authorial voice, by not asking a question." Here Kim gave a summary statement of what the author had done, provided positive evaluations, and then made suggestions about how to revise based on her developing understanding of the compositional goals set by the teacher and her own strategies for meeting those goals. Such iterative passes at review criteria strengthen a learner's repertoire for addressing criteria, supporting the longer trajectories of learning beyond the product at hand.

Such feedback demonstrates the kinds of written responses we have found youth providing one another across studies and grades. Furthermore, it was not uncommon to find students giving more extensive and specific feedback. For example, another student in the same class directed the author's attention to particular aspects of the text and provided specific comments for revision: "The organization of this essay is rather unique. The author did a great job. Rephrasing the explanations would be helpful, as the phrase 'This proves my point because' is used various times throughout the whole essay." Regarding the reasoning and support of the essay, he wrote:

> The author stated two fantastic reasons that prove their point, and explained them very well. The third reason, however, is off. "There really isn't a chupacabra." Does not seem like a reason to me, as this is the opinion of the author. The author also stated in the same paragraph, "This proves my point because it tells me that the coyotes been making the killings instead of the chupacabra. . . ."

In these comments, the reviewer references specific points in the text for revisions, such as moving sentences into different paragraphs. Further, the peer's comments on reasoning and support reflect the criteria the teacher initially established and demonstrate how students provided specific feedback for revision by taking up the environment's interactive affordances in an intentional way. During review in the *Scholar* platform, students are provided criterion-specific textboxes to the right of the text they are reviewing (see Chapter 1, Figure 1.17 in this volume). The option to submit feedback does not become active until they have provided written feedback for each criterion. The alignment of the peer responses with the review criteria shows the affordance of using an online tool that directs students to provide feedback about the aspects of text the instructor has designated.

That said, we offer a word of caution about the rubrics instructors construct in such a system. Magnifico, Woodard, and McCarthey (2014) have found that when rubrics are overly scripted—written to direct the outcome of each aspect of a composition rather than to prompt and guide learning—they can function to limit students' creative and critical impulses in responding to a prompt. These initiating texts can begin to "coauthor" the work for students (see also Prior, 2008; Wilson, 2006), shaping a narrow range of acceptable responses that limit students' intellectual engagement with the course material. That is, teachers who value students' thoughts and discoveries must be careful to avoid overly directive rubrics—it is easy to turn open-ended essay responses into summary-driven recitation tasks.

Rubric criteria that elicit information can provide particularly effective guides for students as they give and respond to meaningful feedback on their texts. After students wrote biographical sketches in Ms. Allen's fifth-grade class, Carolyn provided scores for each criterion but also made suggestions about how the author might attain a higher score while focusing on the effort the author put into the text. She wrote,

> In your body paragraphs you told me a lot of information about Amelia Earheart. I learned a lot more then I did before I read your project. I gave you a three because you put a lot of effort into your body paragraphs.

Regarding the conclusion for which the teacher prompted in her criteria: "Does the conclusion sum up what the paper was about? Does the writer leave you thinking with a statement or question?" Carolyn wrote, ". . . To get a 3 you should put more details instead of 2 sentences. I don't want to know how old she is now I want to find out what did they find, when did she start flying an airplane, why did she want to be a pilot." By attending to the qualities of the text, Carolyn was offering feedback to help her peer improve her text. The author's final text reflected uptake of Carolyn's suggestions, including providing additional details about Amelia Earhart in the body and extending the discussion in the conclusion. Such revision suggests that Carolyn's request for more details may have prompted additional research into the biographical information regarding Amelia Earhart's life and influence. At a minimum, the author engaged in a recursive round of revision and representation of his understanding of this particular historical figure and the extended practice in composing biographies.

More sophisticated revisions can be seen with older students. In an AP US history class, for example, students were asked to choose from a list of videos and write a "concise 3-page essay" about the film. Mr. Daniels created five criteria for students to use in their texts and for peers to review. They included a scale from 0–4 on each of the criteria: title, introduction, main body, conclusion, and readability. Connie wrote one version of the text, received three reviews, and then revised her final text titled "From a Droplet to a Waterfall: Why the AP World History Course Should Consider *The Power of One*." From the original version to the final, she added 400 words and changed 37% of the text.

Most relevant to the recursive feedback capabilities in *Scholar* was the way in which she took up her peers' suggestions. For example, all three reviewers noted that her original title, "From a Droplet to a Waterfall" needed more explanation. They also pointed out throughout their comments that she needed to provide "more mapping," one of the terms the teacher used in the description of the criteria for students to connect their film reviews to the AP course. In response to these suggestions, Connie added the subtitle "Why the AP World History Course Should Consider *The Power of One*" and added three specific connections to the course. These connections included the statement, "Another point the film fails to address is how the apartheid affected humanity on a global scale, an important connection to make in an AP World History class." She wrote in both the body and the conclusion the statement, "However, if it is decided to be adapted into the AP World

History program, students should be aware that a certain amount of creative license was taken to further develop a plotline and therefore create a more successful movie." Connie also incorporated very specific suggestions of her peer reviewers, including a student who suggested she discuss "big ideas." She wrote, "While many of the core facts and ideas are correct, there are flaws considering the 'big picture' ideas of the film," and she added an entirely new paragraph to elaborate on this idea. Finally, reviewers responded to her initial conclusion by suggesting that she combine two paragraphs and tell a lesson that was learned, both of which she did in her revised conclusion.

Similar to what we found in Ms. Miller's eighth-grade classroom in which students revised when more than one peer made a similar suggestion (Magnifico, Woodard, & McCarthey, 2014), Connie revised when two of the three reviewers made a similar point. Connie's revised texts reflect one of the important aspects of recursion—actually taking up the provided feedback and incorporating new ideas into her revisions and understandings. Connie made responsive changes to her text, and her revisions resulted in a more detailed text well suited for her audience and the learning task at hand.

Reflective Self-Reviews Promote Recursion

While Connie took up the feedback suggested by her peers, we do not have direct evidence regarding why she made the textual changes she did nor do we know if she internalized the feedback. However, we had access to this reflective process in Ms. Allen's fifth-grade classroom where students were writing essays comparing and contrasting the novel and play versions of *Stargirl*, a popular young adult novel. After composing their initial comparison, the automated system in the *Scholar* platform sent students' drafts to two classmates' *Scholar* in-boxes for a first round of feedback. After revising their drafts based on that feedback, they conducted a second recursive turn in the form of self-reviews. In the self-reviews, students elaborated on what changes they had made in their texts and how they responded to peer feedback. The following self-reviews highlight the range of ways students responded to their peers both in the revisions they made and in their own assessments of their work.

In responding to the feedback she had received on organization, Ava wrote a typical, somewhat generic self-review comment, "I revised after looking at my comments and fixed what they had suggested, and switched up how I did my transitions." Another student, Tisha, indicated that she was not going to take up one peer's feedback about adding quotes but that she would include a second peer's advice to provide more evidence. Many students composed similar reflective self-reviews that parsed out their revision decision making. Tisha wrote:

> Reviewer 1 gave me a 5 and said that I had good supporting details but I need to work on getting quotes. I don't agree that I need quotes because

we never wrote done any quotes. I think that it was good advice but I don't think I need some of that stuff in my piece. Reviewer 2 gave me a 3. The reviewer said that I need some more supporting evidence and I agree with that that I should put in what I noticed about the book and play. I am going to give more evidence in my piece. I gave myself a 5 because I think that I did a good job of supporting what I am thinking.

In this example, we see a student reflecting on the feedback and articulating what she agreed with and what she found valuable; these appear to be crucial steps in considering what authors might revise. These self-reviews not only promote thoughtful revision but also indicate reflection as an important recursive element in revision, a step that encourages students to reconsider the success of their decisions.

When students in Ms. Allen's class encountered reviews that conflicted with one another, they looked back at their texts and weighed the evidence. In the following self-review, the student gave examples, defending her use of transitions and specifically noting the ones she used. "One of my reviewers said that I didn't have enough transitions, but the other one said I did. I read through my piece and I thought I had enough transitions. I said things like For example and Another reason." In a final example, we see the value of having students reflect on the feedback they have received and the revisions they considered—for both the teacher and the student. In this reflective log, we see the student grapple with the details that could have been included to address the issues raised by a peer reviewer. The thinking and understanding of the course content that would have otherwise been unavailable to the instructor is also revealed in this reflective turn:

I gave myself a four because I feel that I could compare and contrast better. One place where I could have done that is in the fourth paragraph. I could have said that Hilary was portrayed as mean because she picked on Stargirl. In the book, she did this by just being a mean to her face and once even slapping her. But, in the play she was mean to Stargirl because she sent mean text messages out to her friend group that said "Stargirl sucks!" or other things like that. I think that I could have also supported my ideas better in the third paragraph because I said that the lunchroom scenes were totally out of the play but in fact a lunchroom scenes was in the performance but it was just Stargirl singing at the edge of the stage. I could have said more about what I think they could have done differently.

The self-reviews from Ms. Allen's classroom show how peer feedback can promote reflective activity regarding learning artifacts and the decision-making processes of composition. Going back and forth between their own texts, their reviews, and the feedback they provide peers seemed to build students' understanding of the writing process and how knowledge is produced. This awareness is akin to the processes adult writers across many disciplines engage in as they compose, receive reviews, and revise for publication and dissemination.

Annotations Facilitate Dialogic Sequences

Although dialogue between peers is not synonymous with recursive feedback, it can facilitate recursive turns. Our study comparing students' use of *Scholar*'s annotation tool in three classrooms taught by Ms. Anderson demonstrated the affordances of an interactive technology for spurring text-based dialogic sequences (McCarthey et al., 2013). When writing argumentative essays on whether mythical creatures were a hoax (a project referenced earlier in the chapter), students in each of the three classes used the annotation tool in different ways. Class A used the annotation tool for self-annotations related to conventions—they read their own texts and made notes of spelling and grammatical errors. In class B, students used the annotation tool to point out errors in conventions to their peers. Students in class C engaged in brief dialogues with one another about more substantive issues, such as their peers' argumentative moves. It was in class C where we saw the potential for recursion. For example, a student annotated a peer's text that read, "You sit with your ocean treasure nuggets laughing with your salty sea dogs and straw hat pirate crewmates" and the reviewer commented, "I'm confused, is that relevant to what you are trying to prove?" The author responded in writing in an annotation thread, "This is the attention grabber," harkening back to the teacher's criterion. The author and reviewer engaged in brief dialogue pointing out confusion and offering clarification.

In another pair of authors and reviewers, a student wrote, "at controversial-science.com" and the commenter suggested, "Should be according to," to which the author wrote back, "Thanks for the advise!" In a third dialogue, an author had written about a conspiracy theory, "its large and complex," to which the reviewer added the annotation, "Hoaxers could make it perfect and large and complex." The author responded, "Does that mean even in very short time?" These brief dialogues between peers demonstrate the ways the annotation tool could be used to clarify ideas, to defend authorial decisions, or to build learning-focused relationships. The design of the annotation tool facilitated varied uses that, in turn, supported dialogic sequences. These dialogic sequences hold the potential for recursion if and when the author takes up suggestions to reconsider the text and make revisions.

Community Spaces Assist in Democratizing Relations

Modeled after social network group spaces, the Community space in *Scholar* offers additional ways for instructors and learners to interact around course content. In this group space, both teachers and students may initiate posts or prompts. They may ask questions about course content, reply to others' posts or questions, and share ideas and links to external resources regarding the unit of study with the entire classroom community. The community spaces afford the opportunities for sustained dialogue among peers and teachers, which encourages more democratic relationships. Further, when posting, teachers and students can include photographs, diagrams, or other visual and multi-modal posts that may prompt further dialogue.

In such interactions, teachers and students engage with one another in providing information and feedback related to course content but outside the boundaries of assignments, rubrics, or numerical ratings. In Ms. Harrison's eighth-grade social studies class, for instance, she posted photographs and questions to prompt students to analyze historical events, including a 1950s bomb shelter, the March on Washington, and the shootings at Kent State. Students' responses in the Community space varied from one or two sentences to multi-paragraph insights reflecting on the time period and events. Ms. Allen used the space similarly, posting course texts for students to respond to one another informally. In one posted text about the American Revolution, we can see how informal exchange facilitated connections beyond the text and course content. Ms. Allen began with the prompt, "Read the text below. Then, post a comment in Community in which you add an important fact about the American Revolution that you know but which is not included in the text." This prompt asks students to use what they know and to be critical readers. Students' responses differed from what one might find in a typical essay assignment and built on the "short response" opportunity. For example, one student wrote, "The people who supported the American Revolution were sometimes called "Whigs" (a political party), and the anti-Revolution people were sometimes called "Tories" (a term based on a philosophy in Britain)," thus adhering strictly to the assignment. However, another student added a critique of the article, saying, "I think they should have added more detail on how un-prepared the Colonial soldiers were compare to the well trained British militia. It was quite surprising that we won the first few battles. We were not very fit for battle." A student went beyond producing a known fact to give an opinion. The potential for dialogue was taken up in an instance when one student wrote, "The american soldiers fought dirty. They didn't follow the 'rules of war'. They killed the officers first and camouflaged themselves and shot from trees. The British soldiers weren't used to fighting with camouflaged enemies so that's one of the reasons why they lost." A peer responded by writing, "This is such a frivolous thing to say, but I find it a tad amusing you use the term 'fighting dirty.'" This exchange among peers shows how Community allowed students to respond informally to an article and to one another in a brief period of time.

In addition to use in K–12 schools, the *Scholar* platform is being used presently in a range of courses in higher education, as both a component of the course and as the central hub. In a psychology course on human development and technology, for instance, the 101 graduate students are asked to join the professor and teaching assistants in accumulating resources in reflection of the course content. In the Community space, they are invited to create at least five updates that apply the course content to a current technological advancement or argument. They are also asked to respond to a small number of their peers. The timing of these posts and responses is not regulated; rather, the invitation into the Community space works to position these students as fellow contributors.

The students followed suit by posting updates with links to outside multimodal resources and reflections. In their reflections and in the threaded comments that followed, students made reference to course content across the semester as well as to their own professional and personal relevant experiences. In one update that included a short YouTube video of a neurologist discussing social media and hormonal, behavioral, and genetic neurological stimulants, the student, Jorge, included three rhetorical questions and one direct question to his peers. He asked: "Question to all: what unconscious behavior do you see with the evolution of technology?" His peers responded with personal anecdotes, references to other texts they had read previously, and counterarguments to the video and to each proposition laid out in the threaded responses. One peer, Marilisse, cross-posted links to two studies that challenged some of her peers' responses to the topic, stating,

> I posted the following links as a comment to a different update, but they may also correlate. . . . [P]art of this may also be connected to creativity, since being distracted + dopamine may help with thinking through creative solutions.

Heidi, another peer, responded thanking the group for their discussion and sharing how it was helping her reframe her assumptions about brain functioning and technology.

What we have been able to see in classrooms is the potential for an online tool to initiate collaboration and disrupt the top-down, one-way development that characterizes much of contemporary teaching in classrooms. The places where students took advantage of the space in Community show how traditional content and discourse patterns may be challenged and that students might begin to demonstrate agency. Changing classroom norms to allow students to question others and become more active learners is a demanding task, yet the examples where students take risks to comment on one another's texts show that there is potential for change.

Discussion: Recommendations for Designing for Recursive Feedback

Examples from our studies show how teachers and students take up many of the affordances offered by the online writing environment *Scholar*. With access to a digital writing and review space, teachers increased the number of opportunities for peer-to-peer feedback in their instructional sequences. In fact, several teachers with whom we have worked initiated the use of peer review in their instruction as they began to use the platform. Along with increased access to peer review, students also gained access to an annotation tool for dialogue regarding specific text features and a community space to post open-ended comments. Each of these afforded students ways to engage with one another and to provide feedback, and students expressed interest both in using the tools and in providing feedback to one another. Students also used self-reviews to consider their own writing, agree or disagree with peers, and reflect on changes they might make in subsequent texts. These examples illustrate the potential for recursive feedback in using online writing environments and provide direction for how teachers might use the components of an environment like *Scholar* to create more democratic classroom practices that encourage horizontal relationships and rich dialogue.

As we know from previous studies, access to computers alone does not revolutionize classroom learning (e.g., Cuban, 1986, 2010; Warschauer, 2011). Further, any reform of classroom learning is a locally bound, complex process (e.g., McLaughlin & Talbert, 1990; Reiser et al., 2000; Spillane, 1999), and thus, access to tools like *Scholar* does not ensure that teachers will engage in new classroom practices. Making recursive feedback in educational spaces— be it in schools, higher education institutions, or informal educational spaces such as MakerSpaces—a routine practice will require a reimagining of the processes of learning and evaluation and a shift in relationships within those spaces.

The examples from these studies highlight the potential for substantial differences in classrooms when teachers do engage in peer response and revision regularly (Magnifico, Woodard, & McCarthey, 2014). Encouraging collaboration and cooperation by using online writing tools has the possibility of developing new relationships between the teacher and the student as well as among peers. The use of *Scholar* as an example of a tool designed to reshape relationships and resituate the learner as the teacher and the teacher as a learner is the precursor of establishing more equitable power relationships. The cases where students were able to take advantage of the flattened hierarchies in Community or engage in multimodal peer review with the annotation tool show how traditional content and discourse patterns may be challenged and how students might begin to demonstrate agency. Changing classroom norms to allow students to question others and become more interactive learners is a demanding task. However, it is a task worth pursuing. The disjuncture between traditional didactic discourses of school and the social "stickiness" that keeps us engaged with new media—always having an audience, anticipating and receiving rapid, multi-perspective responses—will only grow if educators don't take on the challenge of adapting with the times and social practices of new media.

Conclusion

Emerging composing and communication technologies and social practices have great potential for affording recursive feedback systems in educational spaces. These can be realized when e-learning environments are intentionally designed to provide learners with a widened range of formative feedback types and sources—from peers to machines. The focal example of this chapter, *Scholar*, is only one example of a tool that provides increased access to peer review and to machine and machine-mediated feedback (see Schuun et al., 2016; Littleton, Scanlon, & Sharples, 2012). Not only do these environments provide a space for students to write and revise but also the intentional design of environments like *Scholar* facilitates peer interaction, self-reflection, and recursive feedback. Environments such as these have opened up the discursive space in classrooms to allow for a greater variety of student contributions and interactions. These affordances set e-learning environments apart from other online spaces in which adults and youth compose and communicate. Continuing to design spaces that enable multimodal composition processes that promote interaction, reflection, revision, and dialogue holds promise for disrupting limiting educational norms and changing practices both inside and outside classrooms.

Note

1. Throughout this chapter, students' quoted feedback statements are presented as they were written.

References

Andrews, R., & Smith, A. (2011). *Developing writers: Teaching and learning in the digital age*. London: Open University Press.

Applebee, A., & Langer, J. (2006). *The state of writing instruction in America's schools: What existing data tell us*. Albany, NY: Center on English Learning & Achievement, University at SUNY.

Applebee, A., & Langer, J. (2009). What is happening in the teaching of writing? *English Journal*, 98(5), 18–28.

Atwell, N. (2014). *In the middle: A lifetime of learning about writing, reading, and adolescents* (3rd ed.). Portsmouth, NH: Heinemann.

Beach, R., & Friedrich, T. (2006). Response to writing. In C. A. MacArthur, S. Graham, & J. Fitzgerald (Eds.), *Handbook of writing research* (pp. 222–234). New York: Guilford Press.

Beason, L. (1993). Feedback and revision in writing across the curriculum classes. *Research in the Teaching of English*, 27(4), 395–422.

Bienkowski, M., Feng, M., & Means, B. (2012). *Enhancing teaching and learning through educational data mining and learning analytics: An issue brief*. Washington, DC: US Department of Education, Office of Educational Technology.

Brandt, D. (2015). *The rise of writing*. Cambridge: Cambridge University Press.

Calkins, L. (1994). *The art of teaching writing* (2nd ed.). Portsmouth, NH: Heinemann.

Calkins, L., Ehrenworth, M., & Lehman, C. (2012). *Pathways to the common core: Accelerating achievement*. Portsmouth, NH: Heinemann.

Cazden, C. (2001). *Classroom discourse: The language of teaching and learning* (2nd ed.). Portsmouth, NH: Heinemann.

Cho, K., & MacArthur, C. (2010). Student revision with peer and expert reviewing. *Learning and Instruction, 20*, 328–338.

Cope, B., & Kalantzis, M. (2013). Multiliteracies: New literacies, new learning. In M. R. Hawkins (Ed.), *Framing languages and literacies: Socially situated views and perspectives* (pp. 105–135). New York: Routledge.

Cope, B., Kalantzis, M., Abd-El-Khalick, F., & Bagley, E. (2013). Science in writing: Learning scientific argument in principle and practice. *e-Learning and Digital Media, 10*, 420–441.

Cope, W., & Kalantzis, M. (2015a). Assessment and pedagogy in the era of machine-mediated learning. In T. Dragonas, K. J. Gergen, & S. McNamee (Eds.), *Education as social construction: Contributions to theory, research, and practice* (pp. 350–374). Chagrin Falls, OH: Worldshare Books.

Cope, W., & Kalantzis, M. (2015b). Sources of evidence-of-learning: Learning and assessment in the era of big data. *Open Review of Educational Research, 2*, 194–217.

Cuban, L. (1986). *Teachers and machines: The classroom use of technology since 1920*. New York: Teachers College Press.

Cuban, L. (2010). Rethinking education in the age of technology: The digital revolution and schooling in America. *Science Education, 94*(6), 1125–1127. doi:10.1002/sce.20415

Dawson, S., & Siemens, G. (2014). Analytics to literacies: The development of a learning analytics framework for multiliteracies assessment. *International Review of Research in Open and Distributed Learning, 25*(4). Retrieved from http://www.irrodl.org/index.php/irrodl/article/view/1878/3006

Eagle, M., Hicks, D., Peddycord, B., & Barnes, T. (2015). Exploring networks of problem-solving interactions. In *Proceedings of the Fifth International Conference on Learning Analytics and Knowledge* (pp. 21–30). New York: ACM.

Fields, D. A., Giang, M., & Kafai, Y. (2013). Understanding collaborative practices in the Scratch online community: Patterns of participation among youth designers. In M. Kapur, M. Nathan, & N. Rummel (Eds.), *Proceedings of the 10th International Conference on Computer-Supported Collaborative Learning* (pp. 200–208). Madison, WI: International Society of the Learning Sciences.

Garcia, A. (Ed.). (2014). *Teaching in the connected learning classroom*. Irvine, CA: Digital Media and Learning Research Hub.

Gee, J. P., & Hayes, E. R. (2011). *Language and learning in the digital age*. London: Routledge.

Gere, A. R., & Abbott, R. D. (1985). Talking about writing: The language of writing groups. *Research in the Teaching of English, 19*, 362–385.

Graves, D. H. (1983). *Writing: Teachers and children at work*. Portsmouth, NH: Heinemann.

Hall, M. (2015). Composing in public: The ambient audiences of a writing lab. *Journal of Adolescent and Adult Literacy, 59*(3), 309–318.

Hattie, J., & Timperley, H. (2007). The power of feedback. *Review of Educational Research, 77*, 81–112.

Hull, G. A., & Stornaiuolo, A. (2010). Literate arts in a global world: Reframing social networking as cosmopolitan practice. *Journal of Adolescent and Adult Literacy, 54*(2), 84–96.

Ito, M. (2005). Introduction: Personal, portable, pedestrian. In M. Ito, D. Okabe, & M. Matsuda (Eds.), *Personal, portable, pedestrian: Mobile phones in Japanese life* (pp. 1–16). Cambridge, MA: MIT Press.

Ito, M., Gutiérrez, K., Livingstone, S., Penuel, B., Rhodes, J., Salen, K., . . . Watkins, S. C. (2013). *Connected learning.* Cork, UK: BookBaby.

Jenkins, H., Purushotma, R., Weigel, M., Clinton, K., & Robison, A. (2009). *Confronting the challenges of participatory culture: Media education for the 21st century.* Cambridge, MA: MIT Press.

Kalantzis, M., & Cope, W. (2015). Learning and new media. In D. Scott & E. Hargreaves (Eds.), *The Sage handbook of learning* (pp. 373–387). London: Sage.

Kittle, P. (2008). *Write beside them: Risk, voice, and clarity in high school writing.* Portsmouth, NH: Heinemann.

Kline, S., Letofsky, K., & Woodard, R. L. (2013). Democratizing classroom discourse: The challenge for online writing environments. *e-Learning and Digital Media, 10*(4), 378–394. http://dx.doi.org/10.2304/elea.2013.10.4.328

Lammers, J. C., Magnifico, A. M., & Curwood, J. C. (2014). Exploring tools, places, and ways of being: Audience matters for developing writers. In K. Pytash & R. Ferdig (Eds.), *Exploring technology for writing and writing instruction* (pp. 186–201). Hershey, PA: IGI Global.

Leander, K. M., & Vasudevan, L. (2009). Multimodality and mobile culture. In C. Jewitt (Ed.), *The Routledge handbook of multimodal analysis* (pp. 127–139). London: Routledge.

Lessig, L. (2008). *Remix: Making art and commerce thrive in the hybrid economy.* New York: Penguin.

Ling, R., & Campbell, S. W. (2009). Introduction: The reconstruction of space and time through mobile communication practices. In R. Ling & S. W. Campbell (Eds.), *The reconstruction of space and time: Mobile communication practices* (pp. 1–15). New Brunswick, NJ: Transaction.

Littleton, K., Scanlon, E., & Sharples, M. (Eds.). (2012). *Orchestrating inquiry learning.* New York: Routledge.

Lundstrom, K., & Baker, W. (2009). To give is better than to receive: The benefits of peer review to the reviewer's own writing. *Journal of Second Language Writing, 18*(1), 30–43.

Magnifico, A. M., Curwood, J. S., & Lammers, J. C. (2015). Words on the screen: Broadening analyses of interactions among fanfiction writers and reviewers. *Literacy, 49*(3), 158–166.

Magnifico, A. M., McCarthey, S. J., & Kline, S. (2014, April). *Reconsidering peer feedback in argumentative essays. Innovations in peer and teacher feedback during writing instruction: Results from three IES studies.* Paper presented at the annual meeting of the American Educational Research Association, Philadelphia, PA.

Magnifico, A. M., Woodard, R., & McCarthey, S. J. (2014, December). *A Bakhtinian framework for understanding teachers' initiating texts, peer response, and revision.* Paper presented at the Annual Literacy Research Association Conference, Marco Island, FL.

McCarthey, S. J., Magnifico, A., Kline, S., & Kennett, K. (2013, December). *Secondary students' use of two online peer review tools.* Paper presented at the Literacy Research Association, Dallas, TX.

McCarthey, S. J., Magnifico, A., Woodard, R., & Kline, S. (2014). Situating technology—Facilitated feedback and revision: The case of Tom. In K. Pytash & R. Ferdig

(Eds.), *Exploring technology for writing and writing instruction* (pp. 152–170). Hershey, PA: IGI Global.

McLaughlin, M. W., & Talbert, J. (1990). *The contexts of teaching in secondary schools: Teachers' realities.* New York: Teachers College Press.

Mislevy, R. J., Behrens, J. T., Dicerbo, K. E., & Levy, R. (2012). Design and discovery in educational assessment: Evidence-centered design, psychometrics, and educational data mining. *Journal of Educational Data Mining, 4*(1), 11–48.

Murray, D. M. (2004). *A writer teaches writing* (2nd ed.). Boston: Cengage.

National Council of Teachers of Mathematics. (2000). *Principles and standards for school.* Reston, VA: Author.

Natriello, G. (Ed.). (2013). *Adaptive educational technologies: Tools for learning, and for learning about learning.* Washington, DC: National Academy of Education.

Newkirk, T. (2014). *Minds made for stories: How we really read and write informational and persuasive texts.* Portsmouth, NH: Heinemann.

Nygard, A. (2012). Perforating school: Digital literacy in an arts and crafts class. In J. Ávila & J. Zacher Pandya (Eds.), *Critical digital literacies as social praxis: Intersections and challenges* (pp. 87–106). New York: Peter Lang.

Olmanson, J., Kennett, K., Magnifico, A., McCarthey, S. J., Searsmith, D., Cope, B., & Kalantzis, M. (2015). Visualizing revision: Leveraging student-generated between-draft diagramming data in support of academic writing development. *Technology, Knowledge and Learning, 21*(1), 99–123.

Padgett, E. R., & Curwood, J. S. (2015). A figment of their imagination: Online poetic literacy in an online affinity space. *Journal of Adolescent and Adult Literacy, 59*(4), 397–407. doi:10.1002/jaal.453

Piech, C., Huang, J., Chen, Z., Do, C., Ng, A., & Koller, D. (2013, July). *Tuned models of peer assessment in MOOCS.* Paper presented at the 6th International Conference on Educational Data Mining, Memphis, TN.

Prior, P. (2008). A sociocultural theory of writing. In C. A. MacArthur, S. Graham, & J. Fitzgerald (Eds.), *Handbook of writing research* (pp. 54–66). New York: Guilford Press.

Pugalee, D. K. (2005). *Writing for mathematical understanding.* Norwood, MA: Christopher Gordon.

Resier, B. J., Spillane, J., Steinmuller, F., Sorsa, D., Carney, K., & Kysa, E. (2000). Investigating the mutual adaptation process in teachers' design of technology-infused curriculum. In B. J. Fishman & S. F. O'Connor-Divelbiss (Eds.), *Facing the challenges of complex real-world settings* (pp. 342–349). Mahwah, NJ: Lawrence Erlbaum.

Scheffel, M., Drachsler, H., Stoyanov, S., & Specht, M. (2014). Quality indicators for learning analytics. *Educational Technology & Society, 17*(4), 117–132.

Schunn, C. D., Godley, A., & DeMartino, S. (2016). The reliability and validity of peer review of writing in high school AP English classes. *Journal of Adolescent & Adult Literacy, 60*(1), 13–23.

Simmons, J. (2003). Responders are taught, not born. *Journal of Adolescent and Adult Literacy, 46*(8), 684–693.

Smith, A., West-Puckett, S., Cantrill, C., & Zamora, M. (2016). Remix as professional learning: Fostering transformative teacherly identities in CLMOOC. *Education Sciences, 6*(1), 12. doi:10.3390/educsci6010012

Spillane, J. P. (1999). External reform initiatives and teachers' efforts to reconstruct their practice: The mediating role of teachers' zones of enactment. *Journal of Curriculum Studies, 31*(2), 143–175.

Surowiecki, J. (2004). *The wisdom of crowds: Why the many are smarter than the few and how collective wisdom shapes business, economies, societies and nations.* New York: Doubleday.

Warschauer, M. (2011). *Learning in the cloud: How (and why) to transform schools with digital media.* New York: Teachers College Press.

Waters, J. (2014). Adaptive learning: Are we there yet? *Technological Horizons in Education, 41*(4), 1–4.

West, D. (2012). *Big data for education: Data mining, data analytics, and web dashboards: Governance studies.* Washington, DC: Brookings Institution.

Wiliam, D. T., & Thompson, M. (2006). Integrating assessment with learning: What will it take to make it work? In C. A. Dwyer (Ed.), *The future of assessment: Shaping, teaching and learning* (pp. 53–82). Mahwah, NJ: Lawrence Erlbaum.

Wilson, M. (2006). *Rethinking rubrics in writing assessment.* Portsmouth, NH: Heinemann.

Witte, S. D. (2013). Preaching what we practice: A study of revision. *Journal of Curriculum and Instruction, 6*(2), 36.

Yagelski, R. (2012). Writing as praxis. *English Education, 44*(2), 188–204.

6 Collaborative Intelligence
Social Dimensions of e-Learning

Jane Blanken-Webb

This chapter calls for a reimagining of education in light of the idea that human cognition is best understood and approached as a phenomenon that is rooted in social interactions. This utilizes a conception of mind as a network of associations formed through experience in the world (Gee, 2014). Extrapolating from this conception of mind, the work of education becomes a matter of tending this network in order to utilize it more efficiently and effectively toward aims that are inherently social. e-Learning environments provide concrete manifestations of collaborative knowledge networks that both promote opportunities for and reflect back the work of collaborative intelligence, as e-learning environments are constituted within a social web of interactions. A radical departure from traditional notions of education that center on individual achievements reflected in test scores, educational environments that embrace the notion of collaborative intelligence foster dynamic opportunities for learning communities to collectively create, refine, and share knowledge products that embody more authentic processes of human learning and create the conditions for educational growth that will continue long after students complete their courses.

Cognition—and by extension, knowledge—is inherently social. As creatures of language and culture, we make knowledge through social processes. This comes to the fore in a famous study by Bruno Latour and Steve Woolgar (1979), which described the collaborative processes of laboratory scientists and the complex social practices that give rise to scientific knowledge. Historical knowledge also relies on collaborative processes revealed in trails of footnotes—serving as a form of proof that renders an argument or an idea to be valid (Grafton, 1999). In this way, the range and depth of acquired sources render knowledge more durable through a practice of linking texts. For these reasons, it seems that we do a strange and artificial thing in schools when we individualize knowledge processes. Indeed, "closed-book" exams deny the social nature of knowledge. This chapter endeavors to rethink such practices by considering collaborative intelligence and the ways e-learning environments allow for new opportunities to realize the social nature of knowledge.

What Is Collaborative Intelligence?

In order to address what collaborative intelligence *is*, let us first consider what collaborative intelligence is *not*. The opposite of collaborative intelligence is individual intelligence—a focus that is limited to the stuff contained within the boundaries of an individual's brain. A very concrete example that points to the arbitrariness of such a boundary comes to the fore with the case of writing—a technology that extends the minds of individuals' quite literally beyond the head to the printed page. But the notion of collaborative intelligence extends our understanding of mind much further still, pointing to the ways intelligence is inherently linked to and emerges as an outgrowth of social interaction.

An ecological perspective provides a productive counterpoint to the notion of individual cognition, offering a significantly different view of intelligence than we find in limiting the parameters of consideration to the individual head (Hutchins, 2010). "Indeed, one ecologically informed way to understand the relationship between the individual and the collective in a classroom is that the collective *has* to grasp a new concept or skill before any of the individuals can" (Cunningham, 2014, p. 66). Although not all claims of collaborative intelligence offer conclusions that are quite this strong, collaborative intelligence does posit that the use of social interactions is inherent in making meaning and is therefore concerned with the way we make use of social interactions in developing and furthering intellectual pursuits. These social interactions encompass a broad range that includes the very concrete realm of one-on-one interactions between individuals but extends much further to include the abstract realms of ideas, artifacts, social practices, symbol systems, and culture. Drawing on this broad spectrum of social interactions, the notion of collaborative intelligence extends the mind well beyond the individual.

The idea behind collaborative intelligence relies on a network of connections that allow the work of intelligence to unfold and advance. Intelligence, in this sense, is something that emerges—it is an action, a happening. "Discussions of emergence are often accompanied by such illustrative examples as the flocking of sandpipers, the spread of ideas, or the unfolding of cultural collectives. These sorts of self-maintaining phenomena transcend their parts—that is, they present collective possibilities that are not represented in any of the individual agents" (Davis & Simmt, 2003, p. 140). Intelligence, in this view, is therefore not a static entity possessed by an individual, but is indeed an achievement that comes alive in concrete situations. And when collaborative intelligence emerges as an activity, it involves effectively using a network of connections with phenomena well beyond the boundaries of an individual's head.

Collaborative intelligence also draws on the notion of connectionism, which describes approaches used in the fields of artificial intelligence, cognitive psychology, cognitive science, neuroscience, and philosophy of mind that offer a view of the mind as an emergent process of interconnected networks. Jim Gee (2014) describes the basic argument behind connectionism by stating that "the mind is populated by associations formed in our experiences in the world" (p. xiii). Gee elaborates on this point by saying that our minds are "constantly attuned to and tuned by the social and cultural groups to which we belong" (p. xiii). Thus, the mind is formed and ever re-formed in transaction with the world and, being inherently social, is constituted by social practices at a fundamental level. This offers a view of the mind as a networked phenomenon that is distributed among people, practices, and situations but extends even further to things like artifacts, environments, and symbol systems. This has radical implications for our understanding of intelligence—indeed, it also calls for a dramatic reimagining of education.

In an era of Web 2.0, this extension of mind takes on new power and potency through participative alliances formed through interactive platforms like YouTube, Wikipedia, Facebook, and Twitter that empower users to be knowledge producers who create knowledge rather than simply receive it and store it on an individual basis. More significantly still, Web 2.0 many-to-many infrastructuring allows users to share and network knowledge products (see, for example, Jamieson, 2016). This not only exemplifies but also embodies the very definition of collaborative intelligence and brings to light the need to rethink the notion of intelligence by shifting the focus away from the individual and recognizing intelligence as a collaborative phenomenon. In this, the shift from Web 1.0 to Web 2.0 allows us to more fully embrace "the power of the web to harness collective intelligence" (O'Reilly, 2007, p. 22). Thus, we can say that collaborative intelligence describes a feature of our inherently social minds, which comes to the fore and is perhaps amplified through recent developments in technology.

The Meaning of Literacy Competence in a Digital Age

Concerns about the quality of dialogue take on new significance in a digital age in which virtually anyone—and everyone—has the ability to engage. This calls for educators to help students develop new literacies that will enable them to navigate the cacophony of collaboration we now encounter on a daily basis. This also adds a new wrinkle to considerations of collaborative intelligence, as the sheer quantity of social exchanges now permeating the web stands at times to overwhelm the promise of collaborative intelligence while at the same time creating the conditions for collaborative intelligence to potentially take on new heights.

New digital technologies allow for us all to be participators. The ability to share our ideas, impressions, and meanings with the world is literally at our fingertips. Along with this, many new opportunities and challenges abound, as the meaning of literacy competence is blown wide open in a digital age. As stated by Mark (2013), "the range of literacy that the 21st century requires of us is as vast as society's consciousness."

On the surface, this may appear to open up opportunities for democratic ideals to flourish, as (almost) everyone has the opportunity to join the conversation. But we must also recognize that the most popular digital technologies are equipping us "with tools even more simplistic than the Likert scale [such as] YouTube and Facebook's 'like' or 'dislike' options" (Mark, 2013). In this, "numbers carry more weight than the quality of any singular review . . . [and] persistence through frequent comments can bury more thoughtful comments on a comment list into scrolling oblivion" (Mark, 2013). Indeed, it is almost always quantity over quality that rises to the top in digital space. Furthermore, social media often functions as an echo chamber in which people only communicate and interact with those they already agree with—muting, unfollowing, or blocking all others.

Although social media has the potential to cultivate communities of inquiry that stand to promote critical thinking and democratic exchange, the reality is that it often amplifies intense polarizations that exist among us. In the words of Wael Ghonim (2015), "acting on impulses is only one click away." And "because of the brevity and speed of social media, we are forced to jump to conclusions and write sharp opinions in 140 characters about complex world affairs" (Ghonim, 2015). This poses a challenge to core notions of civic responsibility, as it is easy to forget that there are actual people on the other side of our computer screens. And at the same time, the comments we make today stand to last far longer on the Internet than they may uphold within our own thinking, thus having the potential to influence far beyond the moment of a mouse click.

This collaborative cacophony has far-reaching implications for education. Students need to learn how to navigate the web effectively and to develop skills in judging the credibility of sources. Students also need guidance about posting online. This is essential in order to ensure their safety, but it is also important to ensure that students learn to be effective and socially conscious in how they communicate online. "We should be teaching students how to engage in ongoing, stimulating, respectful dialogues, in succinct, IM formats as well as in longer, article formats" (Mark, 2013). A post by Andrew Marcinek (2010) offers insightful advice about "How to Help Students Use Social Media Effectively," suggesting that students examine their motives before posting online by first asking: "Will this help someone in his or her daily practice? Will it engage or entertain someone? Am I just looking to build my following number and increase the activity of my mentions column?" (Marcinek, 2010). Helping students to develop these kinds of strategies is vital in a digital age, as there is an urgent need for educators to "address social responsibility in the context of convergence and collective intelligence" (Mark, 2013).

The meaning of literacy competence is vastly expanded in a digital age. The challenge before educators and students is to effectively harness the immense capacity that comes with connectivity without getting lost in its cacophony. At its best, this collective capacity has the potential to allow us to more fully realize the ideal of democracy that consists of rich interactions that are free and flexible such that our interdependence with others and the groups in which we are embedded are enhanced and continually expanded (Dewey, 1916/1980). But the reality facing us today on the web often involves immense connectivity that does not necessarily promote the kind of intelligence and civic concern necessary in order for this vision of democracy to come to fruition. And because, following John Dewey's philosophy, democracy is integrally linked with education, we are facing a fundamentally educational concern. Thus, a key question before us is this: How can we teach students to be effective in taking advantage of the immense connectivity we are afforded in a digital age such that our societal dialogue is improved through the cultivation of intelligence and civic concern?

Connectivism: Implications for Education

A reimagining of education in light of collaborative intelligence is prominent in the notion of connectivism, first introduced in 2005 with a piece by George Siemens called "Connectivism: A Learning Theory for the Digital Age." In this piece, Siemens critiques the way most learning theories only address the learning that occurs within the individual and "do not address learning that occurs outside of people," indicating "learning that is stored and manipulated by technology" and "learning [that] happens within organizations" (p. 3). Thus, the main point behind connectivism is that we develop the competence we need in order to act by forming connections and rapidly evaluating the "worthiness" of these connections. In this, "the connections that enable us to learn more are more important than our current state of knowing," as learning becomes a matter of actionable knowledge (Siemens, 2005, p. 5). Closely related to this is a piece that also came out in 2005 by Stephen Downes called "An Introduction to Connective Knowledge," in which Downes offers an epistemological account of a type of "new knowledge" that relies on emergent connections to form an underlying framework that informs social and public knowledge.

Connectivism is especially relevant to this book because what is considered to be the first MOOC was a course facilitated by Siemens and Downes in 2008 called "Connectivism and Connective Knowledge" offered through the University of Manitoba (Liyanagunawardena, Adams, & Williams, 2013, p. 204). This course used the principles of connectivism and literally practiced what it preached, supporting a network of learners who engaged with course content as a catalyst for forming connections. These connections might include a wide variety of linkages, such as connections between course participants, with ideas, and with knowledge products (broadly defined). Indeed, the point of the course itself was purely to form such connections.

Although there is much that is praiseworthy about the notion of connectivism, its status as a theory has been called into question. Verhagen (2006) insists that instead of being a theory, connectivism is rather a "pedagogical view." Verhagen also questions whether connectivism is, indeed, espousing something new that is occurring because of the digital age: "Throughout history groups have functioned according to this principle in all manner of social organizational structures, using a division of tasks and a distribution of knowledge" (p. 4). Kop and Hill (2008) conclude,

> A paradigm shift, indeed may be occurring in educational theory, and a new epistemology may be emerging, but it does not seem that connectivism's contributions to the new paradigm warrant it being treated as a separate learning theory in and of its own right.
>
> (p. 11)

And Bell (2011) noted that "connectivism is perceived as relevant by its practitioners but as lacking in rigor by its critics" (p. 98).

Despite the dispute over connectivism's status as a theory, Downes (2010) draws out the robust pedagogical implications of connectivism that are well suited for a discussion of collaborative intelligence:

> . . . to learn is to immerse oneself in the network. It is to expose oneself to *actual* instances of the discipline being performed, where the practitioners of that discipline are (hopefully with some awareness) *modeling* good practice in that discipline. The student then, through a process of interaction with the practitioners, will begin to *practice* by replicating what has been modeled, with a process of *reflection* . . . providing guidance and correction.
>
> (p. 19)

In essence, connectivism offers a view of pedagogy as a conversation "that forms a rich tapestry of resources, dynamic and interconnected, created not only by experts but by all members of the community, including learners" (Downes, 2010, p. 20).

Although concerns have been raised regarding its status as a theory, connectivism expresses significant ideas for education that build on the notion of collaborative intelligence, offering insights that are especially relevant for the affordances of e-learning environments. Thus, there is strong potential for the basic idea behind connectivism to guide a pedagogical vision that is relevant to a digital age. It will be interesting to see whether the notion of connectivism will endure and take shape moving forward. In the very spirit of connectivism itself, it will likely take on more a more robust form through linkages with other theoretical accounts. In particular, there are strong corollaries to be made with inquiries in philosophy of mind that draw on connectionism, discussed earlier.

Connections with pragmatist theory seem fitting. Indeed, Siemens's (2005) description of connectivism expresses a view that is deeply pragmatic:

> Connectivism is driven by the understanding that decisions are based on rapidly altering foundations. New information is continually being

acquired. The ability to draw distinctions between important and unimportant information is vital. The ability to recognize when new information alters the landscape based on decisions made yesterday is also critical. (p. 5)

Thus, it would be fitting to link connectivism with the pragmatist philosophy of John Dewey, as this could join connectivism's emphasis on emergent connections with processes of inquiry, grounding connectivism's vision in a robust educational philosophy (Dewey, 1938/2003). James Scott Johnston (2009) summarizes Deweyan inquiry well: "All inquiry is transformative; inquiry involves discriminating, analyzing, relating; inquiry takes place (in part) in the context of past inquiries, and inquiry is guided by the problems it aims to solve" (p. 8). This linkage is also fitting within this discussion of collaborative intelligence, as inquiry, for Dewey, is an inherently collaborative process—one in which intelligence is central. Indeed, as encapsulated by Dewey (1946), intelligence is "a short name for competent inquiry work" (p. 330). By linking collaboration and inquiry work with an educational vision that takes advantage of the affordances of a digital age, connectivism contributes fruitfully to the vision we need for realizing a new mode of education that more fully embraces collaborative intelligence.

Vignettes of Two Classrooms

The following two contrasting classroom vignettes offer a richer idea about what it means to support collaborative intelligence pedagogically. Both draw on a particular video example, utilized in two different ways. The video, posted on YouTube in 2008 by a user known as "itisnti" (www.youtube.com/watch?v=J_I8Y-i4Axc), offers an explanation and demonstration of Boyle's law. It is one minute and thirty-seven seconds in length, and it features animated text that explains Boyle's law, followed by a demonstration that uses a balloon in a vacuum chamber. Dance music is played throughout the video.

Vignette 1: In this first vignette, students watch the video at home as part of a flipped classroom experience. During class time, students conduct a similar science lab. Guided by a worksheet, students follow step-by-step directions that detail what they should do, observe, and record. Although the lab experience is conducted in groups of two, it is more cooperative than collaborative, as it is highly structured and content driven rather than driven by "the social nature of learning" (Panitz, 1999, p. 8). Perhaps most significant of all, students' knowledge about Boyle's law will be tested in an exam later in the week in which students will be required to "keep their eyes on their own papers." What is of value here is the knowledge that is stored within each individual's head, as it would be an act of cheating to turn to a neighbor for help in remembering an equation or to see how another classmate approaches a problem. Utilizing the notion of a flipped classroom, this may seem a new and innovative approach to education, but the underlying theory of knowledge acquisition within this classroom is no different from the traditional classroom setup in which knowledge is transmitted from teacher to student and what is of value is individual intelligence—the stuff held within an individual's head as demonstrated on an exam.

What is salient in this first classroom vignette is reminiscent of what we find in many traditional classroom schemas: knowledge is approached as a discrete entity that an individual knower possesses, and intelligence is understood as an individual achievement reflected in a test score. There is no recognition in this first classroom vignette that, in receiving content knowledge, students are, as Isaac Newton once expressed, "standing on the shoulders of giants" and therefore are drawing on a cultural inheritance that belies the notion of intelligence as an individual possession or achievement. It is also notable that, in this first classroom vignette, class peers are not understood as a resource for furthering knowledge or intellectual achievements. Indeed, in this case, intelligence is understood as something isolated that resides within the individual heads of solitary students.

Vignette 2: By contrast, we might imagine a classroom example that draws on the same video demonstrating Boyle's law. However, this time let us imagine that the video is not an assignment for students to watch at home but rather a collaborative group project that students create in order to demonstrate how Boyle's law works. In this, students must work together to determine how to best introduce and demonstrate Boyle's law. Going even further, we could imagine that, once the project is created, it is submitted to other class members for a round of review and revision. This kind of peer feedback on project work can be extremely powerful. It is not only motivating for students to submit their best work but also positions them to consider the ways that other students approach similar problems, prompting metacognitive awareness. And unlike submitting a paper or a project for the teacher alone to read and grade, this process calls for collaboration and revision, prompting students to share their work and make improvements in light of peer feedback. In this classroom, conditions are established for supporting collaboration, and social interaction is considered central in developing and furthering intellectual pursuits. In this classroom, peers are treated as a resource for furthering knowledge rather than as competition or as a temptation for cheating. In this classroom, intelligence is understood as something that is distributed across individuals, environments, and situations—something that comes to life in human activity. In this classroom, "intelligence is accomplished rather than possessed" (Pea, 1993). Indeed, in this classroom, intelligence emerges in collaborative activity, and the aim of education is to foster and hone networked connections that facilitate such processes of intelligence.

It is worth noting that it does seem to be the case that the video used in both classroom vignettes demonstrating Boyle's law *was* in fact created as a class project. Evidence of this can be found in the description of the video: "This is a lab I did for my chem class. Try not to be too astounded." Reading the comment thread below the video, we find instances of users discussing the video, including elaboration on the science behind Boyle's law. The best example of this is found in the following comment posted at least a year after the video was first posted (and therefore presumably well after the class had ended):

> it's not a matter of knowing whether or not the temperature is constant so much as it is keeping the temperature constant. a change in temperature will affect the amount of space a gas takes up, distorting the effects of the experiment. we just kept everything at room temperature.

It is also worth noting, however, that not all comments in this thread were as constructive for improving scientific understanding. Many comments related to the dance music played throughout the video, and one commenter ridiculed the project, saying, "its not that great, i know 6th graders who could think of something better." This suggests that while collaboration can be extremely powerful in educational contexts, we would do well to remember that collaboration can lead to many possible outcomes, not all of which are helpful for educational purposes.

General Educational Research Findings

There has been considerable research in education involving peer interaction in learning. Within this literature, there is an important distinction between collaborative learning and cooperative learning. Although the two approaches overlap and inform each other, collaborative learning approaches are more closely aligned with the idea behind collaborative intelligence, but this is not to say that research involving cooperative learning does not also engage collaborative intelligence. "Collaborative and cooperative learning were developed originally for educating people of different ages, experience, and levels of mastery of the craft of interdependence" and "when using one or the other method, teachers tend to make different assumptions about the nature and authority of knowledge" (Bruffee, 1995, p. 12). Thus, while cooperative learning describes a set of processes developed for use with younger students to help them learn to work together successfully, collaborative learning is geared for adolescents and adults and can be helpful in "teaching students to come to terms with doubt" (Bruffee, 1995, p. 15).

Panitz (1999) distinguishes the two by defining cooperative learning as "a set of processes which help people interact together in order to accomplish a specific goal or develop an end product which is usually content specific" (p. 1). Collaborative learning, on the other hand, describes "a personal philosophy, not just a classroom technique. In all situations where people come together in groups, it suggests a way of dealing with people which respects and highlights individual group members abilities and contributions" (Panitz, 1999, pp. 3–4). Whereas there tends to be more structure in the form of teacher intervention in cooperative learning, structure is valued less in collaborative learning and instead asks, "To what extent is getting off topic a valuable learning experience?" (Panitz, 1999, p. 8).

A meta-analysis by Prince (2004) concluded that "collaboration 'works' for promoting a broad range of student learning outcomes. In particular, collaboration enhances academic achievement, student attitudes, and student retention" (p. 227). In this meta-analysis, the author subsumed cooperative learning under the broader category of collaborative learning, although Prince addressed cooperative learning distinctly when cooperation was studied in comparison with competition. This comparison revealed "broad empirical support for the central premise of cooperative learning, that cooperation is more effective than competition for promoting a range of positive learning outcomes" (Prince, 2004, p. 227).

Hattie's (2009) meta-analysis compared cooperative, competitive, and individualistic learning and concludes, "Peer learning can be powerful—whether cooperatively or competitively," as "cooperative learning leads to higher effects than competitive learning, and both are superior to individualistic learning" (p. 214). However, structure is important for effective peer learning—a finding that some may conclude pushes back against Siemens and Downes's totally open and unstructured model that they envisioned in developing the first MOOC (for an important debate related to this issue, see Hmelo-Silver, Duncan, & Chinn, 2007 and Kirschner, Sweller, & Clark, 2006). Interestingly, intergroup competition, relying on cooperation within groups while competing with other groups, is more effective than interpersonal competition and individualistic efforts. And although cooperative learning proves effective in almost all learning situations, it does not prove helpful for rote decoding and correcting tasks (Hattie, 2009).

Effectively Engaging Collaboration

Kuhn (2015) offers greater precision in analyzing collaborative learning by investigating the conditions under which collaboration works best. Questioning whether it is the problem or the collaboration that makes problem-based learning (PBL) effective, Kuhn offers results from analyses involving middle school students (Wirkala & Kuhn, 2011) and college students (Pease & Kuhn, 2011) presented with challenging, ill-structured problems, comparing students who worked individually with those who worked in small groups to solve the problem. Results indicated that "the benefit appears to come from the goal-directed experience of working on the problem rather than from social collaboration" (Kuhn, 2015, p. 48), as equal levels of mastery were reflected in students who worked independently on the problem and those who worked in small groups. But the investigation did not stop there.

Noting that collaboration did not seem to be of benefit when PBL was utilized in situations requiring a unilateral perspective, Kuhn (2015) investigated further, inquiring about situations that utilize bilateral or multilateral perspectives, such as instances of argumentative discourse in which groups take opposing positions on an issue and work to weaken an opposing group's position while upholding their own views in the face of opposition: "In a word, participants in argumentative discourse must engage with other minds in order to succeed" (p. 49). Kuhn studied electronically mediated argumentation by analyzing both intragroup and intergroup exchanges and noted that "participants' talk is not confined to the task content itself; they also engage in talk about their thinking" (p. 49). Notably, when the same participants engaged in writing a persuasive essay assignment individually, their essays exhibited the "most efficient" means for completing the task and lacked the deeper level of argumentation evidenced with collaboration. Kuhn suggests that this deeper level of argumentation came about when collaborative activity spurred metacognitive activity, stating that "socially mediated metacognitive talk may be a key factor in conferring any benefit the collaborative activity provides" (p. 49).

From this, we might conclude that when collaboration gives rise to metacognitive activity we find *a* (if not *the*) preeminent example of intelligence emerging. Indeed, this follows a developmental trajectory Kuhn outlines.

> Developmentally, the origins of collaboration lie in the phenomenon of joint attention that emerges when infants first recognize that they are sharing an object of attention with another (Brownell, 2011; Tomasello & Carpenter, 2007). Increasing monitoring of this early joint attention leads gradually to a meta-communicative awareness (Barron, 2003) through which a child comes to recognize and appreciate the differing perspective of another.
>
> (Kuhn, 2015, p. 51)

This might suggest that recognition of an other—which involves differentiating what is "me" from what is "not me" (Blanken-Webb, 2014)—is the point at which intelligence itself emerges. Yet it is interesting that this is not at all the direction of Kuhn's conclusion. Kuhn takes this developmental trajectory one step further, pointing to the ways that children gradually build on meta-communicative awareness in learning to coordinate the perspectives of others to develop the skills of effective collaboration.

This prompts a key question that is central to considerations of collaborative intelligence: Is collaboration valuable because it promotes the emergence of intelligence, or do we value collaboration because it promotes the skill of collaboration itself? Although we can certainly value collaboration for both of these reasons, Kuhn (2015) offers that the evidence supporting collaboration's value for promoting intelligence is equivocal. "Collaboration is a long way from the silver bullet many educators wish it to be" (p. 51). Therefore, Kuhn determines, "Collaborative cognition thus needs our attention as a research topic first and foremost because it warrants a place as a core component of what educators are today calling 21st century readiness" (p. 51).

No matter whether we value it primarily as enabling grounds for intelligence to emerge or as skill to be honed in itself, collaboration is important in education, and we would do well to take advantage of the affordances of e-learning environments in promoting it. However, in doing so, we must remember that "it is not enough to simply put individuals in a context that allows for collaboration and expect them to engage in it effectively" (Kuhn, 2015, p. 51). Kuhn's insight regarding the role of metacognition in effective collaborative activity may be key in creating the conditions for student collaboration. Given the affordances of e-learning environments for supporting metacognition (see Chapter 7), there are ample opportunities for e-learning environments to promote the overlap between collaboration and metacognition. The question becomes: How can we utilize the affordances of e-learning environments to best support this endeavor?

Collaboration and Metacognition in e-Learning Environments

e-Learning environments allow for an unprecedented level of connectivity. In essence, they offer learners a conversation space that allows for instant feedback as well as asynchronous responses that extend conversations over time, opening up the possibility for learners to reconsider previous statements through processes of social negotiation long after a course is completed. Zheng (2010) picked up on this idea and contends that, in the in face of Web 2.0 technologies, "traditional ID [instructional design] models are deemed less fit for Web 2.0 learning due to their linear, well-structured design approach" (p. 61). Instead, Zheng proposes a new model that is better suited for Web 2.0 learning that features a learner-centered approach that emphasizes interactive social communication and dynamic learning. The aim is to promote "learning that focuses on metacognitive thinking and self-regulation, facilitates knowledge integration and construction of schemas-of-the-moment for ill-structured learning, and delivers an environment by connecting activities with behavior to form a dynamic learning environment in Web 2.0 application" (p. 61). An approach that is well aligned for promoting the emergence of collaborative intelligence, it is significant that Zheng also integrates metacognitive thinking into the proposed instructional design framework for Web 2.0 learning. Indeed, this is a framework that takes advantage of the affordances Web 2.0 technologies is geared to support an overlap between collaboration and metacognition.

A more specific answer to this question is offered in a recent study (Bernard & Bachu, 2015) that developed a multiplayer video game to promote metacognition in computer programming through collaboration. This multiplayer strategy game encourages equal participation, argumentative discussion, and positive interdependence.

> By enforcing equal participation, each player is motivated to understand the problem and analyze the logic in the programming solution; the argumentative discussion means that they must be able to defend their solution to the other players in the team and positive interdependence means that all players must learn if the team is to complete the game successfully and no player is left behind.
>
> (Bernard & Bachu, 2015, p. 295)

This offers "an approach for promoting metacognition in computer programming using collaboration and computer games" (Bernard & Bachu, 2015, p. 277) and provides a compelling example of how we might take advantage of the affordances of e-learning environments for supporting the combination of collaboration and metacognition.

Collaborative Intelligence in e-Learning Environments

There are many ways that e-learning environments support collaborative work—a key feature of the community of inquiry framework Garrison (2011) describes for e-learning. Garrison maintains that forming a community of learners engaged in inquiry processes is needed in order to realize the full potential of e-learning. Drawing on the power of technological advancement "to connect people in personal and public ways," Garrison describes a vision that is "fundamentally changing approaches to teaching and learning" (p. 19). Accordingly, Garrison describes a critical community of learners that encourages "cognitive independence and social interdependence simultaneously" as the "spark that ignites a true educational experience that has personal value and socially redeeming outcomes" (p. 20). And by taking advantage of the affordances of e-learning environments, new approaches are emerging that shift the teaching and learning transaction and enhance the quality of learning outcomes by increasing access to critical communities of learners that go far beyond merely providing access to information (Garrison & Anderson, 1999).

Deepening the discussion, Garrison (2011) identifies three key elements that must be considered when planning and delivering e-learning experiences: social presence, cognitive presence, and teaching presence. The element of social presence adds a new dimension to considerations of collaborative intelligence by pointing to the significance of participants identifying with a group, feeling comfortable communicating purposefully in a trusting environment, and developing personal and affective relationships by expressing their individual personalities through the medium of communication being used

(Garrison, 2009). This adds to our discussion of collaborative intelligence by considering the qualities of interpersonal exchange that allow for effective collaboration. In this, it is not only the fact of dialogue occurring that is significant but also, and perhaps even more significantly, the quality of dialogue is key:

> What sustains a dialogue over time is not only lively inter-change about the topic at hand, but a certain commitment to one's partner; a commitment that might not precede the dialogue, but arises only gradually in the spirit of the engagement.
>
> (Burbules, 1993, p. 15)

Blogging in the Classroom

New technological tools open up new possibilities for learning that emphasize meaningful conversations through digital means. This involves new demands for students to become literate in expanding ways, as digital technologies are now a prime medium for communicating, generating, assembling, and analyzing information. In this, students use digital tools to engage in authentic tasks supporting collaborative experiences and critical thinking by learning from one another. And when implemented effectively, blogs can support this kind of learning while promoting new literacy skills.

A blog is a web publishing tool that allows authors to quickly and easily self-publish their work. This could involve publishing text, artwork, links to other blogs or websites, and much more. Blogs are user-friendly for teachers and students. There are many different blogging choices available that require minimal work to set up—and most are free. Some popular blogging sites used in the classroom are Google's Blogger, WordPress.com, and KidBlog (Walsh, 2016).

> Blogs posts are typically short and updated frequently. Other individuals are able to continuously post comments relating to original blog post. Blogs create online constant collaboration and discussion experiences between students. This ubiquitous approach is highly motivating to students because it involves technology. Blogging also allows for all students to feel comfortable participating, not having the anxiety of speaking out during class discussions. Today, there are over 172 million Tumblr and 75.8 million WordPress blogs in existence worldwide impacting business, politics and society.
>
> (Walsh, 2016)

Today, blogging is becoming increasingly popular in education, as there is a high demand for pertinent experiences with digital technologies in the classroom.

Some blogging ideas for the classroom include (adapted from Walsh, 2016):

- *Classroom discussion/information board.* This can be used for communication purposes with parents and students.
- *Novel unit discussion purposes.* A blog could be used with a novel to enhance the unit and provide a ubiquitous approach to learning for younger students.
- *Student portfolios.* Students can organize their work as digital profiles, and publishing work can be motivating for students to produce high-quality products.
- *Specific subject-area discussion/collaboration space.* Teachers and students can interact to help further their subject-area and writing skills.
- *Debates.* Blogs can be set up for online debates.
- *Peer review.* Pieces of work can be shared with others to edit and review.
- *Artwork/music.* Artwork and music can be displayed for discussion purposes.
- *Writing forum.* Blogs can be used for writing purposes to enhance language development of students.

Testimonial: I have experience using KidBlog in my third grade classroom. This blogging site best suits my user preferences. It is very easy to set up and user-friendly for both me and my students. So far we've used this blogging space to enhance novel units. I typically post discussion questions that correlate with novels we're reading. Students are thoroughly engaged while blogging, typical posts include thorough answers and students seem encouraged to automatically create their own questions that go along with the discussion. Their comments must be approved before others can read or comment on them, which allows me to better monitor their thoughts and comprehension.

(Walsh, 2016)

Using blogs in the classroom can support many positive educational outcomes. These include (adapted from Walsh, 2016):

- Offering students a platform for developing and expanding their language abilities.
- Continuously learning from one another through collaboration.
- Promoting metacognitive abilities by providing a medium for students to see their own work in a public forum.
- Expanding collective knowledge bases through consistent social experiences.
- Encouraging students to take ownership of their education.
- Allowing teachers to effectively differentiate their instruction according to individual student needs.

- Allowing for possibilities of connecting with others globally.
- Supporting a ubiquitous approach to learning in which students are able to learn anytime, anywhere.

But at the same time, there are limitations to using blogs in the classroom that may impede their effective use. For example, the technology supporting blogs is not always available in classrooms and households, and it can be challenging to find the time to effectively structure blog posts and to teach students how to be successful in blogging. Keeping track of students' blogging activities can also be time consuming for teachers. Nevertheless, it is important for teachers to do so in order to ensure that students are effectively engaging with the technology in supporting educational aims.

Studying Collaborative Intelligence in a Digital Age

As an emergent phenomenon, collaborative intelligence presents a challenge to researchers utilizing an experimental approach to predict learning outcomes.

> We cannot build useful theory without establishing causal relationships among phenomena. And we cannot establish causal relationships just through observation. Without being able to establish through experiments, with a high level of certainty, that Factor A or Context B causes Behavior C, we will not be able to build theory, which successfully predicts learning outcomes, that we so desperately need.
>
> (Winn, 2006, p. 56)

However, where traditional educational research methods are less effective for studying emergent phenomena such as collaborative intelligence, e-learning environments allow for new modes of analysis that have the potential to revolutionize educational research due to the level of detail incidentally recorded alongside interactions in digital spaces. These interactions include everything from a mouse click, to a page view, to creating a complete written manuscript. And every interaction leaves behind a trail of data recording everything that happened: what was said, to whom it was said, who viewed it, who responded, who passed it along, and the like—all time-stamped and often geo-located.

Termed *big data*, this type of information allows us to capture a fine-grained level of detail about learning processes that open up new possibilities for educational research. Indeed, big data analytics can trace the social dynamics and provenance of learning, allowing for a powerful mode of analysis that offers a new lens for understanding the intricate workings of collaborative intelligence.

> When learning is designed around social engagement and interaction there is a need to develop new ways of understanding and assessing

student social mobility. Through SLA [Social Learning Analytics], based on data about student connectivity and activity, we might be able to provide a better insight into the social dynamics and networked learning opportunities that . . . social hubs . . . have to offer.

(De Laat & Prinsen, 2014, p. 58)

Thus, e-learning environments provide an unprecedented way to study interactive, collaborative work, as every mash-up, remix, comment, share, like, and page view is recorded in a data trail left behind by such collaborative interactions.

We now have analyzable records of social knowledge work, recognizing and crediting for instance the peer feedback that made a knowledge construct so much stronger, or tracking via edit histories the differential contributions of participants in a jointly created work.

(Cope & Kalantzis, 2015, p. 223)

Using such data traces, Smith et al. (2016) analyzed the posts and remixes of approximately 2,000 educators participating in the National Writing Project's Connected Learning MOOC to articulate the ways and rhythms that ideas and media spread across a distributed learning community. In such projects, Web 2.0 technologies not only facilitate collaborative knowledge work but also provide a very concrete mapping of it that can be analyzed post factum—an analysis that may, indeed, break new ground in understanding the workings of collaborative intelligence.

Conclusion

Recognizing the significance of collaborative intelligence changes the work of education in considerable ways. At the same time, e-learning environments allow for new modes of education. This supports a dramatic reimagining of education that acknowledges the workings of collaborative intelligence. Backing the notion of collaborative intelligence with the affordances of e-learning environments flies in the face of a most central tenet within the traditional schema of education; namely, the notion that learning is fundamentally about mind/memory and is intrinsically individual. The debate here has been famously played out by Kirschner, Sweller, and Clark (2006), who argued that long-term memory is the central and dominant structure of human cognition, and Hmelo-Silver, Duncan, and Chinn (2007), who rebutted with the proposition that learning is not only about content, as "softer skills" such as epistemic practices, self-directed learning, and collaboration are also essential for developing lifelong learners and citizens in a knowledge society. Collaborative intelligence is thus key on the Hmelo-Silver et al. side of the debate, as it posits intelligence as a phenomenon that emerges out of a web of social interactions. And when collaborative intelligence emerges within e-learning environments, this web of interactions becomes quite literal. In this, e-learning environments highlight the need for a new vision of education that recognizes the significance of collaborative intelligence, and such environments also open new doors for educational research due to their affordance of supremely detailed trails of information pertaining to collaborative knowledge processes. This also calls for a dramatic shift in what we value in education, as the strength of networks and the ability to navigate networks effectively become chief among educational concerns. Allowing for dynamic opportunities for learning communities to draw on their collective strength, e-learning environments afford a new conception of education that recognizes the significance of collaborative intelligence and redefines the work of education.

References

Barron, B. (2003). When smart groups fail. *Journal of the Learning Sciences, 12*, 307–359.

Bell, F. (2011). Connectivism: Its place in theory-informed research and innovation in technology-enabled learning. *International Review of Research in Open and Distance Learning, 12*(3), 98–118.

Bernard, M., & Bachu, E. (2015). Enhancing the metacognitive skill of novice programmers through collaborative learning. In A. Peña-Ayala (Ed.), *Metacognition: Fundaments, applications, and trends* (pp. 277–298). New York: Springer.

Blanken-Webb, J. (2014). The difference differentiation makes: Extending Eisner's account. *Educational Theory, 64*(1), 55–74.

Brownell, C. (2011). Early developments in joint action. *Review of Philosophy and Psychology, 2*, 193–211.

Bruffee, K. A. (1995). Sharing our toys: Cooperative learning versus collaborative learning. *Change, 27*(1), 12–18.

Burbules, N. (1993). *Dialogue in teaching: Theory and practice.* New York: Teachers College Press.

Cope, B., & Kalantzis, M. (2015). Interpreting evidence-of-learning: Educational research in the era of big data. *Open Review of Educational Research, 2*(1), 218–239.

Cunningham, C. (2014). *Systems theory for pragmatic schooling: Toward principles of democratic education.* New York: Palgrave Macmillan.

Davis, B., & Simmt, E. (2003). Understanding learning systems: Mathematics education and complexity science. *Journal for Research in Mathematics Education, 34*(2), 137–167.

De Laat, M., & Prinsen, F. (2014). Social learning analytics: Navigating the changing settings of higher education. *Research and Practice in Assessment, 9*, 51–60.

Dewey, J. (1980). Democracy and education. In J. A. Boydston (Ed.), *Middle works of John Dewey* (Vol. 9). Carbondale: Southern Illinois University Press. (Original work published 1916)

Dewey, J. (1946). *The problems of men.* New York: Philosophical Library.

Dewey, J. (2003). Logic: The theory of inquiry. In J. A. Boydston (Ed.), *The later works of John Dewey, 1925–1953* (Vol. 12). Carbondale: Southern Illinois University Press. (Original work published 1938)

Downes, S. (2005). *An introduction to connective knowledge.* Retrieved from http://immagic.com/eLibrary/ARCHIVES/GENERAL/BLOGS/S051222D.pdf

Downes, S. (2010). Learning networks and connective knowledge. In H. H. Yang (Ed.), *Collective intelligence and e-learning 2.0: Implications of web-based communities and networking* (pp. 1–26). Hershey, PA: IGI Global.

Garrison, D. R. (2009). Communities of inquiry in online learning. In P. L. Rogers, G. A. Berg, J. V. Boettcher, C. Howard, L. Justice, & K. D. Schenk (Eds.), *Encyclopedia of distance learning* (2nd ed., pp. 352–355). Hershey, PA: IGI Global.

Garrison, D. R. (2011). *E-learning in the 21st century: A framework for research and practice.* New York: Routledge.

Garrison, D. R., & Anderson, T. (1999). Avoiding the industrialization of research universities: Big and little distance education. *American Journal of Distance Education, 13*(2), 48–63.

Gee, J. P. (2014). *The social mind: Language, ideology, and social practice.* Champaign, IL: Common Ground.

Ghonim, W. (2015, December). Let's design social media that drives real change. *TED Talk.* Retrieved from http://www.ted.com/talks/wael_ghonim_let_s_design_social_media_that_drives_real_change#t-799468

Grafton, A. (1999). *The footnote: A curious history.* Cambridge, MA: Harvard University Press.

Hattie, J. (2009). *Visible learning: A synthesis of over 800 meta-analyses relating to achievement.* London: Routledge.

Hmelo-Silver, C. E., Duncan, R. G., & Chinn, C. A. (2007). Scaffolding and achievement in problem-based and inquiry learning: A response to Kirschner, Sweller, and Clark. *Eductional Psychologist, 42*, 99–107.

Hutchins, E. (2010). Cognitive ecology. *Topics in Cognitive Science, 2*(4), 705–715.

Itisnti. (2008, April 21). Boyle's law science lab [video file]. Retrieved from https://www.youtube.com/watch?v=J_I8Y-i4Axc

Jamieson, J. (2016). Many (to platform) to many: Web 2.0 application infastructures. *First Monday, 21*(6). Retrieved from http://journals.uic.edu/ojs/index.php/fm/article/view/6792/5522

Johnston, J. S. (2009). *Deweyan inquiry: From education theory to practice.* New York: SUNY Press.

Kirschner, P. A., Sweller, J., & Clark, R. E. (2006). Why minimal guidance during instruction does not work: An analysis of the failure of constructivist, discovery, problem-based, experiential, and inquiry-based teaching. *Educational Psychologist, 41*, 75–86.

Kop, R., & Hill, A. (2008). Connectivism: Learning theory of the future or vestige of the past? *The International Review of Research in Open and Distributed Learning, 9*(3), 1–13.

Kuhn, D. (2015). Thinking together and alone. *Educational Researcher, 44*(1), 46–53.

Latour, B., & Woolgar, S. (1979). *Laboratory life: The social construction of scientific facts.* Beverly Hills: Sage.

Liyanagunawardena, T. R., Adams, A. A., & Williams, S. A. (2013). MOOCs: A systematic study of the published literature 2008–2012. *The International Review of Research in Open and Distributed Learning, 14*(3), 202–227.

Marcinek, A. (2010, October 19). How to help students use social media effectively. *Edutopia.* http://www.edutopia.org/blogs/how-to-help-students-use-social-media-effectively

Mark, L. (2013). The meaning of literacy competence in a postmodern age. Retrieved from https://cgscholar.com/creator/works/9368/versions/17323/export?output_format=standard&journal_article[journal_name]=&journal_article[volume]=

1&journal_article[issue]=1&journal_article[issn]=&journal_article[url]=&journal_article[copyright]=&journal_article[page]=1

O'Reilly, T. (2007). What is Web 2.0: Design patterns and business models for the next generation of software. *Communications & Strategies, 1*, 17.

Panitz, T. (1999). *Collaborative versus cooperative learning: A comparison of the two concepts which will help us understand the underlying nature of interactive learning.* Retrieved from ERIC database. (ED448443)

Pea, R. D. (1993). Practices of distributed intelligence and designs for education. In G. Salomon (Ed.), *Distributed cognitions: Psychological and educational considerations* (pp. 47–87). Cambridge: Cambridge University Press.

Pease, M. A., & Kuhn, D. (2011). Experimental analysis of the effective components of problem-based learning. *Science Education, 95*(1), 57–86.

Prince, M. (2004). Does active learning work? A review of the research. *Journal of Engineering Education, 93*(3), 223–231.

Siemens, G. (2005, April 5). Connectivism: A learning theory for a digital age. *Elearnspace*. http://elearnspace.org/Articles/connectivism.htm

Smith, A., West-Puckett, S., Cantrill, C., & Zamora, M. (2016). Remix as professional learning: Educators' iterative literacy practice in CLMOOC. *Education Sciences, 6*(12), 1–19. doi:10.3390/educsci6010012

Tomasello, M., & Carpenter, M. (2007). Shared intentionality. *Developmental Science, 10*, 121–125.

Verhagen, P. (2006). *Connectivism: A new learning theory?* Retrieved from https://www.scribd.com/doc/88324962/Connectivism-a-New-Learning-Theory

Walsh, B. (2016). Blogging in the classroom, *EPSY 408*. Retrieved from https://cgscholar.com/creator/works/9368/versions/17323/export?output_format=standard&journal_article[journal_name]=&journal_article[volume]=1&journal_article[issue]=1&journal_article[issn]=&journal_article[url]=&journal_article[copyright]=&journal_article[page]=1

Winn, W. (2006). Functional contextualism in context: A reply to Fox. *Educational Technology Research and Development, 54*(1), 55–59.

Wirkala, C., & Kuhn, D. (2011). Problem-based learning in K–12 education: Is it effective and how does it achieve its effects? *American Educational Research Journal, 48*(5), 1157–1186.

Zheng, R. Z. (2010). Designing dynamic learning environment for Web 2.0 application. In H. H. Yang & S.C.Y. Yuen (Eds.), *Collective intelligence and e-learning 2.0: Implications of web-based communities and networking* (pp. 61–77). Hershey, PA: IGI Global.

7   Metacognition

Cognitive Dimensions of e-Learning

Jane Blanken-Webb

The process of metacognition adds to the effect, efficiency, and even the meaning of what we do in education. Instead of viewing education as an endeavor to learn content, metacognition adds another crucial dimension to education: reflecting on content. In contrast to traditional didactic pedagogy that emphasizes memorization and recitation, new pedagogies that recognize the crucial role of metacognition in learning foster meaningful experiences that develop higher order skills, such as critical thinking skills, problem-solving abilities, and refined capacities for judgment. This extends our understanding of education itself. For this reason, metacognition is a crucial concept, and it is imperative that we understand its layers of complexity and the ways it functions in human learning. e-Learning environments stand to advance both of these aims in allowing for new modes of pedagogical interaction that can transcend traditional educational environments in supporting and developing metacognitive abilities. By exploring the intersection of metacognition and e-learning environments, we can gain a new lens for understanding metacognition and its significant role in human learning.

This chapter begins with the notion of metacognition, the concept of which encompasses a broad range. The narrowest conceptions of metacognition focus on self-regulation, but the concept can also be applied much more broadly as, for example, explicit articulations of the conditions of any disciplinary practice. In reviewing these conceptions of metacognition, my aim is to clarify the concept in order to show how metacognition intersects with the affordances of e-learning environments, which offer new opportunities for the development and exemplification of metacognitive abilities. This comes to the fore through considerations of online communities of inquiry, critical learning, and multimodal representations. Finally, this chapter will consider the implications of e-learning environments for researching metacognition and concludes by considering the relationship between metacognition and e-learning environments.

What Is Metacognition?

Commonly referred to as thinking about thinking, metacognition involves thinking at a higher level of abstraction, which improves thinking and learning. This comes across in John Dewey's conviction that "understanding, comprehension, means that the various parts of the information acquired are grasped in their relations to one another—a result that is attained only when acquisition is accompanied by constant reflection upon the meaning of what is studied" (Dewey, 1933, p. 177). In this, metacognition is implicit. Furthermore, the occurrence of metacognition (or reflection) allows for subsequent reflective thought to grow out of such instances, supporting future inquiry (Dewey, 1933/2003, p. 114).

Conceptualizing metacognition as thinking about thinking provides a good place to start introducing the term. Metacognition is a type of thinking (or cognition) that has mental activity itself as its object. As Peña-Ayala (2015) explains, "Metacognition is a term used to identify a kind of cognition oriented to monitor and regulate cognition engaged in a given mental activity (e.g., listening, reading, memorizing)" (p. v). When metacognition is conscious, it might include examples such as asking things like: Do I understand this? How likely am I to remember this? or perhaps, Is there a better way for me to organize or present my ideas?

Metacognition is complex in its depth and scope and can be described from many different analytic lenses. Because of this, metacognition has famously been referred to as a "fuzzy" structure (Efklides, 2006). Reference to metacognition as fuzzy has prompted a fair amount of discussion, which was recently reviewed and fruitfully extended by Peña-Ayala and Cárdenas (2015) in an analysis that offers an original contribution that draws on a comprehensive literature review about metacognition. (Other comprehensive summaries of the literature on metacognition include Akturk and Sahin, 2011; Beran et al., 2012; Lai, 2011; and Schraw and Gutierrez, 2015.)

The fundamental components of metacognition are generally considered to be knowledge and regulation. Used in conjunction, these related abilities allow for higher order metacognitive capacities that are necessary for critical thinking, problem solving, and refined judgment making. e-Learning environments offer opportunities to foster these abilities in ways that are not only new but also, even more significantly, transcend what we do in traditional educational environments by embedding support for metacognition within the design of the learning environment. Thus, in what follows, my aim will be to highlight and explore the intersection of metacognition and e-learning environments in order to draw out the concept of metacognition further and to provide clarity in understanding the ways that e-learning environments afford educational experiences that foster and refine metacognitive abilities.

Components of Metacognition

By and large, the literature on metacognition focuses on metacognitive knowledge, regulation, and monitoring. Indeed, these components supply the fundamental aspects of metacognition, which make possible higher order metacognitive abilities, such as critical thinking and problem solving. These components are often separated into two broad categories: knowledge (i.e., self-knowing) and regulation (i.e., self-monitoring). Although it is helpful to understand these aspects discretely, it is also important to keep in mind that they support and reinforce each other. Hence, Flavell (1979) argued that having metacognitive experiences of monitoring and regulating cognition allow for the development and refinement of metacognitive knowledge. Reciprocally, Schraw (1998) cites several empirical studies that demonstrate cognitive knowledge appearing to facilitate cognitive regulation. It has been further theorized that these two components of metacognition may be integrated into the form of metacognitive theories, which are systematized cognitive frameworks that individuals construct, representing and organizing the individual's beliefs about knowledge (Schraw & Moshman, 1995). Thus, we can speak broadly about metacognitive knowledge and regulation as structures that determine an individual's understanding about knowledge in general, providing an epistemological framework that organizes and facilitates an individual's way of knowing.

Metacognitive knowledge involves a kind of self-knowing that refers to knowledge about one's own cognitive skills and limitations (Flavell, 1979). There are several different types of metacognitive knowledge, including declarative knowledge, procedural knowledge, and conditional knowledge. Metacognitive declarative knowledge includes knowledge about oneself as a learner and knowledge about factors that might influence performance, whereas procedural knowledge includes knowledge about strategies, and conditional knowledge refers to knowledge about when and why to use particular strategies (Lai, 2011). Metacognitive knowledge is crucial for effective learning, as metacognitive knowledge and strategies enable learners to self-regulate their thinking and learning processes (Schraw & Gutierrez, 2015).

Correspondingly, the other major component of metacognition is metacognitive regulation. As Lai (2011) explains, "Metacognitive regulation is the monitoring of one's cognition and includes planning activities, awareness of comprehension and task performance, and evaluation of the efficacy of monitoring processes and strategies" (p. 2). Much of the research in this area focuses on metacognitive strategy instruction and interventions and details specific strategies to be implemented before, during, and after a "learning episode" (Schraw & Gutierrez, 2015). John Hattie's (2009) meta-analyses pertaining to metacognition considered this dimension of metacognition, addressing metacognitive strategies, study skills, and self-verbalizing and self-questioning. On the whole, as several meta-analyses of the research have shown, implementing strategy instruction and interventions proves to be successful in improving student learning, thus reinforcing the importance of monitoring and self-regulative aspects of metacognition (Bielaczyc, Pirolli, & Brown, 1995; Donker et al., 2014; Driver, Newton, & Osborne, 2000; Hattie, 2009).

Metacognitive knowledge, regulation, and monitoring prove especially important in e-learning environments, where students must be self-directed and able to take responsibility for their own learning, such as in the case of asynchronous environments in which there is no one else immediately present to help monitor and regulate the learning process. Garrison (2003) describes the (asynchronous) online learning environment as "An environment and experience where learners have the opportunity to reflect and engage in meaningful discourse with metacognitive awareness and who take responsibility to manage and monitor their learning" (p. 57). This view emphasizes the importance of metacognition for supporting and sustaining e-learning practices, an area of research that is still emerging, as there is a "paucity of research and instrumentation associated with studying metacognition in online learning contexts" (Akyol & Garrison, 2011, p. 183). Garrison (2011) considers metacognition and self-regulated learning as two sides of the same coin that make up the notion of cognitive presence, a critical component of his conception of successful e-learning. In this, metacognitive knowledge and regulation comprise the building blocks that make possible higher order metacognitive functioning.

Higher Order Metacognitive Functioning and Online Communities of Inquiry

Building on the fundamental components of metacognitive knowledge and regulation allows for higher order metacognitive functioning, such as critical thinking skills, problem-solving abilities, and refined capacities for judgment making. All of these skills utilize meta-level analysis of object-level phenomenon; that is, a higher level of abstraction from the object level—such as an idea or even something more fundamental such as a sound or a sentence. The distinction here between the object level and the meta level is that at the object level the object itself is the focus of thought, whereas the meta level involves reflection on this object of thought. This distinction comes alive in Dewey's (1933/2003) discussion of thinking versus reflective thinking, where thinking involves whatever "goes through our heads," whereas in reflective thinking thoughts have a consecutive order based on the consequences of previous thought: "thoughts grow out of one another and support one another" (p. 183)—they are units linked together based on reflection. This linkage of thought through reflection utilizes meta-level awareness.

Considerations of higher order metacognitive functioning open up the discussion further and offer a broader view of metacognition as "a complex concept that relates to the higher order thinking that enables students to understand, analyze, and control their own thought processes" (Bernard & Bachu, 2015, p. 278). These higher order capacities are essential for and promoted by communities of inquiry. "An educational community of inquiry is a group of individuals who collaboratively engage in purposeful critical discourse and reflection to construct personal meaning and confirm mutual understanding" (Garrison, 2011, p. 2). While communities of inquiry need not be situated in online environments, e-learning environments are significant in supporting communities of inquiry because they provide connectivity across the globe as well as asynchronous mediums of discussion that can keep conversations alive across time and space in archived, searchable interfaces.

Inquiry-based learning is fueled by student interest, as learners take initiative and ownership of their own learning process. The inquiry process commences when a student asks a question; that is, when a student identifies something that he or she wants to know more about. Unlike traditional learning environments in which teachers ask questions and students recite answers that have an established value of being "right" or "wrong," inquiry-based learning rearranges this process. In inquiry-based learning, students ask questions, and teachers are poised to help students as they pursue these questions in working to create satisfactory resolutions to their inquiries. Successful inquiry relies heavily on metacognitive activities, such as evaluating the reliability of the source for information, which often is not straightforward and can be challenging for learners at all levels.

e-Learning environments are well suited for this approach to learning for many reasons—not the least of which is because there is so much readily available information online for students to select and examine as they pursue their course of inquiry. The unprecedented level of access to networked information available today makes concrete the fact that we don't need to rely on experts who know the answers because we are in a position to go out and not only find answers but also to create our own novel solutions in order to resolve our inquires.

But even more than an abundance of networked information, online environments connect people to one another and allow for collaboration with others in the inquiry process. Collaboration is a key feature of the inquiry approach to learning, as it develops thinkers who are both independent and interdependent, collaborative learners. According to Garrison (2011), "These [features of independent and interdependent learning] are the very core values and conditions of a worthwhile educational experience" (p. 19). And given "e-learning's unique capabilities to support asynchronous, collaborative communication in a dynamic and adaptable educational context" (Garrison, 2011, p. 19), e-learning environments provide an ideal context for realizing the learning potential of the community of inquiry approach.

There are many examples of e-learning approaches that draw on inquiry-based learning (e.g., Casey & Bruce, 2011; De Jong, 2006; Edelson, 2001; Farmer, 2004; Garrison, 2011; Kim & Hannafin, 2004; Swan, Garrison, & Richardson, 2009; Chapter 8 in Woolf, 2010). This is fitting considering that "Inquiry-based learning is often described as a philosophical and pedagogical response to the changing needs of the information age" (Casey & Bruce, 2011,

p. 78). However, Casey and Bruce point out that the roots of inquiry learning are much deeper than this idea proposes, and they point to John Dewey's philosophy for the fullest articulation of inquiry-based learning (see Dewey, 1899/2003, 1916/1980, 1938/2003a, 1938/2003b).

Drawing on Dewey's philosophy, Casey and Bruce (2011) identified a five-part spiral cycle comprising inquiry learning. These stages include (1) asking questions, (2) investigating solutions, (3) creating, (4) discussing discoveries and experiences, and (5) reflecting on newfound knowledge and continuing the cycle by asking new questions for further inquiry (Bruce & Bishop, 2002). As detailed next, metacognition is central in moving this process along, as metacognitive activities are arguably at play at every stage of this process.

Most clearly, we can see metacognition's inherent role in the reflection stage of the inquiry process. The act of reflection involves taking a step back from a created work or idea and considering it from a meta-level perspective. In this, the learner takes inventory and makes observations in order to decide whether inquiry has reached its culmination. Reflection provides a direct example of metacognition through considerations such as: Does the work satisfy the original question? In what ways does the work *work*? Are there new questions that the work evokes? Indeed, the stage of reflection, by its very definition, serves as a prime example of metacognition.

However, beyond the direct example of this stage of reflection, metacognition is central to this process as a whole in moving each stage of inquiry forward. For example, investigation involves constant monitoring between the object and the meta levels, as investigation is guided by the overarching implicit question of whether and how the object under investigation moves the inquiry forward. The same can be said about the stage of creation in that the implicit question of whether and how a particular brush stroke, phrase, or movement, for example, relates to the inquiry as a whole is always in play.

The stage of discussing discoveries and experiences within a community of inquiry also opens up considerations of metacognition in significant ways, as it brings to the fore recognition of metacognition as socially situated and socially constructed. In this, perhaps there is something about the very nature of being in a community with others that inherently lends itself to meta-level awareness, as being in a community of inquiry necessarily means that there are others looking at and interacting with our work. Indeed, awareness of an "other" in and of itself calls for recognition at a meta level.

Akyol and Garrison (2011) demonstrate that metacognitive behaviors are observable within online communities of inquiry through analyzing an online discussion board from several weeks of an online course. This study revealed not only evidence of metacognitive behaviors but also demonstrated evidence of different types of metacognitive actives. A related study (Hurme et al., 2015) investigated the role of socially shared metacognition in mathematical problem solving through qualitative content analysis of computer notes. The results indicate that when socially shared metacognition emerges within a computer-supported collaborative learning context, groups were successful in solving problems. In contrast, groups that did not exhibit socially shared metacognition were not successful in problem solving. Hurme et al.'s (2015) study extends these considerations even further in helping us understand how socially shared metacognition functions within computer-supported collaborative learning contexts. "In the group where socially shared metacognition emerged, a group member regulated the ongoing problem solving and the other group members acknowledged metacognitive message and developed it further" (Hurme et al., 2015, p. 273).

However, in addition to revealing how socially shared metacognition functions within computer-supported collaborative learning, Hurme et al. (2015) demonstrate that technology-mediated environments do not necessarily guarantee that metacognitive actives will emerge. This is an important message to heed throughout this discussion. Indeed, e-learning environments that support online communities of inquiry, for example, can go a long way in attempts to foster individual and socially shared metacognition, but that does not mean that metacognition will necessarily occur or that we will be able to empirically measure it when it does occur.

Nevertheless, we can recognize that self-corrective thinking is inherent throughout this process and within a community of inquiry, as questioning and self-critique is as much a responsibility of individuals as it is for the group as a whole. Thus, we can see that metacognition needs to be a central feature within communities of inquiry, a point that Garrison strongly picks up on by stating that "metacognition is core to successful inquiry" (Garrison, 2011, p. 50). Garrison continues,

> Metacognition has been generally accepted as consisting of two components—awareness (knowledge) and implementation strategies (control). Awareness allows the learner to monitor the learning process and then to actively manage the inquiry process. In short, metacognition provides the knowledge and strategies to monitor and regulate effective inquiry.
> (Garrison, 2011, p. 50)

Thus, we can see that metacognition is necessary in order for the community of inquiry approach to learning to be successful.

However, in e-learning environments, we can go even further with this idea by considering not only how metacognition serves online communities of inquiry but also how online communities of inquiry might serve metacognition by supporting its functioning. In this vein, prompts for reflection might be built into the interface for a community of inquiry, for example, or a stage of review and revision could be a feature built into a workspace prior to release for publication. In these ways, metacognition is not only needed for successful inquiry but also can indeed be fostered by the e-learning platform that situates the community of inquiry itself.

The role of metacognition at the point of creation raises an interesting consideration if we are to follow Dewey's philosophy all the way through to his later works, especially *Art as Experience* (1934/2003). In this text, Dewey distinguishes *an* experience from experience in general—the major distinction being the quality of relation between self and world in which "everything overlaps and merges." This overlapping and merging of self and world within experience suggests that the point of creation (as theorized by Dewey) would involve an experience of complete immersion such that distinctions between the object and the meta levels would merge. Yet, at the same time, the *work* involved in creation is essentially the management of parts in relation to the whole. Although aesthetic experience (or *an* experience) may not allow for particular points within the stage of creation to be distinguished as either cognition or metacognition, there is little doubt that metacognition is vitally at play within the stage of creation—even if it functions at an unconscious level.

This consideration becomes even more interesting when creation occurs within e-learning environments that build support for metacognitive functions directly into their interface. A prime example of this can be found within the Creator space of *Scholar*, a collaborative knowledge platform (cgscholar.com). The Creator space is essentially a writing platform that allows for integration of text with images, video, audio, and the like (see Figure 7.1). There is a main window in which a work is created—much like a standard word processor. But alongside this main window are various forms of support for metacognitive functions, including:

- Structure of the work in which the author can fill in and organize major headings that link to their corresponding sections within the work
- Feedback offered against successive versions of the work: peer, instructor, self-reflective, and machine feedback

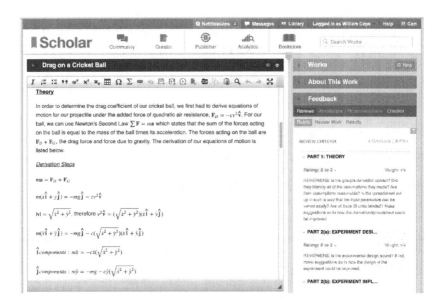

Figure 7.1 Cognition (*left*); rubric prompting metacognition (*right*)

This built-in metacognitive support facilitates the organization of the work along several different dimensions, including evaluative, informational, structural, and temporal. Although this placement of metacognitive support does not guarantee that all users will take full advantage of this feature, what is novel here is that the interface is crafted in such a way as to encourage and facilitate metacognition. The fact that this level of metacognitive support is built into the learning environment far surpasses the possibilities of traditional learning environments that would require the intentional placement of rubrics and notepads alongside a workspace in order to approximate a replication of what this interface automatically sets up from the beginning. In this way, e-learning environments can be designed in ways that inherently support and allow for the refinement of metacognitive functioning.

The *Scholar* platform is designed to support a peer-review process. This facilitates the community of inquiry model, as writers are both independent and interdependent. That is, a writer might create an independent work that will be submitted to the community for a stage of review so that revisions can be made before publishing the work. This stage of review and revision formalizes metacognitive processes, as it sets up a structure in which those involved in the community review and reflect on one another's work—a process that is inherently metacognitive. The fact that this functionality is built into the learning environment is significant for supporting metacognition because it sets up a framework for a writing process that maximizes the potential for engaging in metacognition at every stage of the writing process within an online community of inquiry.

Critical Learning

Another idea that relies heavily on higher order metacognitive functions is James Gee's (2007) notion of critical learning. Critical learning engages critical thinking, problem solving, and judgment making and can be manifested in many different types of learning contexts, including e-learning environments.

> Critical learning, as I am defining it here, involves learning to think of semiotic domain spaces that manipulate (if I can use this term without necessary negative connotations) us in certain ways and that we can manipulate in certain ways . . . the child can learn how to think about, and act on, semiotic domains as a larger design space composed of clusters (families) of more or less closely related semiotic domains.
>
> (Gee, 2007, p. 36)

Hence, critical learning is a mode of learning that involves coming to recognize systems of interactions that follow certain maneuvers or rules that govern how things play out. By recognizing this system of interactions, learners can reflect on ways this system influences their own actions by determining the limits that both constrict and make possible maneuvers within that system. Also, understanding the design principles that underlie the game is one strategy to play the game better. This opens up potential for this system of interactions to be critiqued, and it allows for novel maneuvers to emerge that stand to refine the system itself. This notion of critical learning takes the basic notion of thinking about thinking to a new level as it builds on the foundation that metacognitive knowledge and regulation make possible, allowing for meta-level thinking that goes well beyond thinking about one's own cognition by recognizing systems that determine social functioning on a much broader scale.

There are many potential examples of such systems of interactions. Considerations of disciplinary-based systems of interactions can be particularly helpful here, as this perspective enables recognition of diverse ways that metacognition functions within various disciplinary schemas (e.g., the Common Core State Standards Initiative). Hence, the type of metacognition needed in scientific reasoning, for example, is different from the metacognitive activity required in a quite different domain, such as an ensemble musical performance. In this comparison, scientific reasoning calls for testing of hypotheses to determine whether and in what ways they hold up in experimental inquiry. This involves meta-level analysis of what occurs at the object level in order to determine its meaning in relation to the hypothesis. In this example, metacognition functions according to rules of logical inference, producing results that can be measured and validated. An ensemble musical performance, on the other hand, requires a much different type of metacognition. In this example, an ensemble musical performance requires a constant monitoring between what can be considered the object level (the musician's own performance) in relation to a meta-level perspective (the ensemble taken as a whole). In this, there is an ever-present need for monitoring the relation between these two levels—the implicit question being: How is what I'm doing fitting in with what is going on around me? This kind of metacognitive functioning does not operate only according to logical inference but rather according to aesthetic perception and judgment, which calls for a much different type of metacognitive functioning. Yet it is interesting that in both examples reflection and adjustment are key, even though the timing of such metacognitive functioning might be different in the case of musical performance versus scientific reasoning.

These two very different systems of disciplinary-specific interactions operate in ways that are quite distinct. Yet in both cases, there are domain-specific procedures or "rules" that determine how the system operates, incorporating things like accepted methods for problem solving and specific applications of critical thinking or judgment making. This system of interactions invites opportunities for Gee's (2007) notion of critical learning to come into play, as learners engaged in either scientific inquiry or ensemble musical performances, for example, could draw on even higher levels of metacognitive abilities through recognition of this system of interaction and potentially critique or refine the system itself by coming up with novel maneuvers.

Critical learning can occur in many different types of learning environments, but e-learning environments can be designed in ways that are particularly good at supporting critical learning. In this, e-learning environments stand to allow for the high-level metacognitive actives central to critical learning that do not rely on teachers to direct the possibilities within a system of interactions. In this way, e-learning environments have the potential to transcend what is possible within traditional educational environments for supporting high-level metacognitive activity.

Metacognition and Video Games

Gee (2007) opens up the world of video games to education by demonstrating the complex learning that takes place within their structures. Metacognition is key in this mode of learning, and Gee demonstrates this by taking readers through game scenarios presented in *Pikmin.* As players advance through various areas within the game, they build up knowledge of the game as a system and demonstrate this knowledge by determining which moves to make and when in order to successfully overcome a challenge posed within the game. That is, learners come to understand the design space as a "system of inter-related elements making up the possible content of the domain" (Gee, 2007, p. 32). Understanding the game as a system in and of itself is an example of meta-level thinking, but this kind of knowledge opens up the possibility for more pronounced metacognition to emerge, such as critique of the game or coming up with novel moves or strategies. In this, video game players are "learning to think reflectively about the internal design grammar" (Gee, 2007, p. 35).

Moreover, Gee (2007) points out that there is an external design grammar at play in the practice of video games. This refers to recognizing the video game as a particular social practice, as children play video games in communities, and identities are formed in and around game play. This external design grammar of the game can also be reflected on and critiqued. Thus, video games open up many possibilities for the development of meta-level thinking and critical learning.

Of course, video games do not inherently ensure that this kind of learning will unfold. Some people will be more willing to take up the challenge of engaging as critical learners than others, but the point is that

> good games—and the games get better in this respect all the time—are crafted in ways that encourage and facilitate active and critical learning and thinking (which is not to say that every player will take up this offer).
> (Gee, 2007, p. 38)

Furthermore, the social practices surrounding the video games also promote reflection and meta talk pertaining to the design of the game. Again, this is not to say that every video game player will take up this offer for meta-level reflection within these communities, but nevertheless, video games and their surrounding social practices provide rich environments for the cultivation and refinement of metacognitive abilities. However, along these lines, it is notable that some of Gee's (2007) (and his group's) follow-up work on the idea of community in affinity spaces has shown that a real sense of community often is not present—even in spaces that are devoted to playing a particular game (Hayes & Duncan, 2012).

In a related study, Bernard and Bachu (2015) consider the use of multiplayer video games. This study combines the affordances of video games with an online community of inquiry and develops an approach for promoting meta-cognition in computer programming. The authors identify four dimensions of metacognitive skills that are required by programmers, including being able to understand and interpret a problem, determining the steps to solve the problem and the correct sequence of steps, choosing the best solution in light of self-knowledge about individual skill level, and verifying whether the solution is correct. The authors then developed a multiplayer strategy game that engages these dimensions of metacognition and encourages equal participation, argumentative discussion, and positive interdependence.

> By enforcing equal participation, each player is motivated to understand the problem and analyse the logic in the programming solution; the argumentative discussion means that they must be able to defend their solution to the other players in the team and positive interdependence means that all players must learn if the team is to complete the game successfully and no player is left behind.
>
> (Bernard & Bachu, 2015, p. 295)

This offers "an approach for promoting metacognition in computer programming using collaboration and computer games" (Bernard & Bachu, 2015, p. 277) and presents a compelling example of how we might take advantage of the affordances of e-learning environments for supporting metacognition.

Metacognition and Multimodal Representations

Another dimension of metacognition that builds on the foundation established with metacognitive knowledge and regulation involves the metacognitive functioning in multimodal representations. This affords a view of metacognition as cognition that stands in relation to other cognitions. An example offered by Winne and Baker (2013) illustrates that "computing the roots of a quadratic expression can be carried out algebraically or graphically. In choosing one method, a learner exercises cognitive control. Monitoring depends on conditional knowledge. Cognitive control depends on procedural knowledge" (pp. 2–3). Thus, more foundational metacognitive abilities involving knowledge and regulation allow for learners not only to make sense of multimodal representations but also to select the best mode of representation for a given purpose (see Chapter 4 in this volume for more on this topic).

This kind of metacognition is extremely important for the development of mind, a point that Elliot Eisner has argued throughout his career. "Some meanings are 'readable' and expressible through literal language; still others demand other forms through which meanings can be represented and shared" (Eisner, 2002, p. 230). For this reason, Eisner argues for the importance of helping students to be "multi-literate" in order have access to the full range of meanings made available through culture: "Literacy, as I use the term, is the ability to encode or decode meaning in any of the forms of representation used in the culture to convey or express meaning" (Eisner, 1994, p. x). Thus, Eisner contends that one of the major aims of education is to develop "students' ability to access meaning within the variety of forms of representation that humans use to represent the contents of their consciousness" (Eisner, 1994, p. x). Metacognition is central to this discussion, as it is necessary for determining the mode of representation that is best suited to a particular meaning and for enabling students to think within a variety of forms of representation that can stand in relation to one another.

Although Eisner stressed the importance of education in the arts for enabling students to gain meaningful access to a wide variety of representational media, his approach can fruitfully be extended through considerations of e-learning environments. Many e-learning environments are well suited for incorporating multiple modes of representation. Integrated digital platforms allow for text to stand alongside image, audio, or video, for example, thus empowering learners to draw on metacognitive capacities in representing meaning in multimodal ways. In this, e-learning environments support this vital dimension of metacognition in ways that surpass the possibilities of paper and pen.

One example of this is The Geometer's Sketchpad, which "allows teachers and students to model mathematical concepts and change those models at will. This promotes metacognitive abilities in helping student to think in ways that relate numeric, tabular, and graphical representations" (Brand, 2014). The Geometer's Sketchpad allows for "dynamic geometry," which involves "interactively manipulating mathematical diagrams while maintaining their fundamental definitions" (The Geometer's Sketchpad, 2014). This allows for a broad range of educational applications that support metacognitive thinking through multimodal representations, as it allows for mathematical visualization, generalization, conjecturing, and problem solving. "*The Geometer's Sketchpad* has developed into a powerful and concept-rich tool for math investigations. The tools and supporting materials allow elementary through high school students to move beyond hearing and seeing mathematics. Students can 'do and understand'" (Brand, 2014).

Teaching and Learning with Digital Concept Maps

Another example of supporting metacognition with e-learning environments involves using digital concept maps. Concept maps are a graphical representation of knowledge that show relationships among ideas. Concept maps engage metacognition's fundamental components of knowledge and regulation and could also be implemented in conjunction with metacognitive strategy instruction, such as those discussed in Schraw and Gutierrez (2015). In addition to graphically representing knowledge, concept maps help students relate new concepts to previously learned concepts, which allows for deeper and more meaningful understanding. Although concept maps are not limited to digital space, there are distinct advantages to digital concept maps, as they allow for embedding other resources and offer sharing capacities that transcend the capacities of pen and paper.

There are many different web apps available that support concept mapping, and Popplet, a particular iOS app created in 2011, can be readily utilized in classrooms. Popplet is designed to allow users to capture and organize their ideas. Although typical concept maps only support using text, Popplet offers the advantage of including images and videos in addition to text. Popplet also allows users to share concept maps online either as completed products or as works in progress. This allows students to work collaboratively to capture ideas visually and recognize the relationships among ideas, all of which support metacognitive functioning in substantial ways.

Using Popplet collaboratively enables two or more users to work together to add content to the same Popplet page.

> This is an excellent option for students working together on group assignments as they all have equal access to the assignment. When students add a box to the project, it automatically adds the student's name to the box so that it is clear who contributed what to the project.
>
> (Fajks, 2014)

Once completed, Popplet concept maps can be exported in several formats (e.g., PDF, JPEG, or PNG files). Alternatively, users can easily share links for their concept maps with others or even use the embed code provided to add a Popplet concept map directly to another webpage.

"Another advantage of using a piece of technology like Popplet, as opposed to using a traditional paper and pencil version of a concept map, is that students can [more readily] provide peer feedback on each others' assignments" (Fajks, 2014). And if students share their Popplet projects on social media, then they will have the opportunity to receive feedback from an even wider audience representing many different perspectives. This can be motivating for students to do their best work, as their knowledge product would be designed for public use rather than merely being an assignment to submit to the teacher alone.

Fajks (2014) offers several examples for effectively using Popplet in classroom environments. One novel suggestion involves using Popplet concept maps for creating and organizing ideas for an essay.

> For example, for an essay on a book or movie review project, the teacher can create a Popplet project template for each student that contains a

video box in the center with a summary of the book or movie, surrounded by boxes with the text "who, what, when, where, and why." Students can then add boxes containing the information requested. Once those questions are answered, they can use that information to form a structure for their essay paragraphs.

(Fajks, 2014)

Another suggestion for using Popplet might involve organizing historical research.

Each student could be assigned a different European explorer and compare their goals, obstacles, motivations and consequences of European exploration and colonization of the Americas (Noska, 2012). The students can color code the research that they gather and post (green boxes for economic consequences, red boxes for religious consequences, etc.). After each student has completed their research Popplets, the projects can be gathered and individually placed on a Google Slide presentation and shared with all students. Students can then read each others' projects, learn from them, and comment on them with constructive peer feedback.

(Fajks, 2014)

One final example includes a variety of uses.

I recommend using Popplet for a variety of uses in the classroom. It is an easy way for students to brainstorm essay topics since they are able to connect and arrange ideas on screen. It should also be used when teaching new concepts, such as science vocabulary, and relating it to prior knowledge. I strongly recommend using Popplet collaboratively since students learn better when they teach content to each other and they will grow as they receive constructive feedback and alter their concept maps. Popplet concept maps should also be shared through social media platforms to get a more worldly view and make the learning more meaningful since those with differing perspectives can offer new insights on the maps.

(Fajks, 2014)

Concept maps offer a strong pedagogical example for supporting metacognition. By concretely embodying relationships among ideas, concept maps inherently function at a meta level. But going even further, they can be utilized pedagogically in ways that exploit metacognition even more through incorporating collaboration with others and the use of multimodal representations. Here is where possibilities abound for taking advantage of the affordances of e-learning environments because digital environments excel in allowing for multimodal meaning making and collaborative intelligence in ways that fundamentally support metacognition (see also Chapter 4 and Chapter 6 in this volume).

Implications for Researching Metacognition

Exploring the intersection of metacognition and e-learning environments allows for a view that breaks new ground in researching and understanding the complexities of metacognition and its significance for education. In addition to opening up our understanding of metacognition in new ways, e-learning environments also allow for new ways to measure metacognition—a feat that has long proven difficult. There are two main approaches to measuring metacognition: self-reports, such as interviews or questionnaires, and objective behavior measurements, such as systemic observation and think-aloud protocols. e-Learning environments, however, open up the possibilities for investigating and measuring metacognition immensely and are advancing research on metacognition in significant ways.

One challenge cited in studying metacognition via a think-aloud protocol deals with the limitations of the traditional classroom environment.

> While think aloud protocols are useful in the laboratory conditions, they are not functional in the classroom environment because when students are asked to think aloud while they are performing a task, it is necessary that they leave their typical learning environment.
>
> (Akturk & Sahin, 2011, p. 3734)

This constraint does not apply to e-learning environments, which can embed opportunities for students to provide this kind of feedback seamlessly (e.g., annotation tools). However, it is worth considering that the kind of information students provide in annotations is not the same kind of data that think-alouds elicit. Nonetheless, this is one key area in which e-learning environments stand to transcend constraints posed by the traditional classroom environment in the measurement of metacognition in addition to metacognition's facilitation.

Another way that e-learning environments open up new possibilities for measuring metacognition is through transcript analysis of activity within online communities of inquiry. This was confirmed in a study (Akyol & Garrison, 2011), which was the first of a two-part study of metacognition within collaborative online learning environments (Akyol & Garrison, 2011; Garrison & Akyol, 2013). Qualitative transcript analysis was also successfully utilized by Hurme et al. (2015) in exploring socially shared metacognition in mathematical problem solving.

Data mining presents another key opportunity for measuring metacognition within e-learning environments. This mode of research concretely identifies and operationalizes specific behaviors that are theorized to represent metacognition (Winne & Baker, 2013). Developing a model of operationalized metacognitive behaviors allows for opportunities to study that model in fine-grained detail and can also be "applied to new sets of data to study relationships between a behavior and other 'snap shot data'" (Winne & Baker, 2013,

p. 6). One recent application of educational data mining to study metacognition involves modeling metacognitive activities in medical problem solving (Lajoie et al., 2015). This study captured user interactions and compared them to an expert model in order to adapt instruction to the specific needs of the learner.

> The expert model fosters metacognition as learners are supported in formulating plans, monitoring their progress, and adaptively engaging in strategic actions while problem solving. The novice-expert overlay model individualizes feedback by highlighting similarities and differences between their respective solution paths.
>
> (Lajoie et al., 2015, p. 330)

In this, e-learning environments allow researchers not only to measure metacognition but also to go even further than this in implementing learning interventions aimed to improve metacognitive functioning.

Conclusion

New connections between metacognition and e-learning environments are emerging, generating far-reaching ways in which metacognition not only sustains e-learning practices but also designs e-learning practices to support metacognitive activities. In this, there is a reciprocal relationship between e-learning practices and metacognition, as metacognitive abilities are necessary in order for e-learning practices to be effective, but at the same time, e-learning environments are emerging that uniquely support metacognitive functioning, thus promoting the development and refinement of metacognitive abilities. Accordingly, e-learning environments themselves can allow for metacognitively rich learning experiences that do not rely on teachers alone to direct and facilitate metacognition. Indeed, e-learning environments allow for us to transcend what is possible within traditional schemas of education by facilitating the conditions for learners to make metacognitive leaps on their own.

References

Akturk, A. O., & Sahin, I. (2011). Literature review on metacognition and its measurement. *Procedia-Social and Behavioral Sciences, 15,* 3731–3736.

Akyol, Z., & Garrison, D. R. (2011). Assessing metacognition in an online community of inquiry. *The Internet and Higher Education, 14*(3), 183–190.

Beran, M. J., Brandl, J., Perner, J., & Proust, J. (Eds.). (2012). *Foundations of metacognition.* Oxford: Oxford University Press.

Bernard, M., & Bachu, E. (2015). Enhancing the metacognitive skill of novice programmers through collaborative learning. In A. Peña-Ayala (Ed.), *Metacognition: Fundaments, applications, and trends* (pp. 277–298). New York: Springer.

Bielaczyc, K., Pirolli, P. L., & Brown, A. L. (1995). Training in self-explanation and self-regulation strategies: Investigating the effects of knowledge acquisition activities on problem solving. *Cognition and Instruction*, *13*(2), 221–252.

Brand, M. (2014). The Geometer's Sketchpad: "I do and I understand," *EPSY* 408. Retrieved from https://cgscholar.com/creator/works/16844/versions/31017/export?output_format=standard&journal_article[journal_name]=&journal_article[volume]=1&journal_article[issue]=1&journal_article[issn]=&journal_article[url]=&journal_article[copyright]=&journal_article[page]=1link]

Bruce, B. C., & Bishop, A. P. (2002). Using the web to support inquiry-based literacy development. *Journal of Adolescent and Adult Literacy*, *45*(8), 706–714.

Casey, L., & Bruce, B. C. (2011). The practice profile of inquiry: Connecting digital literacy and pedagogy. *e-Learning and Digital Media*, 8(1), 76–85.

De Jong, T. (2006). Technological advances in inquiry learning. *Science*, *312*(5773), 532–533.

Dewey, J. (2003). The school and society. In J. A. Boydston (Ed.), *The middle works of John Dewey 1899–1924*. (Vol. 1). Carbondale: Southern Illinois University Press. (Original work published 1899)

Dewey, J. (1980). Democracy and education. In J. A. Boydston (Ed.), *The middle works of John Dewey 1899–1924* (Vol. 9). Carbondale: Southern Illinois University Press. (Original work published 1916)

Dewey, J. (2003). How we think. In J. A. Boydston (Ed.), *The later works of John Dewey 1925–1953* (Vol. 8). Carbondale: Southern Illinois University Press. (Original work published 1933)

Dewey, J. (2003). Art as experience. In J. A. Boydston (Ed.), *The later works of John Dewey 1925–1953* (Vol. 10). Carbondale: Southern Illinois University Press. (Original work published 1934)

Dewey, J. (2003a). *Logic: The theory of inquiry*. In J. A. Boydston (Ed.), *The later works of John Dewey 1925–1953* (Vol. 12). Carbondale: Southern Illinois University Press. (Original work published 1938)

Dewey, J. (2003b). Experience and education. In J. A. Boydston (Ed.), *The later works of John Dewey 1925–1953* (Vol. 13). Carbondale: Southern Illinois University Press. (Original work published 1938)

Donker, A. S., De Boer, H., Kostons, D., van Ewijk, C. D., & Van der Werf, M.P.C. (2014). Effectiveness of learning strategy instruction on academic performance: A meta-analysis. *Educational Research Review*, *11*, 1–26.

Driver, R., Newton, P., & Osborne, J. (2000). Establishing the norms of scientific argumentation in classrooms. *Science Education*, *84*(3), 287–312.

Edelson, D. C. (2001). Learning-for-use: A framework for the design of technology-supported inquiry activities. *Journal of Research in Science Teaching*, *38*(3), 355–385.

Efklides, A. (2006). Metacognition and affect: What can metacognitive experiences tell us about the learning process? *Educational Research Review*, *1*, 3–14.

Eisner, E. (1994). *Cognition and curriculum reconsidered* (2nd ed.). New York: Teachers College Press.

Eisner, E. (2002). *The arts and the creation of mind*. New Haven, CT: Yale University Press.

Fajks, K. (2014). *Teaching and learning with Popplet concept maps, EPSY 556*. Retrieved from https://cgscholar.com/community/profiles/kfajks/publications/45830

Farmer, J. (2004). Communication dynamics: Discussion boards, weblogs and the development of communities of inquiry in online learning environments. In R. Atkinson,

C. McBeath, D. Jonas-Dwyer, & R. Phillips (Eds.), *Beyond the comfort zone: Proceedings of the 21st ASCILITE conference* (pp. 274–283). Perth, WA: ASCILITE.

Flavell, J. H. (1979). Metacognition and cognitive monitoring: A new area of cognitive-developmental inquiry. *American Psychologist, 34*(10), 906–911.

Garrison, D. R. (2011). *E-learning in the 21st century: A framework for research and practice.* London: Taylor & Francis.

Garrison, D. R. (2003). Cognitive presence for effective asynchronous online learning: The role of reflective inquiry, self-direction and metacognition. *Elements of Quality Online Education: Practice and Direction, 4,* 47–58.

Garrison, D. R., & Akyol, Z. (2013). Toward the development of a metacognition construct for communities of inquiry. *The Internet and Higher Education, 17,* 84–89.

Gee, J. P. (2007). *What video games have to teach us about learning and literacy* (revised and updated ed.). New York: Palgrave Macmillan.

Hattie, J. (2009). *Visible learning.* London: Routledge.

Hayes, E. R., & Duncan, S. C. (2012). *Learning in video game affinity spaces.* New York: Peter Lang.

Hurme, T.-R., Järvelä, S., Merenluoto, K., & Salonen, P. (2015). What makes metacognition as socially shared in mathematical problem solving? In A. Peña-Ayala (Ed.), *Metacognition: Fundaments, applications, and trends* (pp. 259–276). New York: Springer.

Kim, M., & Hannafin, M. (2004). Designing online learning environments to support scientific inquiry. *Quarterly Review of Distance Education, 5*(1), 1–10.

Lai, E. R. (2011, April). *Metacognition: A literature review. Pearson's Research Reports.* Retrieved from http://images.pearsonassessments.com/images/tmrs/Metacognition_Literature_Review_Final.pdf

Lajoie, S. P., Poitras, E. G., Doleck, T., & Jarrell, A. (2015). Modeling metacognitive activities in medical problem-solving with BioWorld. In A. Peña-Ayala (Ed.), *Metacognition: Fundaments, applications, and trends* (pp. 323–343). New York: Springer.

Noska, D. (2012). Learning to use Popplet in your classroom. *Darcy Noska's MSU Teaching Portfolio.* Retrieved from http://msuportfolio2.weebly.com/popplet-in-the-classroom.html

Peña-Ayala, A. (Ed.). (2015). Metacognition: Fundaments, Applications, and Trends. New York: Springer.

Peña-Ayala, A., & Cárdenas, L. (2015). A conceptual model of the metacognitive activity. In A. Peña-Ayala (Ed.), *Metacognition: Fundaments, applications, and trends* (pp. 39–72). New York: Springer.

Schraw, G. (1998). Promoting general metacognitive awareness. *Instructional Science, 26*(1–2), 113–125.

Schraw, G., & Gutierrez, A. P. (2015). Metacognitive strategy instruction that highlights the role of monitoring and control processes. In A. Peña-Ayala (Ed.), *Metacognition: Fundaments, applications, and trends* (pp. 3–16). New York: Springer.

Schraw, G., & Moshman, D. (1995). Metacognitive theories. *Educational Psychology Review, 7*(4), 351–371.

The Geometer's Sketchpad. (2014). The sketchpad story. *McGraw-Hill Education.* Retrieved from http://www.dynamicgeometry.com/General_Resources/The_Sketchpad_Story.html

Swan, K., Garrison, D. R., & Richardson, J. (2009). A constructivist approach to online learning: The community of inquiry framework. In C. R. Payne (Ed.), *Information technology and constructivism in higher education: Progressive learning frameworks* (pp. 43–57). Hershey, PA: IGI Global.

Winne, P. H., & Baker, R. S. (2013). The potentials of educational data mining for researching metacognition, motivation and self-regulated learning. *JEDM-Journal of Educational Data Mining, 5*(1), 1–8.

Woolf, B. P. (2010). *Building intelligent interactive tutors: Student-centered strategies for revolutionizing e-learning.* Burlington, MA: Morgan Kaufmann.

8 Differentiated Learning

Diversity Dimensions of e-Learning

Samaa Haniya and Sol Roberts-Lieb

Introduction

One of the biggest challenges in education systems around the world is to provide appropriate educational opportunities for all learners, especially given growing recognition of diversity in schools. Whether this diversity is related to linguistic, cognitive, cultural, immigration status, socioeconomic, gender, body, or personality traits, it needs to be well recognized in the design of learning opportunities.

From a cognitive perspective, there are many students who are identified with special needs and others who are identified as gifted students. In addition, gender differences between male and female and straight and gay could possibly influence the conditions of student learning. Even learners from the same family would learn things differently from other members of the family (Kalantzis & Cope, 2012). From another perspective, at the intersection of globalization and digitization, students experience the effects of mobility as a consequence of migration and human movement, as well as the unprecedented flow of digital information, leading to a daily experience of heterogeneity within contemporary society (Appadurai, 2013; Rizvi & Lingard, 2010).

It is been estimated that "one in five children in the United States today has an immigrant parent, and young children under six in immigrant families are the fastest growing segment of the child population" (Oakes & Lipton, 2007, p. 7). This increasing rate of student diversity as a consequence of immigration to the United States adds the dimension of language diversity to classrooms (Grant & Sleeter, 2007). Moreover, classrooms may have students from multiple ethnic groups and races who must be acknowledged as sources of experience and identity. Socioeconomic status also plays an important factor in student achievement. Students who come from a low socioeconomic status may have fewer educational resources at home and potentially attend schools with fewer academic resources.

Moreover, a generation of learners is growing up in a digital world where they have more access to a wide variety of information through various digital media tools. Each person is now capable of developing his or her own digital identity and thus specific kinds of learning preferences. Some students would prefer visual learning while others may like auditory learning; another group may prefer kinesthetic learning (learning by doing). With this range of diversity in mind, students need to have different educational support and scaffolding tailored to suit their abilities, needs, backgrounds, and experiences. The big challenge for teachers, then, is how to ensure educational equity in such a complex educational environment, ensuring that all students receive the necessary support. Failing to achieve this goal may exacerbate the risk of students being left behind and holding back their educational progress. The resulting consequences of this unequal learning produces an achievement gap among students while putting their educational success at risk (Oakes & Lipton, 2007).

Based on data released from the US Department of Education, almost one-fifth of students between the ages of 16 and 24 did not graduate from high school in the 2012–2013 school year (DePaoli et al., 2015). This graduation rate is lower among different student populations, such as students of color, low socioeconomic status, English language learners, and differently abled students, creating an alarming educational achievement gap. Often, students coming from these backgrounds are not provided appropriate learning opportunities that suit their needs. This is particularly the case when teachers use a one-size-fits-all teaching strategy oriented to "average" students. According to a report released by the Bill and Melinda Gates Foundation and written by Bridgeland, DiIulio, and Morison (2006), almost half of the students who drop out of schools find schools' subjects and classroom activities boring and not engaging. They experience little motivation to keep learning (Bridgeland, DiIulio, & Morison, 2006).

Following the one-size-fits all approach not only affects struggling students but also all students to the extent that their learning preferences and aptitudes are different. Whether the student is gifted or less successful in school, able-bodied or disabled, poor or rich, local or international, male or female, or white or a student of color, all will be affected if their needs are not fully met. The only way to reach out to the different educational needs of each individual and provide a high quality of learning is via applying a differentiated learning approach.

In this chapter, we will explore the concept of differentiated learning and how this may be facilitated by technology devices and digital media. We will present an overview of its current literature and introduce a model of how to use differentiated instruction at a scale we call choice-based instruction. Our discussion and final remarks will focus on how educators in the field can build successful models of differentiated instruction that will help their students develop knowledge and skills according to their interests.

What Is Differentiated Learning?

Differentiated learning is a philosophy that values what students know and who they are before they come to the classroom and works with them to achieve what they need to learn. It is a mind-set to actively engage students in meaningful activities and real-world concepts. Taking this approach, instruction aims to demonstrate better understanding, maximize content knowledge, and improve the learning skills of a wide range of learners. Traditionally, educators use a didactic approach where all students learn the same thing (content) in the same way (process) with the same assessments (product) in the same space (learning environment) following the one-size-fits-all approach. All students read the same book, listen to the same lecture, and do the same exercise at the same time and in the same place without paying attention to varied individual needs (Kalantzis & Cope, 2016).

Instead of assuming sameness or homogeneity, education should calibrate educational options for each individual to suit their needs and interests. Unlike the didactic approach, differentiated learning integrates multiple paths of learning in the classroom to make school curriculum and instruction the best fit for different types of learners. Such a responsive teaching approach requires a deeper level of understanding of "whom we teach" and "how we teach" (Tomlinson, 2014; Tomlinson & McTighe, 2006). Students' unique patterns of readiness, interest, experiences, and modes of learning should be considered when planning educational programs and activities. Then, in the processes of implementation, instruction must be flexible as it is constantly adapted and modified to balance student needs and learning progress.

In these ways, differentiated learning does not merely focus on the logistics of teaching students at different learning levels and interests, it goes beyond this simple notion to include the learner's own voice and self-identity. Pedagogical reformers have frequently advocated recognizing these differences of students' identities, along with interests and motivation. One of the first pedagogical reformers who emphasized students' identities or "inner voices" was Maria Montessori (1912), who developed the Montessori method. Montessori believed that education is a natural process nurtured by creating an environment where students can realize their interests through free play and engage in individual and/or group activities of their own choice. This kind of lightly guided learning allows learners to have a better sense of who they are and how others look at them in the social interactions of the classroom. Thus, identities can be produced to align with evolving trajectories of emotional growth, social development, and academic success. Similarly, in the early decades of the twentieth century, John Dewey called for a pedagogical reform built on the idea of experiential learning, with a focus on educating the whole child (Dewey, 1938). Dewey valued the individual experience and learning identity as essential to true learning and to enable students to contribute to society more effectively. In both Dewey's and Montessori's approaches, it is recognized that learners come to school with some prior knowledge, experiences, and cultural identities. Teachers as facilitators encourage learners to extend these experiences in the classrooms via active and discovery learning strategies. Sharing identity and expressing one's own voice can help the learner to build on his or her own personal experiences.

These approaches also align with the critical pedagogy theory of Paulo Freire (1970). Freire explicitly discusses the significance of "conscientization," a process of thinking to develop a critical awareness of one's self-identity and sociocultural context through a set of organized reflections and actions with others and society. A key aspect of this approach is to look at education as a means of consciously shaping the person's own identity in relation to society. Learners are challenged to bring their self-identities to school, to be articulated there as different ways of thinking, knowledge production, creativity, innovation, and interaction. This view would imply a move away from passive education based on abstract concepts unconnected to life experience and to a more active learning that facilitates a deep conceptual understanding on the basis of self-identity, experience, interest, content knowledge, and society.

Kalantzis and Cope (2016) called for a reflexive/inclusive pedagogical reform that aligns with the affordances of new media and aims to promote productive diversity in education. This proposed pedagogy is built on four main principles that honor differentiation as follows: (1) the design principle: with the support of new media resources, this pedagogy recognizes learners as designers of their own knowledge and teachers as facilitators; (2) the collaborative principle: to encourage knowledge sharing of multiple perspectives in the learning process, creating a collaborative and dynamic learning environment; (3) the differentiation principle: recent new media tools such as big data and learning analytics allow students to do different things in different ways by adapting learning activities to suit each learner's needs; and (4) the comparability principle: new media tools allow designing assessments that accommodate the different interests, activities, and trajectories of each learner.

Translating the philosophy of differentiated learning into action can be a challenging effort—unless, that is, appropriate tools are combined with congruent and well-designed pedagogical strategies. As we will go on to show, recent technology innovations may facilitate differentiated learning by providing tools that manage its intrinsic complexity.

Differentiated Learning in the Digital Media Age

From apps on mobile phones to tablets and laptops to computing and gaming devices, our lives are surrounded by digital media. This growing ubiquity of digital media tools has led to a paradigm shift in the ways we learn and acquire knowledge. In particular, digital media help to facilitate differentiated learning by providing multiple learning opportunities for teachers to engage their students in a productive way (D'Arcy, Eastburn, & Bruce, 2009; Kalantzis & Cope, 2012). This creates the space for multiple perspectives where learners engage in learning dialogues in ways that they were unable to do before. School textbooks are not the only way to deliver information now that students have access to a variety of information resources anytime and anywhere at the click of a mouse. Instead of accepting knowledge provided by teachers and textbooks in a didactic approach, in technology-mediated learning environments, students may supplement what is provided with knowledge they construct on their own in a participatory, connected culture (Jenkins et al., 2009). Learning is about knowledge creation that comes from making connections and interactions with diverse students discussing, evaluating, arguing, and criticizing big ideas that need to be taught (Siemens, 2005). Widespread open education resources, such as Khan Academy and MOOCs, have opened the door for students to maximize learning opportunities according to their needs. Some teachers are also taking advantage of such approaches by flipping the typical school script (Bishop & Verleger, 2013). They may ask students to watch a series of videos on a particular topic at home and allocate class time for discussion and interaction to work individually or in groups. More and more applications are being developed to create customized, learner-specific environments that appeal to and support learners' unique needs and preferences.

These developments are complemented by the emergence of learning analytics tools that make it easier than before to precisely detect the strengths and weaknesses of each individual student (Cope & Kalantzis, 2015). There is no need for teachers to waste time on paper-and-pencil assessment tools to keep track of students' progress. Students' works are stored in the cloud, allowing teachers to simply click a button to see what students are doing in the moment and to review their progress over time.

Types of Learning: Differentiated, Individualized, Adaptive, and Personalized

As educational technologies advance, new pedagogical processes have emerged, such as adaptive and personalized learning, which differentiate learning for each student (NMC Horizon Report, 2015). Differentiated learning is an umbrella term that applies to learning or instruction that can be calibrated to meet students' learning preferences and needs. In what follows, we will provide definitions, analyze similarities, and contrast the key differences among several commonly used terms: individualized, adaptive, differentiated, and personalized learning.

Differentiated instruction is a process by which educators modify their instruction to suit the different learning styles and abilities of students. According to Grant and Bayse (2014), the academic goals for all of students remain the same; however, the educator has the ability to deploy a range of options to connect with each student, based on what has worked in the past for that student or similar students. Differentiated instruction addresses "how" instruction is done rather than the "what" or content of instruction. In the following sections, more examples will be provided to demonstrate how to differentiate instruction.

Grant and Bayse (2014) postulate that individualized learning, which is similar to tutoring in that both feature a one-to-one relationship, focuses on the "when" of instruction or the appropriate pace of learning for an individual student. Whether digitally facilitated or face-to-face, the goals and content of all students are the same, the difference being the rate at which students work through the material. This approach is used to reduce the number of students who are bored because they already know the material or frustrated because it is too hard for them. In the latter case, this approach provides additional time for students who are unfamiliar with the concepts or are struggling with the content.

An adaptive learning system aims to provide a personalized learning resource for students, especially learning content and user-preferred interfaces for processing their learning (Yang, Hwang, & Yang, 2013). What this means is that the content and even the assessments are customized to direct students to achieve to the best of their abilities by modifying the assessment and/or providing additional content based on their answers. For example, if a student answers a question deemed to be incorrect, the technology can provide another question that is considered easier or it could provide a hint explaining why that selection was incorrect. Adaptive learning uses data generated during the learning process to provide content to students based on their measurable performance. Most often this is done automatically through technologies integrated into a learning management or intelligent tutoring system, such as adaptive release. The technology enables the process of incremental release of curriculum content without teacher intervention. The use of these systems is a low burden on the teacher, although there is a high barrier to entry unless the content is purchased from a vendor with all the selections included. Adaptive learning systems can be acquired in one of two ways. The first is to acquire the engine that runs the system. This is the brain that provides the analytics and delivers content based on student performance. The second way is to acquire the content and the engine together. In some STEM fields, for instance, intelligent tutors or educational games merge engine and curriculum content into a single package. However, such systems require high levels of technical expertise and considerable resources to create—taking the process of curriculum design away from teachers.

Finally, there is Grant and Bayse's (2014) concept of personalized learning. To examine personalized learning, one must look at the ecosystem of learning, not just the "how" or the "why." Personalized learning is customized to students' desires and talents. Their interests (content), their skills, their abilities (pace and process), and their motivation all relate to the individual and may be completely different from others in the class.

Of the types of differentiated learning, personalized learning may align best with the interests and identity positions of students, and it also requires considerable skill and cultural sensitivity on the part of educators.

In this chapter, we will focus on technology-enabled differentiated learning and instruction and point to some cases where individualized or personalized learning may be implemented to leverage these affordances of differentiated learning.

Digitally Differentiated Learning Across Multiple Contexts

There is a growing body of educational policy and research that emphasizes the importance of adopting differentiated learning facilitated via technology to transform learning and enhance students' educational gains. The US Department of Education developed a new National Education Technology Plan in 2016, advocating for transformational learning experiences for all learners regardless of their backgrounds and educational levels. One of its leading statements of principles reads as follows:

> Technology can enable personalized learning or experiences that are more engaging and relevant. Mindful of the learning objectives, educators might design learning experiences that allow students in a class to choose from a menu of learning experiences—writing essays, producing media, building websites, collaborating with experts across the globe in data collection—assessed via a common rubric to demonstrate their learning. Such technology-enabled learning experiences can be more engaging and relevant to learners.
>
> (US Department of Education, 2016, p. 10)

As described here, effective use of technology might transform learning from the conventional view of one size fits all to more engaging, differentiated, and personalized learning.

The research bears out the validity of such policy aspirations. For example, Zheng et al. (2016) conducted a meta-analysis to examine the effect of using new technologies such as the one-to-one laptop program on teaching and learning in K–12 school settings. The authors revealed that the integration of such technology creates a positive effect on teaching and learning, transforming pedagogy from a teacher-centered approach to a collaborative environment that respects students' diversity. The overall results of this study suggest that the appropriate use of technology leads to a positive improvement in student's educational outcomes in literacy, mathematics, and science.

A meta-analysis released by the US Department of Education has shown similar results. In synthesizing more than 1,000 empirical studies in diverse settings, including K–12, higher education, and corporate training with diverse populations of students, the authors found that improved student learning outcomes in online-supported instruction is better than traditional face-to-face instruction. Although this study provides evidence of the effectiveness of using online learning over face-to-face instruction, much of this success is related to the teaching techniques of differentiation. One of the key findings noted that "giving learners control of their interactions with media and prompting learner reflection" to accommodate their individual needs led to a positive effect on students' learning (Means et al., 2009, p. xvi).

In special education, differentiated learning in digitally mediated environments plays an important role in helping learners who are differently abled to learn more easily and effectively in classrooms. The National Center on Universal Design for Learning (2012) developed a set of principles to grant equal learning opportunities to meet the needs of differently abled learners and those who have been typically marginalized in "averaged" learning. The first principle in universal design for learning is to provide students with multimodal knowledge presentations in order to make the curriculum content accessible (CAST, 2011). A second standard focuses on providing students with multiple options and digital tools to express their own ideas and demonstrate their understanding. The third standard advocates multiple resources for differently abled students to be engaged and motivated to learn.

Currently, there are different kinds of assistive resources in the form of hardware and software to support productive learning for differently abled students. Through these tools, teachers can develop an appropriate educational plan to suit the individual learning needs for each learner. Integrating well-designed educational games, thoughtful educational apps, captioned YouTube videos, social media networking, interactive e-books, and smart technology devices can help differently abled learners to learn better (Bryant, Bryant, & Ok, 2014). For instance, those who have physical difficulties may use an advanced keyboard with custom keyboard overlays. Equipped with an on-screen avatar presenting content in American Sign Language, this keyboard will also allow students with hearing impairments to overcome their physical challenges and learn like others. This keyboard can also help students with visual impairments by magnifying the on-screen text and images (US Department of Education, 2016, p. 19). Moreover, learners with movement impairments that prevent them from going to regular schools can now take classes online that cover the same curriculum ground as face-to-face classes.

English language learners can also benefit from adopting differentiated learning in digitally mediated learning environments. Because of their limited English proficiency, it is often a challenge for these learners to express their ideas and opinions in the same way as native English speakers. Taking advantage of the abundant learning opportunities that digital technologies provide expands the reach and accessibility of these students to express themselves through multiple pathways, such as multimodal knowledge presentations and online interaction among peers and teachers (Kalantzis et al., 2016; Wen, Looi, & Chen, 2012). Presenting knowledge and content in multiple modes, such as images, videos, soundtracks, or e-texts, helps students to demonstrate a better understanding of the instruction. English language learners may also feel reticent to share their ideas in front of the class. However, online forums, blogs, and social network applications bridge this barrier by providing opportunities for them to freely communicate and connect with peers in a more comfortable way. Encouraging English language learners to draw on their self-identities and cultural values can generate diverse ideas on the discussed topic to be shared with the whole class, thus creating an enriched learning environment in a participatory culture (Jenkins et al., 2009; Kalantzis & Cope, 2016; Wen, Looi, & Chen, 2012).

Differentiating Instruction

Differentiated instruction (see Figure 8.1) is defined as tailoring instruction to meet individual needs (Tomlinson, 2000). Technology, such as learning management systems, on-demand training like lynda.com, and online collaborative tools such as wikis and blogs, empower educators to create differentiated instruction classrooms.

To meet the needs of each individual, an educator first needs to know what the learners' strengths are and how they learn and then modify the lesson to meet those needs. This begins with an initial assessment, which includes asking questions related to the lesson content, how the student prefers to learn, what strengths the student has, and what weaknesses or areas of improvement the student has. On this basis, the educator develops a plan to differentiate the lesson (Burggraf, 2005). Once an educator has completed the initial assessment, he or she can differentiate the lesson across four main components: content (what they

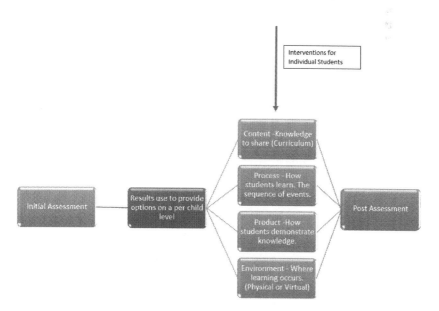

Figure 8.1 Differentiated instruction workflow

learn), process (how they learn), product (how they show what they learned), and learning environment (where they learn) (Tomlinson, 2000). Although modifying curriculum to meet individual styles does take additional work, it addresses the issues of varied learning styles. An advantage to this approach is that educators can begin with just a small lesson or module; they don't need to switch the entire class overnight to a differentiated model. Kari Wehrmann (2000) relates differentiated instruction to the process of running a marathon. Educators don't wake up one day and decide to jog 20 miles. Educators begin by adding activities gradually, not increasing the workload dramatically. This approach allows educators to test new ideas and see how students relate to the modified lesson without converting an entire class and then waiting for results.

Creating a lesson plan or learning module that enables differentiated learning follows familiar learning design processes, with several additional aspects to consider. An educator should start from the same place and objectives and then follow the conventional phases. For instance, teachers could use the steps outlined in *The New Teacher's Companion* by Gini Cunningham (2009): set a purpose; introduce the key concepts, topic, and main idea; pull students into the excitement of learning; and make the learning relevant. These form the objectives or the big idea of the lesson. Once the big idea is known, educators can figure out how to assess the different experiences and interests that students bring to the table. This diagnostic assessment should consist of what content they know, how they learn, and what their motivations are. After completing this initial assessment, educators can then devise groups and activities that appeal to the strengths of different groups of students or individual students. The essential aspect of differentiated learning and instruction is that, while educators are allowing flexibility for students' learning styles, all students are moving along the same path to achieve the same course objectives.

The path to differentiated learning begins with conducting an assessment; moves on to differentiating content, process, product, and the learning environment; and concludes with a post-assessment of student outcomes and an evaluation of the methods used throughout the class. Based on concepts described by Tomlinson and Moon (Tomlinson & Moon, 2013, p. 2), Figure 8.1 illustrates the Differentiated Instruction workflow process including the four different types of interventions or changes an educator can make to the class to appeal to individual learner's needs. These include changes to the Content, Process, Product, and Learning Environment.

Conducting an Initial Diagnostic

Rock et al. (2008) break differentiated instruction into five different quality indicators: the teacher variable, the content variable, the learner variable, the instruction variable, and the assessment variable. After working through the first two indicators (teacher and content), the learner variable addresses the ways in which educators create a lesson that benefits each learner. Choices should be offered only after a pre-assessment or learning skills inventory is complete. This will provide educators with a diagnosis of their students' strengths, weaknesses, and abilities while also giving them insight into how they think and learn. These individual results can then be collated to provide educators with the range of needs that should be accounted for when selecting the choices students can make to differentiate their learning. The ranges also help place students into like-minded or opposite-minded groups to ensure the differentiated approach being used is successful.

This assessment should not be used to provide points or a grade for the course. Rather, it is only intended to help judge the aptitude of both the individual student and the class as a whole. This allows educators to create custom options to meet student needs while reducing the overall workload or by providing options that will not benefit students. The cycle of assessment should be constant as the educator moves from one piece of content to another. Remediation can be offered as needed, or if students are excelling, then additional content or challenges can be added.

The National Research Council (2001) stated that formative assessments should be comprehensive, coherent, and continuous. Such assessment can be used as a baseline for differentiation. Comprehensive assessment, according to Herman (2013), is a system of assessments that are coherent to specified learning goals, and all the components collectively support multiples uses of the skills. In other words, multiple assessments all evaluate the same learning objectives. This helps eliminate biases in one assessment and also allows students who excel in one manner to show their knowledge without being penalized for not being adept at another method. For instance, if the objective was to understand 1980s US history and one student could write a great paper and the other could do an oral report, both could show that they understood the content. The ability to write the paper or to do an oral presentation is not what is being measured in this case.

Coherent assessment is to measure the "right stuff" in the "right way" (Herman, 2010). In differentiated learning facilitated by technology, the nature of coherent assessment is not different from traditional mass-based assessment. The ability to ensure that the assessment tool is measuring the specific objective is complex. It involves trial and error, seeing how others have evaluated this objective, and finally using a variety of instruments to ensure validity in the assessments.

Continuous assessment is a form of formative assessment wherein educators evaluate skill and knowledge throughout the learning module rather than summatively, at the end of the lesson or class. In differentiated instruction, this provides educators with information to alter the way they are teaching, including the processes students are using, the learning environment, and the content, to ensure that learning outcomes are reached.

Without these three types of assessments, educators may not have an opportunity to change their approaches to help students, as most traditional assessment occurs after the lesson or after the course. Technology allows these processes to be more automated and customized. Examples of this include weekly or module-based quizzes that can be taken and retaken by students as many times as they wish until they get the correct answer. Adaptive testing is also critical here where, if students select a wrong answer, then not only will it tell them the correct answer but also will either provide them with a question of lower intensity to help them learn or direct them to additional examples or content to improve their chances of getting it correct on the next attempt.

One method to design a differentiated lesson or module is to start with the objectives. This lesson or assessment design is called backwards design or integrated course design (Fink, 2003). Fink applies this to course design, where instead of thinking about what students will learn, what activities they will do with the knowledge, and then how the teacher assesses that knowledge, educators focus on what learning objectives they want the student to achieve. "Course design by objectives guarantees a high level of student engagement because the process steers you towards student active teaching strategies" (Nilson, 2003, p. 17). Before creating the content and activities, it is necessary to have clear-cut objectives for what students will be able to do, understand, and demonstrate. Once the objectives are clear, educators can determine how to provide the content, what processes should be used to deliver the content, and ultimately how to assess the knowledge. This process ensures that objectives are clear and that they are congruent with the assessment. Although the workload may seem intense to design a differentiated course, spending time on understanding the objectives and how to pre-assess students will ensure that the steps an educator implements for differentiating content, process, product, and learning environment will be more effective.

Differentiating the Content

Content is what we teach, addressing the question: What does the educator want students to learn? This is specific to the discipline being taught and should contain enough content for students to be able to show they have completed the objectives outlined in the lesson plan. The idea of differentiating content is challenging because, if educators offer content differentiation, then how do they fairly assess student learning outcomes?

The core principle of differentiating content is that all students still have access to all the content; it is just presented in a variety of ways (Hall, 2002). Understanding by Design addresses the question of what do we teach and how it relates to standards. "Beset by lists of content standards and accompanying 'high-stakes' accountability tests, many educators sense that both teaching and learning have been redirected in ways that are potentially impoverishing for those who teach and those who learn" (Tomlinson & McTighe, 2006). If educators begin to differentiate the content, then students may not be prepared to pass a standardized test. Standardized tests focus on certain content areas that in a differentiated environment may not be covered or covered to the same extent for all students. If the course is designed according to differentiated instruction characteristics, then the content students learn is the same, just presented in different ways, and there may be additional content made available to those who want or need it. Tomlinson and McTighe (2006) further state that differentiated instruction may be paired with Understanding by Design to ensure that the diverse needs of learners are met while still providing the content to perform well on standardized tests. Here is an example of differentiating the content while keeping the overall objectives the same. If the class in question is accounting, then educators may have students who struggle with basic math while others understand the basics of accounting already. Educators can provide links to basic math instruction for those who need it while offering advanced accounting practices to those who have mastered the basics. Knowing who needs what type of information is garnered through the pre-assessment. The bottom line is that all students can access both the basic and the advanced material. However, it is not required for them to do so, nor is their final grade based on how they perform on the extra work. This content is offered either to provide a foundation for the core learning or to provide supplementary knowledge for those who wish to learn more about the subject. The key is to base assessment on the core content, not on any of the extra material provided.

The concept of providing extra content to advanced learners and introductory content to beginning learners is not new. What is revolutionary is the access to digital resources and adaptive learning, which can make content more readily available and make deciding who is ready for the different content automatic. In the past, an educator might need to provide an extra textbook to a student who is ready for advanced math. With the Internet and powerful search engines, an educator can provide a link or terms for a student to search on, thus providing them with instant access.

Differentiating the Process

Process refers to the media of instruction and how these might be differentiated. The process could be a standard classroom with students listening to an educator; it could be in groups; it could in pairs. In many cases, differentiating process can be time consuming, and determining how students learn can lead to more options than are feasible to support. In addition, addressing process often involves aligning the activities of several students, such as in group work. To be successful at differentiating the process, an educator needs to ask pertinent questions during the initial assessment and then present a subset of options for how to learn. This offers students a refined list of choices from which they can select.

Another way to think about process is to consider the timing and pace of instruction and when to assess new knowledge (Subban, 2006). As an example, educators may have new material that a class needs to learn for the next week. They can offer the following methods for students to learn: didactic lecture, study group, video instruction, reading the lecture, interview with an expert, or more. The intent is to cover the same content while allowing students to select from a given menu the experience that matches their styles the best. These options have been available in the past, but with the advent and increased use of technology, this is much more practical for students to use and educators to require. Tools such as YouTube, Google Hangouts, wikis, blogs, and Facebook allow both access to content and the ability to share and create collaboratively. For instance, lectures can be provided in an online on-demand format outside class time. This provides students with multiple chances to review the material. Technology also allows the experts to come to the student. A student may interview an expert halfway around the world whereas that wasn't an option without expensive travel in the past. Another process item is group work. Groups can now be assigned by the computer based on any number of traits provided about the students. This allows more flexibility for the students in groups, and educators can change how groups are constituted without additional work. They can also allow students to work with their groups in person, online synchronously, or online asynchronously. In the past, creating groups was a manual process, and the groups met in person either during class or at a place off-line. Asynchronous group work wasn't effective without these online platforms to share and collaborate on work products.

Differentiating the Product

Traditionally, the assessable product of learning has taken the form of a paper, a quiz, or a presentation. Students may vary in their preferred and best ways to articulate their knowledge. Some may be excellent orally, while others still are excellent writers. By allowing flexibility in how students show their knowledge, educators achieve the assessment objectives without hindering the learner's ability due to lack of skill or ability in one mode of knowledge representation.

To help students know how they will be assessed, an assignment in the form of a project, report, or multimodal text should have a rubric associated with it. This not only offers the learner clarity about learning objectives but also what areas of the assignment the student should focus on. Depending on how the rubric is created, in differentiated instruction, educators may need to modify the rubric to be product-agnostic. The rubric would state what information must be presented, even though the package (document, blog, website, article, etc.) may be different. Or the product may be the same, but the empirical focus of the project may be different. This rubric should be created to have a clear set of criteria to help students understand exactly what is needed (Standford, 2010) relatively independent of the specifics of the product itself, thus allowing scope for student voice and creativity. This may also reduce the educators' workload, meaning that they do not have to create a specific rubric for every possible product that could match the lesson's objectives. This reduces the complexity of grading, as the media in which the product is created are not being assessed but rather how the student achieves what is set forth in the rubric. It also assures a measure of comparability of student work, notwithstanding the differences in the form or content of products.

Differentiating the Learning Environment

A fourth way to differentiate is to alter the learning environment. Prior to the rise of technology and online learning, differentiating the classroom often meant physically altering the arrangement of the classroom, such as changing the layout of desks and chairs, changing the types of furniture, or providing stations focused on learning abilities, whiteboards, temperature, music, and decorations. Tomlinson (2014) states that routines and processes in the classroom must be designed to give all students access to whatever they need for success. Giving students access to whatever they need is not only a matter of providing teaching resources but also considering the structure of the physical classroom. Some students learn better in quiet classrooms, some in loud classrooms, some in groups, and some individually. Arranging the physical space to meet these needs can be cost effective and flexible, allowing for multiple arrangements to meet changing needs.

The online learning environment is analogous to the physical classroom in that it is the place where content is shared and learning is assessed. This is the space where students interact, learn content, and submit their assignments. The major differences occur in the finite nature of the time available in the classroom, the boundaries of the classroom, who is in the classroom, and what technology is available. In the virtual classroom, students may be in the room at different times, with different technology available to assist them. They may also have different limitations, such as time to spend, screen size, Internet connectivity, and external noise in the form of distractions.

Individualizing the learning management systems used in many institutions can also be a challenge, particularly when students are expected to move through the system at the same week-by-week pace. If the educator is using a learning management system, then one way to differentiate is to see if any customization is allowed. This customization comes in many forms, such as allowing students to reposition widgets on their homepages and a capacity to move forward onto new tasks. Learning management systems have traditionally focused on providing generic function rather than on content or process specialized to discipline or topic. This has caused both students and educators to be unhappy with the design and opting for another or supplementary web environment to conduct class. If educators are not using a learning management system, then providing students some sort of space to store files, documents, and collaborate in a manner they are comfortable with helps as well. Instead of using a new tool for collaboration, if students are already using Facebook or Google Hangouts, then using these familiar tools reduces the learning curve. Of course, in using publicly accessible tools, it is essential to ensure that institutional rules are being adhered to as well as compliance with laws designed to protect personal data security. One caveat to this approach is that students may use these tools in ways that educators were not expecting (Tarantino, McDonough, & Hua, 2013). Although this can expand the scope of learning and lead to greater achievement, it can also cause issues of who is the authority and the direction of the overall direction of student experience.

Allowing for student choice in these ways does create additional work. The goal of differentiated instruction is not to have a completely different course for each student. Rather, a differentiated experience speaks to the strengths of each student while at the same time orienting learning to the mastery of shared learning objectives.

Differentiating Learning Opportunities at Scale

Differentiated learning is driven by student interest and aptitude. Although differentiated instruction is not new, technology makes differentiated learning more practical by both reducing the burden on educators and appealing to student needs.

In this section, we provide examples on how to enable differentiation at scale. When an educator has a small number of students, creating individualized or differentiated lesson plans is a manageable task. If this is expanded to 30 students, 50, 100, or beyond, then it is nearly impossible without greatly increasing teacher or technology support to enable this.

We propose an approach to differentiated instruction that we call choice-based instruction, which uses technology to allow students to choose the learning path that meets their needs. Choice-based instruction combines the best of having a set list of activities to do and providing individual choice. As we mentioned earlier, assessment is still a key to being successful here. Just because students may want to make a choice, they may not have the ability to use that choice.

The following example is a simplistic view of how to put this practice in motion. Although it does take time to set up the choices and create a balanced rubric, the unlimitedness of the choices is reduced, which reduces the complexity of grading.

Example

The teacher finishes teaching students about the American Civil War and wants to assess their knowledge.

Standard classroom: Each student must write a 10-page, double-spaced, 12-point font term paper with sources.

Differentiated classroom: Each student chooses how to show his or her knowledge and demonstrate content mastery about the American Civil War in any format.

Choice-based instruction classroom: Each student must choose one of the following options to show his or her knowledge of the American Civil War:

- Write a 10-page, double-spaced, 12-point font term paper with sources.
- Make a video illustrating your knowledge. You must also cite sources.
- Watch a Civil War movie and compare and contrast the movie with the events of the day. Cite your sources.

History of the American Space Program Grading Rubric – Standard

Please write a 1,000 word essay on a topic relating the history of the American Space Program. The paper must be double spaced, 10 point Times New Roman Font, with a table of contents, and appropriate supporting references.

Score Levels	Content	Conventions	Organization	Presentation
4	• Is well thought out and supports the solution to the challenge or question • Reflects application of critical thinking • Has clear goal that is related to the topic • Is pulled from a variety of sources • Is accurate	• No spelling, grammatical, or punctuation errors • High-level use of vocabulary and word choice	• Information is clearly focused in an organized and thoughtful manner • Information is constructed in a logical pattern to support the solution	• Format enhances the content • Presentation captures audience attention • Presentation is organized and well laid out
3	• Is well thought out and supports the solution • Has application of critical thinking that is apparent • Has clear goal that is related to the topic • Is pulled from several sources • Is accurate	• Few (1 to 3) spelling, grammatical, or punctuation errors • Good use of vocabulary and word choice	• Information supports the solution to the challenge or question	• Format is appropriate for the content • Presentation captures audience attention • Presentation is well organized

(Continued)

Figure 8.2 Standard rubric

Score Levels	Content	Conventions	Organization	Presentation
2	• Supports the solution • Has application of critical thinking that is apparent • Has no clear goal • Is pulled from a limited number of sources • Has some factual errors or inconsistencies	• Minimal (3 to 5) spelling, grammatical, or punctuation errors • Low-level use of vocabulary and word choice	• Project has a focus but might stray from it at times • Information appears to have a pattern, but the pattern is not consistently carried out in the project • Information loosely supports the solution	• Format does not suit the content • Presentation does not capture audience attention • Presentation is loosely organized
1	• Provides inconsistent information for solution • Has no apparent application of critical thinking • Has no clear goal • Is pulled from few sources • Has significant factual errors, misconceptions, or misinterpretations	• More than 5 spelling, grammatical, or punctuation errors • Poor use of vocabulary and word choice	• Content is unfocused and haphazard • Information does not support the solution to the challenge or question • Information has no apparent pattern	• Presentation appears sloppy and/or unfinished • Format does not enhance content • Presentation has no clear organization

Figure 8.2 (Continued)

History of the American Space Program Grading Rubric – Choice – Based

Please create a product showing your knowledge on one area the American Space Program. The product must be of an appropriate length to cover the topic in detail and have supporting references as appropriate. You may choose from one of the following products: a video, a presentation, a written paper, a skit, or a product of your choosing with teacher consent.

Score Levels	Content	Conventions	Organization	Presentation
4	• Is well thought out and supports the solution to the challenge or question • Reflects application of critical thinking • Has clear goal that is related to the topic • Is pulled from a variety of sources • Is accurate	• High-level use of vocabulary and word choice	• Information is clearly focused in an organized and thoughtful manner • Information is constructed in a logical pattern to support the solution	• Format chosen is extremely effective in sharing knowledge. • Multimedia if used is used to clarify and illustrate the main points • Format enhances the content • Presentation captures audience attention • Presentation is organized and well laid out
3	• Is well thought out and supports the solution • Has application of critical thinking that is apparent • Has clear goal that is related to the topic • Is pulled from several sources • Is accurate	• Good use of vocabulary and word choice	• Information supports the solution to the challenge or question	• Format chosen is effective in sharing knowledge effectively. • Multimedia if used is used to illustrate the main points • Format is appropriate for the content • Presentation captures audience attention • Presentation is well organized

(*Continued*)

Figure 8.3 Choice-based rubric

Score Levels	Content	Conventions	Organization	Presentation
2	• Supports the solution • Has application of critical thinking that is apparent • Has no clear goal • Is pulled from a limited number of sources • Has some factual errors or inconsistencies	• Low-level use of vocabulary and word choice	• Project has a focus but might stray from it at times • Information appears to have a pattern, but the pattern is not consistently carried out in the project • Information loosely supports the solution	• Format chosen is not effective in sharing knowledge effectively. • Multimedia if used loosely illustrates the main points • Format does not suit the content • Presentation does not capture audience attention • Presentation is loosely organized
1	• Provides inconsistent information for solution • Has no apparent application of critical thinking • Has no clear goal • Is pulled from few sources • Has significant factual errors, misconceptions, or misinterpretations	• Poor use of vocabulary and word choice	• Content is unfocused and haphazard • Information does not support the solution to the challenge or question • Information has no apparent pattern	• Format chosen is a poor fit for sharing knowledge effectively. • Multimedia if used is overused or underused • Presentation appears sloppy and/or unfinished • Format does not enhance content • Presentation has no clear organization

Figure 8.3 (Continued)

As acknowledged earlier, if students don't have the ability to make a video, then that choice would not be appropriate for them. This can be remedied by providing links to online training, group training, or by eliminating that choice based on assessments. In the example provided, the rubric would focus on content and not form. Figures 8.2 and 8.3 provide two rubrics that illustrate the difference between traditional and choice-based instruction rubrics. The intent of the assignment was to gauge student's knowledge of the history of America's space program. The first rubric is requesting a paper to be written that describes the content needed, the format needed, and how the paper should be written. The second rubric is product agnostic, meaning a student could submit a video, a painting, a paper, or even a song and the same rubric would be used. This allows students to make choices without increasing the burden on an educator by requiring them to create different grading schemes. As you can see, the main difference between the two rubrics are in the Conventions and Presentation categories. These minor changes to the rubric, allow a greater flexibility in choice for the students. While many may still chose a traditional written essay, this opens the door for those who are more proficient or can better express themselves in a different medium.

Challenges to Differentiated Learning

Differentiated learning has its critics. In her recent article on the pros and cons of differentiated instruction, Crystal Lombardo (2015) lists four cons for differentiated instruction: a larger workload on teachers in the design of instruction, the task of managing learners when they are working at different paces, lack of a clear schedule, and difficulty in evaluating teacher effectiveness. That students learn at different paces is natural, but in a classroom context, this makes planning for shared activities more difficult, as students may be working on different concepts with some ahead of the curve and others behind. The main downside, and one reiterated in teacher testimonials, is that it is a "tougher workload for teachers." Knope (2012) supports this concept, arguing that

> ... a great deal of preparation is necessary to successfully use differentiated learning. The larger the class size, the more overwhelming it can become. A great deal of staff development is necessary to help train those new to it and to mentor and manage the experienced teachers.

One response to mitigate these challenges is to implement differentiated instruction through choice-based instruction. This approach provides a common set of choices for students that reduces the demands on the instructor for grading a variety of work products, reduces the ways that material can be delivered and consumed, and reduces the number of processes to be used to work through mastery of the material.

Conclusion

Differentiated learning is the recognition that every student comes from a background of unique life experiences and will develop knowledge and skills based on their specific interests. The advent of new learning technologies has made the concept of differentiated learning practical and achievable at scale. While traditional education training taught educators the didactic, lowest common denominator approach, new technologies allow for instant access to knowledge, social learning, and continuously adjusted individualized plans of education. Recent research and educational policies emphasize the significance of adopting differentiated learning facilitated by technology to enhance teaching and learning for all learners in different contexts and without a dramatic increase on educator load.

To ensure effective implementation of differentiated learning in digitally mediated environments, we have shown specific practical guidelines on how to differentiate learning across its four main components. Simply, educators need to differentiate the content (what students learn), process (how they learn), product (how they show what they learned), and learning environment (where they learn). Overall, adopting differentiated learning in schools would respect the uniqueness of different students' experiences and provide different educational options for each individual to suit his or her needs and interests.

References

Appadurai, A. (2013). *The future as cultural fact: Essays on the global condition*. Brooklyn, NY: Verso Books.

Bishop, J., & Verleger, M. (2013, June). *The flipped classroom: A survey of the research*. Paper presented at the 120th ASEE Annual Conference and Exposition, Atlanta, GA.

Bridgeland, J. M., DiIulio, J. J., Jr., & Morison, K. B. (2006). *The silent epidemic: Perspectives of high school dropouts*. Washington, DC: Civic Enterprises.

Bryant, D. P., Bryant, B. R., & Ok, M. W. (2014). Assistive technology for individuals with learning disabilities. In G. Lancioni & N. Singh (Eds.), *Assistive technologies for people with diverse abilities* (pp. 251–276). New York: Springer.

Burggraf, K. (2005). *Best practices in education: Differentiated instruction*. Retrieved from http://www.dayonepublishing.com/Educational/DifferentiationCard/DiffCard.pdf

CAST. (2011). *Universal design for learning guidelines version 2.0*. Wakefield, MA: Author.

Cope, B., & Kalantzis, M. (2015). Sources of evidence-of-learning: Learning and assessment in the era of big data. *Open Review of Educational Research, 2*(1), 194–217.

Cunningham, G. (2009). *The new teacher's companion: Practical wisdom for succeeding in the classroom*. Alexandria, VA: ASCD.

D'Arcy, C. J., Eastburn, D. M., & Bruce, B. C. (2009). How media ecologies can address diverse student needs. *College Teaching, 5*(2), 1–7.

DePaoli, J. L., Fox, J. H., Ingram, E. S., Maushard, M., Bridgeland, J. M., & Balfanz, R. (2015). *Building a grad nation: Progress and challenge in ending the high school dropout epidemic. Annual update 2015*. Washington, DC: Civic Enterprises.

Dewey, J. (1938). *Experience and education*. New York, NY: Touchstone Books.

Fink, L. D. (2003). *Creating significant learning experiences: An integrated approach to designing college courses.* San Francisco: Jossey-Bass.

Freire, P. (1970). *Pedagogy of the oppressed* (M. B. Ramos, trans.). New York: Continuum.

Grant, C., & Sleeter, C. (2007). Race, class, gender, and disability in the classroom. In J. A. Banks & C.A.M Banks (Eds.), *Multicultural education: Issues and perspectives* (6th ed., pp. 63–84), Hoboken, NJ: Wiley.

Grant, P., & Bayse, D. (2014). *Personalized learning: A guide for engaging students with technology.* Eugene, OR: International Society for Technology in Education.

Hall, T. (2002). *Differentiated instruction.* Retrieved from http://www.principals.in/uploads/pdf/Instructional_Strategie/DI_Marching.pdf

Herman, J. (2010). *Coherence: Key to next generation assessment success.* Retrieved from https://www.cse.ucla.edu/products/policy/coherence_v6.pdf

Herman, J. (2013). *Formative assessment for next generation science standards: A proposed model.* Retrieved from http://www.ets.org/Media/Research/pdf/herman.pdf

Jenkins, H., Purushotma, R., Weigel, M., Clinton, K., & Robison, A. (2009). *Confronting the challenges of participatory culture: Media education for the 21st century.* Cambridge, MA: MIT Press.

Kalantzis, M., & Cope, B. (2012). *New learning: Elements of a science of education* (2nd ed.). New York: Cambridge University Press.

Kalantzis, M., & Cope, B. (2016). New media and productive diversity in learning. In S. Barsch & S. Glutsch (Eds.), *Diversity in der Lehrerinnenbildung* (pp. 310–235). Münster, Germany: Waxmann.

Kalantzis, M., Cope, B., Chan, E., & Dalley-Trim, L. (2016). *Literacies* (2nd ed.). Cambridge: Cambridge University Press.

Kalcevic, N. (2014, November). *Build a new box: Choice-based art.* Paper presented at the Arkansas Art Educators Conference, North Little Rock, AR.

Knope, A. (2012, February 25). Differentiated learning: The pros and cons. *Teacherlinx.* Retrieved from http://teacherlinx.com/#!/lesson/4605/differentiated-learning-the-pros-and-conshttp://teacherlinx.com/

Lombardo, C. (2015, August 15). Pros and cons of differentiated instruction. *Vision launch.* Retrieved from http://www.visionlaunch.com/pros-and-cons-of-differentiated-instruction/

Means, B., Toyama, Y., Murphy, R., Bakia, M., & Jones, K. (2010). *Evaluation of evidence-based practices in online learning: A meta-analysis and review of online learning studies.* Washington, DC: US Department of Education.

Montessori, M. (1912). *The Montessori method: Scientific pedagogy as applied to child education in "the children's houses."* London: Heinemann.

National Center on Universal Design for Learning. (2012). *The three principles.* Retrieved from http://www.udlcenter.org/aboutudl/whatisudl/3principles

National Research Council. (2001). *Knowing what students know: The science and design of educational assessment.* Washington, DC: National Academy Press.

New Media Consortium. (2015). *NMC horizon report 2015: Higher education edition.* Retrieved from http://cdn.nmc.org/media/2015-nmc-horizon-report-HE-EN.pdf

Nilson, L. B. (2003). *Teaching at its best: A research-based resource for college instructors.* Bolton, MA: Anker.

Oakes, J., & Lipton, M. (2007). *Teaching to change the world* (3rd ed.). Boston: McGraw Higher Education.

Rizvi, F., & Lingard, B. (2010). *Globalizing education policy.* New York: Routledge.

Rock, M. L., Gregg, M., Ellis, E., & Gable, R. A. (2008). REACH: A framework for differentiating classroom instruction. *Preventing School Failure: Alternative Education for Children and Youth, 52*(2), 31–47.

Siemens, G. (2005). Connectivism: A learning theory for the digital age. *International Journal of Instructional Technology and Distance Learning, 2*(1), 3–10.

Stanford, P., Crowe, M. W., & Flice, H. (2010). Differentiating with technology. *TEACHING Exceptional Children Plus, 6*(4), n4.

Subban, P. (2006). Differentiated instruction: A research basis. *International Education Journal, 7*(7), 935–947.

Tarantino, K., McDonough, J., & Hua, M. (2013, Summer). Effects of student engagement with social media on student learning: A review of literature. *The Journal of Technology in Student Affairs*. Retrieved from http://www.studentaffairs.com/ejournal/Summer_2013/EffectsOfStudentEngagementWithSocialMedia.html

Tomlinson, C. A. (2000). *Differentiation of instruction in the elementary grades*. Retrieved from ERIC database. (ED443572)

Tomlinson, C. A. (2010). *Student assessment strategies* [Presentation]. Retrieved from http://www.caroltomlinson.com/2010SpringASCD/Rex_SAstrategies.pdf

Tomlinson, C. A. (2014). *The differentiated classroom: Responding to the needs of all learners* (2nd ed.). Arlington, VA: Association for Supervision and Curriculum Development.

Tomlinson, C. A., & McTighe, J. (2006). *Integrating differentiated instruction & understanding by design: Connecting content and kids*. Alexandria, VA: Association for Supervision and Curriculum Development.

Tomlinson, C. A., & Moon, T. R. (2013). Assessment and student success in a differentiated classroom. Alexandria, VA: ASCD.

US Department of Education. (2016). *Future ready learning: Reimagining the role of technology in education*. Retrieved from http://tech.ed.gov/files/2015/12/NETP16.pdf

Wehrmann, K. S. (2000). Baby steps: A beginner's guide. *Educational Leadership, 58*(1), 20–23.

Wen, Y., Looi, C. K., & Chen, W. (2012). Supporting teachers in designing CSCL activities: A case study of principle-based pedagogical patterns in networked second language classrooms. *Educational Technology & Society, 15*(2), 138–153.

Yang, T.-C., Hwang, G.-J., & Yang, S. J.-H. (2013). Development of an adaptive learning system with multiple perspectives based on students' learning styles and cognitive styles. *Educational Technology & Society, 16*(4), 185–200.

Zheng, B., Warschauer, M., Lin, C. H., & Chang, C. (2016). Learning in one-to-one laptop environments: A meta-analysis and research synthesis. *Review of Educational Research*. doi:10.3102/0034654316628645

Contributors

Tabassum Amina is a doctoral student in the Department of Education Policy, Organization, and Leadership at the University of Illinois at Urbana–Champaign. She holds a Master of Arts degree in sociology and education. Her current research explores online learning in developing countries, with a particular focus on women's participation in MOOCs. Her previous research has investigated the nongovernment education sector in Bangladesh.

Jane Blanken-Webb is a postdoctoral researcher with the University of Eastern Finland and previously held the position of IES postdoctoral fellow at the University of Illinois at Urbana–Champaign. Her work has been published in journals such as *Educational Theory,* the *Journal of Aesthetic Education,* and *Philosophical Studies in Education.* She holds a PhD in social and philosophical foundations of education from the University of Illinois at Urbana–Champaign. Her research draws on the philosophy of John Dewey and engages educational questions involving intersections with educational technologies, aesthetic education, and citizenship education.

Bill Cope is a professor in the Department of Educational Policy Studies at the University of Illinois. He is principal investigator in a series of major projects funded by the Institute of Educational Sciences in the US Department of Education and the Bill and Melinda Gates Foundation researching and developing multimodal writing and assessment spaces. From 2010–2013, he was chair of the Journals Publication Committee of the American Educational Research Association. Recent books include *The Future of the Academic Journal* (with Angus Phillips, eds.; Elsevier, second edition, 2014), and *Towards a Semantic Web: Connecting Knowledge in Academic Research* (with Kalantzis and Magee; Elsevier, 2010).

Samaa Haniya is a PhD student in the Department of Education Policy, Organization, and Leadership at the University of Illinois at Urbana–Champaign. She holds a Master of Education degree in Curriculum and Instruction from the University of Illinois at Urbana–Champaign and received the university's Max Beberman Academic Achievement award in 2008. Prior to joining the doctoral program, she was a faculty member in the humanities department at Parkland College in Champaign, Illinois, where she taught Arabic language classes. Her primary research interests involve digital learning in higher education, students' interaction in online learning communities, digital equity, instructional design, and program evaluation.

Mary Kalantzis is dean of the College of Education at the University of Illinois at Urbana–Champaign. She was formerly dean of the faculty of education, language, and community services at RMIT University in Melbourne, Australia, and president of the Australian Council of Deans of Education. With Bill Cope, she is coauthor of *New Learning: Elements of a Science of Education* (Cambridge University Press, second edition, 2012) and *Literacies* (Cambridge University Press, second edition, 2016), and co-editor of *Ubiquitous Learning* (University of Illinois Press, 2009) and *A Pedagogy of Multiliteracies* (Palgrave, 2015).

Katrina Kennett is a doctoral student in curriculum and instruction with a specialization in writing studies at the University of Illinois at Urbana–Champaign. Her research interests include the digital composing process and multimodal literacy pedagogy. She taught high school English and continues to work with teachers and districts as they incorporate technologies into the classroom.

Alecia Magnifico is an assistant professor of English at the University of New Hampshire, where she teaches courses on English teaching, digital literacies, and research methods. Her research interests focus on understanding, supporting, and encouraging writing and collaboration across contexts and audiences. A former middle school teacher, she also enjoys working with teachers and students to design learning spaces, curricula, and assessments that engage multiple tools and literacies. She is coauthor of *Conducting Qualitative Research in Learning in Online Spaces* (Sage, 2017), and recent articles have appeared in *Literacy* and the *Journal of Adolescent and Adult Literacy*.

Sarah McCarthey is a professor in the Department of Curriculum and Instruction and director of teacher education at the University of Illinois at Urbana–Champaign. She was co-editor of *Research in the Teaching of English* with Mark Dressman and Paul Prior from 2008–2013 and is codirector of the University of Illinois Writing Project with Scott Filkins. Her latest work focuses on teachers' writing practices and professional development in writing and has been published in *Pedagogies: An International Journal*, *Written Communication*, and *Journal of Writing Research*.

Sol Roberts-Lieb is the associate director of pedagogy strategy and industry relations for the Center for Innovation in Teaching and Learning at the University of Illinois at Urbana–Champaign and an EdD student in the Department of Education Policy, Organization, and Leadership. He holds a master's degree in liberal studies focusing on technology impact and assessment from the University of Illinois at Springfield. His research interests include differentiated instruction and ways to help teachers learn how to personalize learning to meet students' varying skills and abilities at all levels.

Adam Rusch is a PhD student in the Department of Education Policy, Organization, and Leadership at the University of Illinois at Urbana–Champaign. He holds degrees of Master of Arts in communication and Master of Science in library and information science. His research interests include informal learning practices in online communities, finding ways to bring the energy of informal learning into higher education institutions, and developing learning management systems.

Anna Smith is an assistant professor at Illinois State University, following an IES postdoctoral fellowship in writing and new learning ecologies at the University of Illinois at Urbana–Champaign. She serves on the board of the Writing and Literacies Special Interest Group of the American Educational Research Association. She is coauthor with Richard Andrews of *Developing Writers: Teaching and Learning in the Digital Age* (Open University Press, 2011) and has recent articles in the *English Journal, Literacy, Education Sciences,* and *Journal of Literacy Research.* Her research interests include writing development, transliteracies, educational technologies, and the intersection of teaching and learning. Her scholarly work is buttressed with 17 years of work in public schools as a teacher, district-level literacy specialist, and teacher educator.

Index